INTERPRETING THE SCRIPTURES

INTERPRETING THE SCRIPTURES

BY KEVIN CONNER
and
KEN MALMIN

Published by City Bible Publishing
9200 NE Fremont
Portland, Oregon 97220

Printed in U.S.A.

City Bible Publishing is a ministry of City Bible Church and is dedicated to serving the local church and its leaders through the production and distribution of quality materials.

It is our prayer that these materials, proven in the context of the local church, will equip leaders in exalting the Lord and extending His kingdom.

For a free catalog of additional resources from City Bible Publishing please call 1-800-777-6057 or visit our web page at www.citybiblepublishing.com.

ISBN 0-914936-20-4

Dedication

To our loving wives, Joyce and Glenda, who have faithfully supported us in life and particularly in the production of this text.

and

To those students of Portland Bible College with whom we have enjoyed sharing these principles.

and

To all those who have a hunger to know the meaning of Scripture.

PREFACE

Every sincere Bible scholar realizes that it is absolutely essential to have Biblical keys and principles which will unlock the Scripture in order to bring forth the wisdom and knowledge that God has placed within the pages of His Word.

I am grateful for such a book as this that clearly lays out keys of interpreting the Scriptures. I believe that those readers who are interested in knowing the secrets of God which are locked up in His Word will greatly benefit by reading this text.

However, we must remember that the Word of God still requires the anointing of the Holy Spirit to reveal truth to our spirits. The principles herein will help to release to our minds an understanding of God's Word as the Holy Spirit quickens our spirits.

We are indebted to Kevin J. Conner and Kenneth Malmin for the countless hours spent in preparing *Interpreting the Scriptures* for all those who hunger and thirst after an opened understanding of the Sacred Word, the Holy Bible.

Rev. K.R. (Dick) Iverson
Pastor — Bible Temple
President — Portland Bible College

FOREWORD
INTERPRETING THE SCRIPTURES

It is recognized by Christians around the world that God has spoken in His Word; the Sacred Scriptures. However, what is not so clear is what He meant by what He said. On this point the opinions are innumerable. Unfortunately these differences have been used to divide the Body of Christ into many varied factions. Seeing the evil of divisions, it is the conviction of the authors that one of the root causes of theological differences lies in the field of hermeneutics. Since all proper doctrine arises out of the interpretation of Scripture, it is logical that at the root of doctrinal differences lies hermeneutical differences. Hermeneutics and its application becomes then the central issue of doctrinal divisions. Generally speaking, Bible believing Christians are united in accepting the facts of revelation and inspiration. However, the major divisions concern interpretation and application. The problem is not over *revelation and inspiration* so much as it is over *interpretation and application.*

The authors of this text do not regard themselves as infallible hermeneuticians. The Lord Jesus Christ alone is that. But, at the same time, it is evident that the Lord Jesus gave to the early apostles definite "keys" of interpretation, which they used in interpreting the Old Testament in writing infallible Scripture. It is with a burning desire to rediscover what might be called "Apostolic Hermeneutics" that this book is written.

The foundational proposition upon which this text is built may be stated as; "The *literary methods* used in *writing the Scriptures* give rise to the *principles* of *interpreting the Scriptures."* In other words, the way a thing is put together indicates the way it can be taken apart. Hence, the way the Bible was written indicates the way it should be interpreted. The universe is maintained by the laws of God. Man does not make these laws; he only discovers them. As long as he does not violate these laws, he can use them to find blessing. So it is in the field of hermeneutics. There are Divine laws, principles of interpretation, hidden in the Scriptures. As the interpreter discovers these, he will be able to use them to discover the meaning of Scripture. On the other hand, a violation of these principles will bring misunderstanding and confusion. According to ***Proverbs 25:2, "It is the glory of God to conceal a thing: but the honour of kings is to search out a matter."***

This comprehensive textbook presents a unique approach in several of its areas, particularly in its evaluation of history, its definition of the foundational elements in interpretation and its presentation of hermeneutical principles.

We have purposely designed this text to reach the levels of both teacher and student. It is our prayer that the reader will find this book helpful and will experience as much joy in using these principles as we have found in presenting them. Any correspondence concerning this text will be welcomed. May the Spirit of Truth guide us all in rightly dividing the Word of Truth.

The Authors

Kevin J. Conner
Ken Malmin

Portland Bible College
7626 N. E. Glisan Street
Portland, Oregon 97213
U.S.A.

TABLE OF CONTENTS

*All the Principles have the same four divisions.

Chapter 1
AN INTRODUCTION TO HERMENEUTICS

I. THE DEFINITION OF HERMENEUTICS

A. Literal Definition

Webster's dictionary defines hermeneutics as, "The science of interpretation, or of finding the meaning of an author's words and phrases, and of explaining it to others; exegesis; particularly applied to the interpretation of the Scriptures."

Modern theologians define hermeneutics as both "the science and the art of Biblical interpretation." It is (1) a *science* because it is concerned with principles within an ordered system. It is meant to derive and classify the principles necessary for the proper interpretation of Scripture. It is also (2) an *art* because it is concerned with applying the principles derived. The application of these principles cannot be mechanical, but must involve the skill of the interpreter.

B. Classical Definition

The classical background of the word "hermeneutics" is found in Greek and Roman mythology. Hermes (Greek), or Mercury (Roman), was the god of science, speech, writing, invention, and art. He was the messenger and interpreter for the gods, conveying their communications to mortals. Mercury is referred to in ***Acts 14:8-18,*** where the men of Lystra, ignorantly assuming Paul and Barnabas to be gods, referred to Paul as Mercury, "because he was the chief speaker," and called Barnabas Jupiter, the father of Mercury. In Greek culture every interpreter (HERMENEUS) supposedly inherited some of the mystic qualities of Hermes, the god of literature and patron of eloquence.

C. Scriptural Definition

The heart of hermeneutics is centered in the word "interpretation." This word is used in both the Old and New Testaments as follows:

1. **Old Testament Hebrew and Chaldee**

a. PATHAR — to open up; (fig.) interpret; explain (a dream).
Translated: interpret, interpreted, interpreter, interpretation ***Genesis 40:8, 16, 22; 41:8, 12, 13, 15***

b. PITHRON — interpretation; explanation.
Translated: interpretation ***Genesis 40:5, 8, 12, 18***

c. MELIYTSAH — an aphorism; also a satire, interpretation.
Translated: interpretation ***Proverbs 1:6*** taunting (proverb); ***Habakkuk 2:6***

d. LUWTS to make mouths at; to scoff; hence (from the effort to pronounce a foreign language), to interpret or (gen.) to intercede; to treat as a scorner or foreigner.
Translated: Generally—scorner, mocker.
Figuratively—interpreter ***Genesis 42:23; Job 33:23,*** ambassadors ***II Chronicles 32:31,*** teachers ***Isaiah 43:27***

e. SHEBER — a fracture; a breaking; a solution (of a dream).
Translated: Generally—to break, broken
Figuratively—interpretation ***Judges 7:15***

f. PESHAR (Chaldee) — interpretation; explanation.
Translated: interpret, interpreting, interpretation ***Daniel 2:4, 5, 6, 7, 9, 16, 24, 25, 26, 30, 36, 45; 4:6, 7, 9, 18, 19, 24; 5:7, 8, 12, 15, 16, 17, 26; 7:16; Ecclesiastes 8:1*** (Hebrew)

g. TIRGAM — to throw over; transfer; translate.
Translated: interpreted ***Ezra 4:7***

Together, these words show interpretation to be an opening up, a breaking, explanation, solution, and a translation. They are used predominantly in reference to the interpretation of dreams, although they are also used in relation to visions, proverbs, foreign languages, and various symbols.

2. **New Testament Greek**

a. HERMENEUO — to interpret; explain in words; expound; translate.
Translated: being interpreted, by interpretation, being by interpretation ***John 1:38, 41, 42; 9:7; Hebrews 7:2***

b. HERMENEIA — interpretation; explanation (of obscure utterances), (metonymically—the power or faculty of interpreting.
Translated: interpretation ***I Corinthians 12:10*** (some mss.—DIERMENEIA); ***14:26***

c. DIERMENEUO — to interpret or explain thoroughly; to interpret fully; to unfold the meaning of what is said; explain; expound; to translate into one's native language.
Translated: expounded ***Luke 24:27***
by interpretation ***Acts 9:36***
interpret ***I Corinthians 12:30; 14:5, 13, 27***

d. DIERMENEUTES — a thorough interpreter; one who interprets or explains fully.
Translated: interpreter ***I Corinthians 14:28*** (some mss.—HERMENEUTES)

e. DUSERMENEUTOS — hard to interpret; difficult to be explained; hard to be understood.
Translated: hard to be uttered ***Hebrews 5:11***

f. METHERMENEUO — to translate into the language of one with whom communication is desired; to interpret.
Translated: being interpreted, by interpretation ***Matthew 1:23; Mark 5:41; 15:22, 34; John 1:42; Acts 4:36; 13:8***

g. EPILUSIS — a loosing; a solution; an explanation; (metaphorically, interpretation).
Translated: interpretation ***II Peter 1:20***

Together, these words show interpretation to be an explanation of obscure utterances, a translation into one's own language, an expounding, an interpreting or explaining thoroughly, a loosing, and a solving. These words are used (1) of Christ's thorough *exposition* to the two disciples on the road to Emmaus the things concerning Himself in the Law, the Psalms, and the Prophets (the whole of the Old Testament); (2) of the *translation* of names and phrases from Hebrew and Aramaic to Greek; and (3) of the *interpretation* of unknown languages.

II. THE SCIENCE OF HERMENEUTICS

We have defined hermeneutics as the science and art of interpretation. It is a *science* because it can reduce interpretation, within limits, to a set of rules. It is an *art* in that the application of the rules remains complex, requiring a skilled interpreter. Hermeneutics is the pivotal point of all science because it is the bridge of communication. We will now consider the necessity and importance of hermeneutics under the following two headings: *General Hermeneutics,* including all forms of communication; and *Bible Hermeneutics,* dealing with God's communication to man.

A. General Hermeneutics

General hermeneutics refers to the various sets of rules which are used in the interpretation of the materials presented through the many forms of communication. Communication is the transmission and reception of thoughts and feelings in a medium common to both sender and receiver. All forms of communication, including speech,

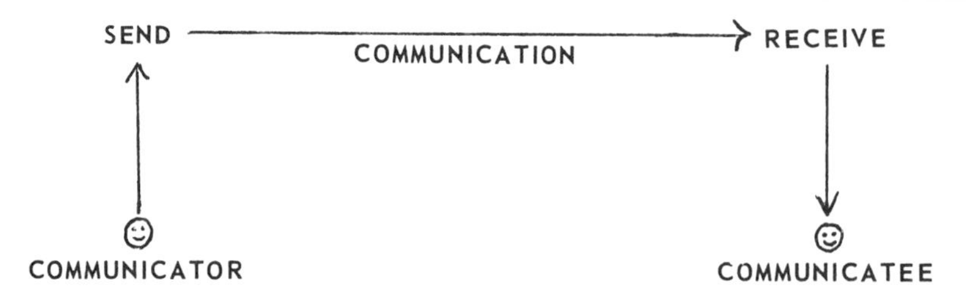

literature, and the arts, present subject matter which interpretation by the proper application of the rules of general hermeneutics. When something hinders clear understanding in the process of communication, there arises the need for interpretation.

Whenever communication is to take place, it must be recognized that a gap in understanding may exist between the communicator and the receiver. For communication to be successful, there must be a common medium between the two in order that this gap may be bridged. The rules of interpretation supply us with the materials with which the bridge can be built. Between the sender and receiver there lies a vast field of experience which may contain differences that cause understanding gaps. In other words, both sender and receiver has his own frame of reference around the message being relayed. The following is an illustration of the field of experience, consisting of the frames of reference of both the sender and receiver, in relation to communication:

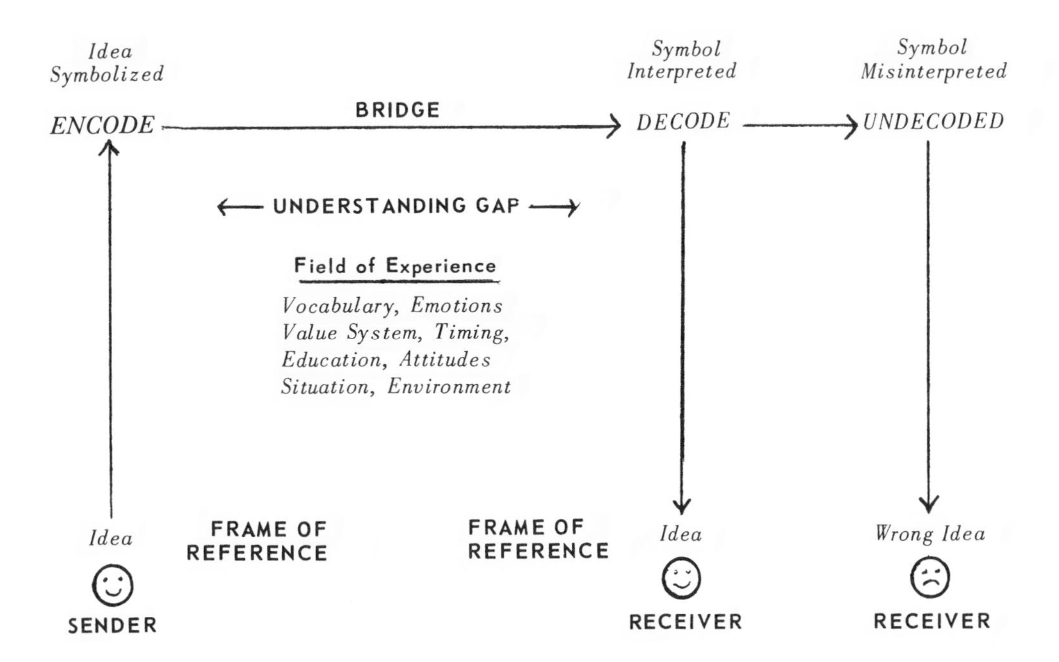

Whenever man communicates, the exercising of interpretation becomes necessary. Whether it is art, music, law, history, poetry, or philosophical and religious literature; all these forms of communication require interpretation.

1. **Art**—Modern art, whether painting or sculpture leaves the untrained observer bewildered as to its significance. Thus arises the need for art experts.
2. **Music**—Many compositions of the great composers of past days require the interpretative skill of a music expert.
3. **Law**—In the United States, the Legislative branch of government makes the laws while the Judicial branch interprets them. It is the sole duty of the Supreme Court to interpret the Constitution, thus showing the need for law experts.
4. **History**—Every person interprets history in the light of his own philosophical and theological predispositions. Before history can be interpreted, all the facts must be gathered by the history expert.
5. **Poetry**—The unique nature and structure of poetic language demands knowledgeable interpretation by the poetry expert.
6. **Literature**—The profoundly abstract nature of most philosophical and religious literature calls for the ability of an enlightened interpreter. The prominence of sacred books such as the Veda, the Buddhist Canon, the Egyptian book of the Dead, and the Koran, has given birth to their respective schools of interpretation. Hence, the need for the literature expert.

The above illustrations point out the necessity and importance of General Hermeneutics. If experts are needed in all these areas in order to make each form of communication effective, how much more so is there a need for Biblical Hermeneutics.

B. **Biblical Hermeneutics**

General Hermeneutics is the science of interpreting the communication of man to man. Biblical Hermeneutics is the science of interpreting the communication of God to man. This Divine communication has come to man in the form of sacred literature—the Bible.

It is certain that God has spoken to man in His Word: Jesus—the Living Word; and the Bible—the Written Word. But what has He said? The primary purpose of Biblical Hermeneutics is to ascertain what God has said in the Scriptures and to determine its meaning. We derive no benefit from the fact that God has spoken unless we understand what is meant by what He said.

As previously noted, there is an understanding gap between the minds of the communicator and receiver which must be bridged in order for an effective transfer of ideas to take place. If this is true concerning man to man communication, how much more it applies to communication from the infinite God, who is omniscient, to the mind of finite man, whose frame of reference is limited.

It must also be recognized that God communicated His truth through human writers utilizing their frames of reference. This serves to doubly necessitate the proper interpretation of Scripture. (Both God to man; and God through man, to man).

THE COMMUNICATION OF SCRIPTURE

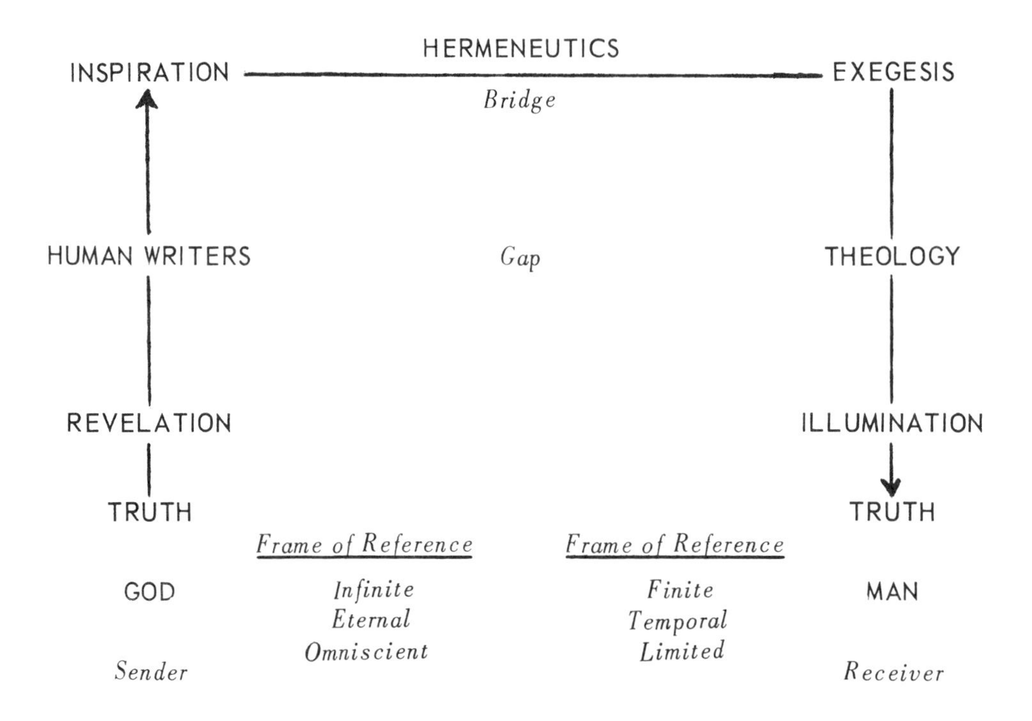

It is necessary and important to interpret Scripture because it is communication from Divinity to Humanity. In addition, it is necessary because the Scriptures were written, under inspiration, by approximately thirty five different authors from all walks of life, over a period of about 1600 years (from Moses to John), and in three different languages. These facts make the Bible unique in its need for interpretation.

Another factor which makes interpretation necessary is the variety of methods by which God has spoken to and through man.

*''In many **separate** revelations—each of which set forth a **portion** of the Truth—and in **different ways** God **spoke** of old to (our) forefathers in and by the prophets.''* ***Hebrews 1:1*** Amplified New Testament.

*''God, who at **sundry times** and in **divers manners spake** in time past unto the fathes by the prophets''* ***Hebrews 1:1*** King James Version.

*''In **many parts** and in **many ways** . . .''* ***Hebrews 1:1*** Berry Interlinear.

Ways God Has Spoken

a. **DREAM**—A succession of images, thoughts, or emotions passing through the mind during sleep. ***(Numbers 12:6; Joel 2:28; Matthew 1:20)***

b. **VISION**—Something presented to the mind through other than natural means of sight while awake; seeing with the eyes open in the spiritual world; a supernatural appearance that conveys a revelation. ***(Numbers 12:6; Joel 2:28; Acts 2:17; Acts 9:10, 12)***

c. **ANGEL OF THE LORD**—Generally spoken of as a theophany, which is a manifestation and revelation of the Lord Jesus Christ before His incarnation; a manifestation or appearance of God to man. ***(Genesis 18; Exodus 3; Judges 6 and 13)***

d. **SIMILITUDE**—A shape, form of, model or pattern; a resemblance or likeness similar to the real; a person or thing resembling a counterpart. ***(Deuteronomy 4:12, 15, 16; Daniel 10:16; Hosea 12:10; Romans 5:14; Hebrews 7:15)***

e. **FIGURE**—A form or shape as determined by outlines; the external shape or outline of something; to represent or express by figure of speech; emblematic of the real. ***(Romans 5:14; Hebrews 9:9, 24; 11:19; I Peter 3:21)***

f. **TYPE**—A thing embodying qualities characteristic of a particular person; the mark or impression of something; a figure or representation of something to come; a prophetic representation, foreshadowing, prefiguring. ***(Romans 5:14; I Corinthians 10:6, 11)***

g. **SHADOW**—A faint and imperfect representation; an imitation of something having form without substance; a dark figure or image cast on a surface by a body intercepting the light; a foreshadowing. ***(Colossians 2:17; Hebrews 8:5; 10:1)***

h. **EXAMPLE**—A part of something, taken to show the character of the whole, a pattern or model, as of something to be imitated or avoided; an instance, sample, or specimen serving for illustration. ***(I Corinthians 10:6, 11; Hebrews 4:11; 8:5; II Peter 2:6; Jude 7)***

i. **PATTERN**—An original or model considered for, or deserving of imitation; anything designed as a model; the first thing or being of its kind; the original model from which a thing is made. ***(Exodus 25:9; I Chronicles 28:11, 12, 19; I Timothy 1:16; Hebrews 8:5)***

j. **SIGN**—A token used in place of that which it represents; a signal to draw attention to something; a mark or a symbol having a specific meaning. ***(Exodus 3:12; Isaiah 7:11, 14; Matthew 12:39; John 20:30)***

k. **SIGNIFYING OF THE HOLY SPIRIT**—To indicate by a mark; to speak by sign-language; to represent the real with a symbol. ***(John 12:33; 18:32; 21:19; Acts 11:28; Revelation 1:1)***

l. **ALLEGORY**—A comparison sustained through numerous details; a symbolic narrative presenting an abstract or spiritual meaning using material forms; a story in which people, things, and happenings have another meaning, usually a moral lesson. ***(Galations 4:24)***

m. **MYSTERY**—That which is secret and can be known only to the initiated; truth which can be known only by revelation. ***(Ephesians 1:9; 3:9; 5:32; I Timothy 3:16; Revelation 1:20)***

n. **DARK SAYING**—A hidden saying, the meaning of which must be discovered; a knot of speech which must be unraveled; an obscure utterance which must be clarified. ***(Numbers 12:8; Psalms 49:4; 78:2; Proverbs 1:6; Daniel 8:23)***

o. **RIDDLE**—A puzzling question framed so as to require ingenuity in answering it; an enigma needing solution. ***(Judges 14:12; Ezekiel 17:2)***

p. **PROVERB**—A short didactic saying embodying a truth; a sentence briefly and forcibly expressing some practical truth. ***(Proverbs 1:6; Luke 4:23; II Peter 2:22)***

q. **PARABLE**—A short story conveying some truth or lesson by a comparison; an earthly story with a heavenly meaning. ***(Matthew 13:3, 10, 13, 34, 35; Mark 3:23; Luke 8:10)***

r. **VOICE OF WORDS**—The audible voice of the Lord in actual words; audible communication, utterance. ***(Genesis 3:8; Numbers 7:89; Deuteronomy 5:22-28; I Kings 19:12, 13; Psalms 103:20; Daniel 10:6, 9)***

s. **PROPHECY**—To speak under inspiration concerning the present (forthtelling) or concerning the future (foretelling); to either proclaim or predict. ***(Numbers 12:6-8; I Peter 1:10-12; II Peter 1:20, 21)***

t. **WRITING**—To communicate through inscriptions; to use letters for characters as visible symbols of ideas and words. ***(Exodus 31:18; 32:16; I Chronicles 28:19; II Chronicles 35:4; Daniel 5:5)***

Even a cursory glance at the above list will serve to underscore the need for interpretation of the Word of God. In addition, there are many other factors which lead to the conclusion that the interpretation of Scripture is of utmost importance. These fall into two main groupings:

u. **SYMBOLIC GROUP**—This includes areas such as interpretation of names, significance of numbers, and all other symbols. These require special interpretation, and will be dealt with later.

v. **FIGURES OF SPEECH GROUP**—Included here are metaphors, similes, hyperboles, idioms and others. Refer to Bullinger's *Figures of Speech Used in the Bible.*

III. HERMENEUTICS AND OTHER BIBLICAL SCIENCES

It is necessary that the Bible scholar have an understanding of the inter-relatedness of the various Biblical sciences. Hermeneutics is not to be viewed as a solitary science, but rather as a link in a chain of related sciences. The major Bible sciences are the study of the Canon (Canonology), Historical Criticism, Textual Criticism, Hermeneutics, Exegesis, and Biblical Theology.

A. **Canology**—The word "canon" simply means "a rod, rule, or measuring stick." This science has to do with determining which sacred books measure up to the standard of Divine inspiration. By Divine inspiration we mean that God inspired the very thoughts and words of Scripture, utilizing the writer's frame of reference yet without corrupting the communication.

The books which measure up to this standard are to be recognized as "God-breathed"—the very Word of God ***(II Timothy 3:16).*** These would include the sixty-six books of the Authorized Version of the Bible. The Apocrypha is excluded.

B. **Historical Criticism**—The word "criticism" is not used here, nor in the following section, in the negative destructive sense. Rather it is used to connote discernment. This science deals with the authorship, date, historical circumstances, authenticity of contents, and literary unity of the books.

C. **Textual Criticism**—The word "textual" refers to the actual wording of a book. This science does not attempt to undermine the inspiration of Scripture but rather to determine as accurately as possible the original wording of the inspired text. This process is complicated by the fact that the original manuscripts no longer exist. Those copies which do exist are many and vary in quality. This requires keen discernment on the part of the textual critic.

D. **Hermeneutics**—This science is not concerned with inspiration (Canonology), background (Historical Criticism), or the wording of the books (Textual Criticism), but instead is concerned with determining the principles by which the books may be interpreted.

E. **Exegesis**—The word "exegesis" comes from a Greek word (exhegesisthai) meaning "to guide or lead out." It refers to bringing out the meaning of any writing which might otherwise be difficult to understand. This science involves the *application* of the rules of hermeneutics. While hermeneutics provides us with the tools, exegesis refers to the actual *use* of these tools; hermeneutics supplies the *principles* of interpretation, while exegesis is the *process* of interpretation. Exegesis, then, can be thought of as applied hermeneutics.

F. **Biblical Theology**—The word "theology" comes from two Greek words (theos = God and logos = word), and means literally, "the study and discourse of God." The science of Biblical theology involves the compilation, categorization, and summarization of Biblical doctrines. It formulates conclusions on a Biblical subject by considering all the Scripture relative to that subject.

A definite progression can be seen in these six related Bible sciences (As noted by Ramm, p. 10):

1. The study of the canon determines the inspired books.
2. The study of historical criticism gives us the framework of the books.
3. The study of textual criticism determines the wording of the books.
4. Hermeneutics gives us the rules for the interpretation of the books.
5. Exegesis is the application of these rules to the books.
6. Biblical theology is the result.

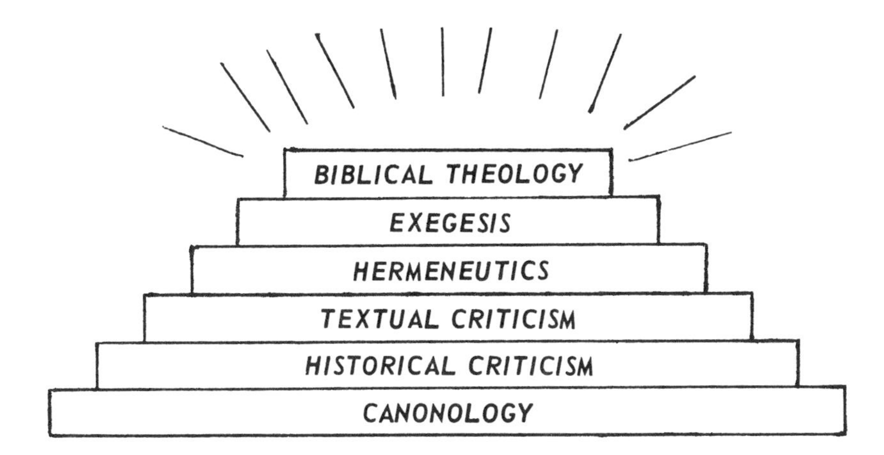

These six sciences can be easily divided into two groups of three: the first group deals with the infallible materials the Bible student has available; the second group is concerned with his use of these materials. Both groups are units; threefold cords which should not be broken ***(Ecclesiastes 4:12).*** Canonology, historical criticism, and textual criticism are bound together and provide the Bible student with a solid basis upon which he can build. These three are then completed by the second group. Hermeneutics provides the guidelines for exegesis, which in turn sets the stage for Biblical theology.

Proper application of God's Word is dependent upon proper interpretation of it. All exposition, preaching, and teaching must, therefore, be based on the appropriate exercise of the principles of hermeneutics, exegesis, and Biblical theology.

IV. HERMENEUTICS AND CHURCH DIVISIONS

It is important to recognize that many of the divisions within Christianity have arisen, not only out of carnality or sectarianism, but also because of differences in the field of hermeneutics. It must be understood that one's theological viewpoint is determined primarily by his hermeneutics. Thus a difference in hermeneutics will most likely lead to a difference in doctrine.

The issue debated in Christendom is not so much whether God has spoken (though many skeptics argue this point); nor is it so much the specific books in which He has spoken. It concerns, rather, the question of what God meant by what He said. The problems that arise, in other words, are not over *inspiration* as much as they concern *interpretation and application*.

It should be noted, however, that it is possible to adhere to the same system of hermeneutics and still reach differing doctrinal conclusions as a result of a difference in exegetical approach.

It can be concluded, then, that one of the most logical and effective means of solving the problem of divisions within Christianity would be to first settle the differences that exist in the principles and application of hermeneutics. If the principles used in the interpretation of Scripture were applied uniformly, there would be a basic agreement in the resultant theology. This, in turn, would eliminate or minimize many of the doctrinal differences which now divide the Body of Christ.

Chapter 2
THE QUALIFICATIONS OF AN INTERPRETER

I. INTERPRETERS

It has already been noted that hermeneutics is both a *science* and an *art*. Having defined the *science* of hermeneutics, it is fundamental that the *art* be considered as well, particularly as it relates to the hermeneutician. Interpretation necessitates the involvement of a person—the interpreter. The *art* of hermeneutics has to do with the applied skill of that interpreter.

The *science* of hermeneutics has suffered much because of the lack of *art* on the part of the interpreter. A mere knowledge of the rules of hermeneutics does not necessarily make the student a good interpreter, just as knowing the rules of a game does not always make one a good player. There are certain qualifications which every interpreter of the Word must have. Otherwise, hermeneutics becomes a source of confusion rather than order. False cults have developed systems of hermeneutics by which the Word of God is misinterpreted, heresy is forced out of truth, and darkness is presented as light.

Interpreters are spoken of in the Scriptures under three categories: legal interpreters, false interpreters, and true interpreters.

A. Legal Interpreters

In ***Acts 13:27*** we read: ***"For they that dwell at Jerusalem, and their rulers, because they knew him not, nor yet the voices of the prophets which are read every sabbath day, they have fulfilled them in condemning him"*** (see also ***John 18:28).*** Generally speaking, the rulers referred to here were the priests, scribes, and Pharisees in the days of Christ. The scribes were the official interpreters of the Old Testament Scriptures. Because of letterism and legalism they misinterpreted the voices of the prophets, and finally crucified Christ with their legal interpretation. This shows that it is possible, sadly enough, to know the letter of the Scriptures, but because of legalistic interpretation, miss Him of whom the Scriptures speak ***(John 5:39, 40).***

B. False Interpreters

The Scriptures also refer to another group of interpreters who are clearly revealed as false.

In ***II Corinthians 4:2,*** Paul refers to those who are guilty of "handling the Word of God deceitfully" (Amplified — "adulterate or handle dishonestly the Word of God").

In ***Ephesians 4:14,*** Paul speaks of those who, in relation to doctrine, use "sleight of men and cunning craftiness, whereby they lie in wait to deceive" (Amplified — "the cunning and cleverness of unscrupulous men, gamblers engaged in every shifting form of trickery in inventing errors to mislead").

In ***II Peter 3:16,*** Peter also refers to these men as those who are unlearned and unstable and wrest (torture on the rack) the Scriptures unto their own destruction (Amplified — "twist and misconstrue to their own utter destruction, just as they distort and misinterpret the rest of the Scriptures").

These references point out that there are those who willfully and deliberately interpret the Scriptures falsely, thus damning their own souls and the souls of those who follow them. These are "ever learning and never able to come to the knowledge of the truth" ***(II Timothy 3:7).***

C. True Interpreters

In Luke 24, Jesus is revealed to us as the perfect interpreter. Verse 27 says, ***"He expounded*** (Greek — interpreted) ***unto them in all the Scriptures the things concerning Himself."*** He is THE Interpreter; one among a thousand ***(Job 33:23).*** Every true interpreter must be patterned after Him. The exhortation of Scripture to the true interpreter is, ***"Study to shew thyself approved unto God, a workman that needeth not to be ashamed, rightly dividing the word of truth (II Timothy 2:15).***

The above categories show clearly that there must be a qualified interpreter; one who has the faculty of interpreting and explaining fully the meaning of the Word of God. These bring us to a consideration of those spiritual and mental qualifications needed by any interpreter of the Holy Scriptures.

II. QUALIFICATIONS

A. The Interpreter Must be Born of the Spirit and the Word *John 3:1-12; I Peter 1:23*

Although Nicodemus was a teacher in Israel, he still needed to be born "from above." It is impossible for anyone to see or understand the things pertaining to the Kingdom of God and the plan of redemption unless he is born of the Spirit. How can one who is not born of the Spirit and the Word comprehend or interpret the Word which was produced by the Spirit? As interpreters of the Word we must be guided in our interpretation by the same Spirit that inspired those who wrote it.

B. The Interpreter Must Have a Passionate Hunger for the Word of God

If one has been truly born again, the first evidence of that birth is hunger. This refers to an intense desire for that which is highly valued. Knowing God through His Word must be of primary importance to the interpreter. Job exemplified this as he spoke of his hunger and love for the Word of God: ***"I have esteemed the words of His mouth more than my necessary food" (Job 23:12).*** David said, ***"and I will delight myself in Thy commandments, which I have loved" (Psalms 119:47).*** Jeremiah expressed the same longing for the Word: ***"Thy word was unto me the joy and rejoicing of mine heart" (Jeremiah 15:16).*** (See also: ***Psalms 19:7-10; Ezekiel 3:1-3; Matthew 4:4; Revelation 10:8-10.)*** A highly valuable practice for the interpreter is the rapid reading of the whole Bible. This helps give him a thorough acquaintance with the Word as a whole.

C. The Interpreter Must Possess an Attitude of Humility

The attitude of humility is a quality essential to spiritual insight. Pride and arrogance bring spiritual blindness, making the discovery of the true meaning of God's Word impossible. The religious leaders of Christ's day were haughty and proud. Though holding the Scriptures in their hands, they were blind to the true interpretation of them. They rejected and crucified the very Christ to which the Scriptures pointed ***(Acts 13:27).*** The Scriptures exhort us to possess ***"lowliness of mind" (Philippians 2:3); "humility of mind" (Acts 20:19);*** and ***"humility" (I Peter 5:5).*** We are to ***"receive with meekness the engrafted word" (James 1:21).***

D. The Interpreter Must Possess an Attitude of Reverence and Respect for the Word of God

One of the greatest safeguards against mishandling the Word of Truth is to maintain a wholesome reverence for God's Word. If the interpreter recognizes the awesomeness of the Book he is interpreting, there will be less tendency to handle it lightly . A proper respect will act as a restraint against using the Word to project his own ideas. David said, ***"Then shall I not be ashamed, when I have respect unto all Thy commandments" (Psalms 119:6).***

E. The Interpreter Must Accept the Total Inspiration of the Scriptures

According to Paul, in ***II Timothy 3:16, "All scripture is given by inspiration of God . . . ."*** The Holy Spirit inspired the Word; it was "God-breathed." The Holy Spirit breathed into human vessels the very thoughts and words He wanted written. The Word flowed through those human channels involving, but not violating, their emotions, education, experiences, and personalities. Yet the Holy Spirit guarded and preserved each phrase, thought, and word from any error, omission, or inaccuracy. According to Peter, in ***II Peter 1:21, ". . . holy men of God spake as they were moved by the Holy Ghost"*** (see also ***I Peter 1:10-12***). If the interpreter does not accept the total inspiration of the Scriptures, it will be impossible for him to properly interpret them.

F. The Interpreter Must Approach the Word of God in True Faith

Hebrews 11:3 tells us ***"Through faith we understand . . ."*** Reason alone cannot perceive and grasp the Divine communication. It is, unfortunately, possible to have eyes and not see; ears and not hear; a heart and yet not perceive ***(Matthew 13:10-17; Isaiah 6:9,10).*** It was because the religious leaders depended on reason alone that they could not comprehend the sayings of Christ ***(Matthew 16:1-4; Mark 12:18-27; John 9:39-10:6).*** An overdependence on reason will result in faulty interpretation and misunderstanding. Faith, however, is not contrary to reason, but rather above it. Faith brings understanding to the heart which reason alone could never acquire. ***"But without faith it is impossible to please Him: for he that cometh to God must believe that He is, and that He is a rewarder of them that diligently seek Him" (Hebrews 11:6).***

G. **The Interpreter Needs a Renewed Mind**

In ***Romans 12:2*** the command is given; ***"be ye transformed by the renewing of your mind . . . "*** (see also ***Ephesians 4:23).*** The natural and carnal mind is at enmity with God and is not subject to His law. It cannot understand the things of the Spirit of God. Only the regenerated mind can feel at home in the Scriptures ***(I Corinthians 2:14-16; Romans 8:5-7; Philippians 2:2,3).***

H. **The Interpreter Needs to Depend Upon the Holy Spirit's Illumination**

It is necessary that the interpreter receive illumination from the Holy Spirit. The Spirit inspired the Word and it is He who must interpret that Word. This occurs through illumination. The Bible is primarily a spiritual book, and spiritual things must be spiritually discerned ***(I Corinthians 2:7-16).*** The interpreter must recognize the theological difference between (1) Revelation, (2) Inspiration, and (3) Illumination.

1. **Revelation** is **imparted truth** which could not be discovered by natural reasoning. The Bible is the written revelation of God. In it God has revealed Himself; that is, His nature, character and being. All that may be known of God in this life is founded in and upon the Scriptures. They are the only inspired and infallible authority for all Christian faith and practice.
2. **Inspiration** describes the **process** by which the revelation was recorded. The Scriptures are in infallible revelation because of inspiration. God brought infallible revelation through fallible men without violating their personalities ***(II Peter 1:20, 21; II Timothy 3:16).*** Revelation is the substance and inspiration is the process by which that substance is Divinely communicated.
3. **Illumination** is the **perception** of truth brought about by the influence of the Holy Spirit. Many times the word "revelation" in the New Testament actually refers, theologically, to illumination ***(Ephesians 1:17, 18).*** The believer today simply receives illumination of the revelation given by inspiration. Illumination is the supernatural opening of the understanding to receive that which is revealed in Scripture. Inspiration was infallible; Illumination is fallible. The Holy Spirit knows what He meant when He inspired the Word; we, therefore, need His illumination. We must be sensitive to the Spirit, for it is His ministry to lead us into all truth ***(John 15:26; 16:12, 13).*** The agent of inspiration becomes the agent of illumination and interpretation.

I. **The Interpreter Needs to Maintain a Spirit and Attitude of Prayer**

Those who wrote the Bible were all men of prayer. Much of the Word was communicated to them by the Spirit of God while they were in an attitude of prayer. Prayer is the method by which man communicates with God. Illumination of the Word will most often come as the interpreter waits upon the Lord in prayer. The apostles of the New Testament said, ***"But we will give ourselves continually to prayer, and to the ministry of the Word" (Acts 6:4).***

J. **The Interpreter Needs to Meditate on the Word**

In meditation upon the Word of God, the Spirit is able to bring holy thoughts to the heart and mind of the interpreter. To meditate means to "ponder; reflect; think deeply; to coverse with oneself." David said of the righteous man, ***"in His law doth he meditate day and night" (Psalms 1:2).*** (See also ***Joshua 1:8; Psalms 119:48, 78, 148.)***

K. **The Interpreter Must be Intellectually Honest**

Jesus said that an honest heart is good ground in which the seed of the Word may grow and bear fruit ***(Luke 8:15).*** If there is not intellectual honesty the interpreter can make the Word say whatever he desires. The dishonest interpreter can make the Scripture support any false doctrine he wishes to disseminate ***(II Corinthians 4:2; II Peter 3:15, 16; Ephesians 4:14).*** The false cults in Christendom, with their corrupt systems of hermeneutics, are not intellectually honest. Rather they twist the words of Scripture to suit their doctrines, deceiving thousands of people.

L. The Interpreter Needs to Recognize the Unity of the Spirit and the Word

The Spirit and the Word agree ***(I John 5:7, 8).*** The Spirit inspired the Word and so will never contradict it. No person can claim illumination by the Spirit in his interpretation of any passage if that interpretation is in conflict with other passages of Scripture. The believer must discern between the spirit of truth and the spirit of error ***(I John 4:1-6).*** The spirit of error can take a verse and purport it to say opposite of that which the spirit of truth is saying; when in reality no verse can be made to contradict another verse. The Spirit will never communicate to the mind of the believer any doctrine or meaning of Scripture which is not already in Scripture itself.

M. The Interpreter Needs to Recognize the Unity and Harmony of the Progressive Revelation of Scripture

1. There is *unity of progression* in the books of the Bible. The Bible is a unity; it is one Book of many books. A survey of the Bible shows clearly that the revelation of God to fallen man has been progressive. The revelation of the plan of redemption moves progressively through the histories of the Old and New Testaments. This leads to the realization that no one book of the Bible is complete in and of itself. Each book needs the other books to supply that which is incomplete in it. Every book has some main emphasis or theme which is only a part of the whole, and which adds to the chain of truth already linked together by the preceding books.

2. There is *harmony of revelation* in the books of the Bible; no book contradicts another. Each adds to and complements the others so that the sixty-six books of the Bible are a unity; a progressive revelation; one harmonious whole. Truth itself is a harmonious whole; the interpreter must, therefore, gather every verse in each book pertaining to a particular subject in order to see what the Spirit has revealed concerning that subject.

N. The Interpreter Must Understand the Relationship Between the Old and New Testaments

The theme of both Old and New Testaments is Jesus Christ and His plan of redemption. The Old Testament should be viewed as preparatory to the New Testament, with the Cross the dividing line between the two. Both testaments must be interpreted in the light of that which took place at the Cross. The dealings of God with Israel and the Gentiles under the Old Covenant must be distinguished from His dealings with them under the New Covenant ***(Jeremiah 31:31-34).***

O. The Interpreter Needs to be Diligent in His Use of Study Resources

The interpreter must avail himself of proven resource materials. It is pseudo-spirituality for an interpreter to boast that he studies only the Bible. Many men of God have produced study resources which are invaluable to the interpreter, and to ignore these aids is to sever oneself from much needed help. The Holy Spirit will not help an intellectually slothful interpreter; the student must not expect the Holy Spirit to do what he can do himself. However, this is not to deny the interpreter's utter dependence upon the Holy Spirit's illumination. A delicate balance must be constantly maintained between the spiritual and the intellectual. Paul exhorted Timothy: ***"Till I come, give attendance to reading, to exhortation, to doctrine" (I Timothy 4:13). "Study to show thyself approved unto God, a workman that needeth not to be ashamed, rightly dividing the word of truth." (II Timothy 2:15).***

P. The Interpreter Needs to Possess a Sound Mind

In ***II Timothy 1:7*** we read, ***"God hath not given us the spirit of fear; but of power, and of love, and of a sound mind."*** A sound mind has several distinct qualities:

1. Well-balanced
   a. Not highly fanciful
   b. Not hasty in judgment
   c. Not given to extremes or vain and foolish notions
2. Quick and clean in perception
3. Acute in intellect
4. Good judgment and reasoning ability
5. Able to communicate clearly

Chapter 3
THE METHODS OF INTERPRETATION

The interpreter of Scripture must constantly keep in clear focus the basic objective of interpretation: discovering the meaning intended by the author when he wrote. Through the centuries the interpreters of Scripture have developed various methods of interpretation. (This development through history will be traced in Chapter 4.) These methods comprised and actually originated as differing approaches to the interpretation of Scripture. As they were developed they became comprehensive systems of interpretation, each possessing its own set of rules. As methods, they each include their own distinctive group of principles.

Some of the most prominent methods will now be briefly defined and evaluated.

I. THE ALLEGORICAL METHOD

A. **Origin:** The allegorical method originated through the union of Greek philosophy and religion. With the rise of philosphy, the Greeks began to realize that they could not interpret their religious writings literally and still hold to their philosophy. If both were taken literally they would be contradictory. Because of their new found loyalty to philosophy they had to conclude, in order to reconcile the two, that their religious writings meant something other than what they literally said. The method they created to do this was allegorism.

B. **Definition:** The allegorical method presumes that beneath the plain and obvious sense of Scripture lies its true meaning. It believes that what the words of Scripture literally say are only external "chaff" which hides the true spiritual "what" of the Word. In allegorization, a passage with obvious literal meaning is interpreted using a point by point comparison, which brings out a hidden spiritual meaning not evident in the plain language of the passage. This method has been applied to the whole of Scripture by allegorists both ancient and modern. As an example of allegorism, Tan (p. 38) cites Pope Gregory the Great's interpretation of the Book of Job: "The patriarch's three friends denote the heretics; his seven sons are the twelve Apostles; his seven thousand sheep are God's faithful people; and this three thousand hump-backed camels are the depraved Gentiles."

C. **Evaluation:** Centuries have proven the allegorical method to be quite inadequate in the interpretation of Scripture. The error of this method begins at its foundational assumption: that what God said in plain language is not really what He meant.

It is a dangerous method in that there are no Scriptural boundaries to guide its implementation. Undoubtedly, this is the reason for the great variety of contradictory theological positions among allegorists. Through the allegorical method Scripture is interpreted apart from its grammatical-historical meaning. What the author was trying to plainly communicate is almost totally ignored and what the interpreter desires to say is forced upon it. Allegorism obscures both the literal and figurative elements in Scripture. By exalting the interpreter's intentions and ignoring the author's intended meaning, the allegorical method fails to reach the basic goal of interpretation and must be discarded.

Extreme typology borders on allegorization. However, it must be recognized that these two are not synonymous. The difference, as cited by Mickelsen (p. 238) quoting K. J. Woolcombe, is that typology is "the search for linkages between events, persons or things within the historical framework of revelation, whereas allegorism is the search for secondary and hidden meaning underlying the primary and obvious meanings of a narrative." The interpreter must also be careful not to confuse the practice of allegorization with the figure of speech called allegory. (For a discussion of the interpretation of allegory refer to Chapter 23, "The Allegorical Principle.")

II. THE MYSTICAL METHOD

A. **Origin:** Closely associated with the allegorical method is the mystical method of interpretation. Some scholars even view them as synonymous. However, here we will consider it on its own. In relation to the interpretation of Scripture, the origin of the mystical method can be traced to the Hagadic method of exegesis developed by the Palestinian Jews in the inter-testamental period. This method involved both allegorical and mystical interpretations of the Old Testament. In being over-anxious to apply Scripture to the lives of the people, interpreters mistook application for interpretation and read into Scripture depths of meaning not plainly there.

B. **Definition:** The mystical method presumes that hidden beneath the surface of the words and their plain sense there lies a multiplicity of meanings. It goes beyond the allegorical method by opening the door to a wide variety of interpretations. Using the mystical method, a passage of Scripture with obvious literal meaning is interpreted to have a number of exalted spiritual meanings. Because of the professed desire to reach beyond the letter into the spirit of the Word, the function of this method has also been called "spiritualization."

As an example of mystical interpretation, Terry (p. 165) refers to Swedenborg's interpretation of ***Exodus 20:13: "Thou shalt not kill."*** In applying a three-fold sense of Scripture to this commandment, he says that its *natural sense* is that murder, hatred and revenge are forbidden; its *spiritual sense* is that "to act the devil and destroy a man's soul" is forbidden; and its *heavenly sense* is that for the angels, hating the Lord and His Word is as murder.

C. **Evaluation:** History has proven the mystical method to be misleading and of little value in the interpreting of Scripture. The error in its foundational assumption goes beyond that of the allegorical method in that it presumes that a Scripture may have any number of meanings. In other words, in authoring Scripture, God meant many things other than those He actually said. The objection to this is, that if God did not mean what He said, then how can the interpreter discover what He did mean? Instead of regarding Scripture as a sensible communication from God, mystics turn it into a riddle and make it say almost anything other than what God meant for it to say. Differing from allegorizers, who tend to follow some of comparison, spiritualizers are more erratic, not bound by any law. They each become a law of interpretation to themselves. By exalting the interpreter's intentions and ignoring the author's intended meaning, the mystical method fails to reach the basic goal of interpretation and must be discarded.

III. THE DEVOTIONAL METHOD

A. **Origin:** Like the mystical, the devotional method of interpretation originated with the Hagadic exegesis of the inter-testamental period. In seeking to apply the Scriptures to their lives, Jewish scribes began to interpret them in the light of their own life situations. In their zeal for application they produced faulty interpretation. In church history this method had its greatest emphasis among the Pietists of the Post-Reformation period. Thus it has also been known as the Pietistic method of interpretation.

B. **Definition:** The devotional method belives that the Bible was written for the personal edification of every believer and that its personalized hidden meaning can only be revealed by the shining of a great inner spiritual light. ***I John 2:20*** is often used as a proof-text for this. It searches the Scripture to discover meaning that will build up the spiritual life. In interpretation that which is most important is not what God said to others, but what He is saying to the interpreter. Thus, to interpret the Scriptures devotionally is to search beyond their plain obvious meaning for spiritual meaning applicable to the beliver's life. As an example of devotional interpretation, some well-meaning Christians have interpreted ***Matthew 10:9, 10, 19*** to mean that in their evangelizing they should neither take any material provision nor make any spiritual preparation.

C. **Evaluation:** Time has proven the devotional method to be quite dangerous as a system of interpretation. The chief danger of this method is that in seeking to apply Scripture personally the interpreter may ignore the plain literal sense of what God was saying to those in that particular historical setting, and thus apply Scripture self-centeredly. Two other weaknesses, noted by Ramm (p. 62, 63), are that devotional interpretation falls prey to allegorization or excessive typology, and may become a substitute for the requisite exegetical and doctrinal studies of the Bible.

However, this does not rule out altogether the devotional, practical and edifying use of the Scripture. Certainly this is a prominent part of and purpose of Scripture, and the Word of God is of no value to the believer unless it is applied to his life practically. The interpreter must recognize that Scripture is meant to be applied devotionally, but that this can only be properly done after it has been interpreted literally and historically. Devotional interpretation must also be harmonized with doctrinal interpretation.

IV. THE RATIONALISTIC METHOD

A. **Origin:** Having its seeds in ancient history, the rationalistic method blossomed during the Post-Reformation period and is still bearing fruit in this modern age. Through recent centuries the seat of rationalism has been in Germany, where the Schools of Higher Criticism have attempted to undermine the authority of Scripture. There are actually many different methods that are here being summed up under this title because of their common characteristics.

B. **Definition:** The rationalistic method presumes that the Bible is not the authoritative inspired Word of God. It interprets Scripture as a human document in the light of human reason. With the rationalist, "Nature is the standard, and reason is the guide." If the Bible can be made to harmonize with the knowledge of the interpreter, then it is to be understood as meaning what it says; but if not, it is to be regarded as mythical, or used by way of accommodation. Thus, a sort of educated modern mentality is used to judge and interpret Scripture. As examples of rationalistic interpretation: to explain away the supernatural, Lazarus is said to have gone into a coma rather than having died, and Jesus is said to have only appeared to have walked on the water; to undermine the authority and veracity of Scripture, historical events such as the crossing of the Red Sea and the transfiguration of Christ are explained as either fanciful exaggerations or contrived myths.

C. **Evaluation:** Several generations have proven this method to be little more than the method of unbelief. In fact, rationalistic exegesis could be better termed "exit-Jesus." Though claiming the title "rational," this method is actually most irrational. It is virtually uninterested in what the writers literally said, but cares only for what the interpreter thinks they should have said. It exalts the god of reason above the authority of the Word of God. By it the interpreter sets himself up as the standard of truth and only sees value in Scripture as it confirms his conclusions. For the interpreter who views Scripture as the inspired Word of God, the rationalistic method in all its various forms must be totally rejected.

V. THE LITERAL METHOD

A. **Origin:** In relation to Scripture, the literal method of interpretation is the oldest in existence. It is said to have originated with Ezra, the Father of Hermeneutics. The progress of its history will be traced in Chapter 4 through the Palestinian Jews, Christ and the Apostles, the School of Antioch, and the Reformers, to the fundamentalist Conservatives of the present day.

B. **Definition:** The literal method assumes that the words of Scripture in their plain evident meaning are reliable; that God intended His revelation to be understood by all who believe; that the words of Scripture communicate what God wants man to know; and that God based the communication of truth on the regular laws governing written communication, thereby intending for it to be interpreted by those same laws. This is not to deny the Holy Spirit's involvement in both the production and the interpretation of the Bible.

The expression "literal sense" may be defined as: the usual, customary, and socially accepted meaning conveyed by words or expressions in their particular contexts. It involves that which a particular word meant to the original writer and readers. It recognizes that a word may have different meanings in different contexts and thus must be interpreted in the light of its contextual usage. It contends that though a word may possibly have several meanings, in any one particular usage it generally will have but one intended meaning.

According to Tan (p. 29), "To interpret 'literally' means to explain the original sense of the speaker or writer according to the normal, customary, and proper usage of words and language." He notes that this method is also called the Grammatico-Historical method because, in order to determine the normal and customary usages of Bible language, the accepted rules of grammar and rhetoric must be considered and the historical and cultural aspects of Bible times must be taken into consideration.

Though we do not totally agree with the results of Tan's application of the literal method, we do endorse his expansion of it (p. 30-35), in the following four areas:

1. **The Literal Sense does not exclude the figurative.** Some interpreters have used the term figurative in opposition to the term literal, as though the figurative meaning of words were opposed to their literal sense. However, in that figurative language is a part of normal communication, it also is encompassed by the literal system of interpretation. Thus, the literal includes the figurative.

2. **The Literal Method does not exclude the spiritual meaning.** Some interpreters have used the term spiritual in opposition to the term literal as though the spiritual meaning of Scripture were opposed to its literal meaning. Under the title of "the spiritual method," some interpreters have spiritualized Scripture to mean something other than what it says. The literal method, though rejecting spiritualization, does admit the spiritual substance and nature of the Scriptures. The Bible is a spiritual book conveying spiritual truth and therefore must be spiritually interpreted. This can be done by accepting as sufficient the illuminated literal meaning of the words.

3. **The Literal Interpretation does not exclude application.** Some interpreters confuse interpretation with application. John Calvin said, "The Word of God is inexhaustable and applicable at all times, but there is a difference between explanation and application, and application must be consistent with explanation." The task of literal interpretation is first to discern the meaning of God's Word, and then, upon that basis, to apply it. A general rule of the literal method is: "There is one interpretation, but many applications."

4. **The Literal Method does not exclude depth of meaning.** Some interpreters believe that the literal method greatly limits the believer in discovering the divine depths of truth latent in Scripture. Indeed, some definitions of this method do, but here it is defined to include depth of meaning within certain necessary limitations. In that God is the virtual Author of Scripture, some truths therein are patent, outward and obvious, while others are latent, inward and hidden. Historical events do have spiritual significance, and certain figures of speech, such as types, symbols, and allegories, do have hidden meaning. However, this meaning is solidly based on the earthly sense of the words and necessitates that interpretation remain within the proper boundaries of truths plainly revealed in God's Word.

C. **Evaluation:** In conclusion, the literal method stands out among the rest as the only sound, safe and sensible approach to the interpretation of Scripture. Each of the other methods have been proven inadequate in that they lack God-given and well-defined boundaries. It is upon this literal method that this text is built.

Chapter 4
A BRIEF HISTORY OF HERMENEUTICS

The student will benefit greatly from a general knowledge of the history of Biblical hermeneutics. History serves to show the origin, progress and development of hermeneutical principles. It gives, as well, a working knowledge of the different periods, schools and methods of Biblical interpretation.

In addition it shows what external and internal pressures were brought to bear upon the interpreter of the Scriptures. One may look at the search by God's people through the centuries to discover what God meant by what He said. A knowledge of the history of Biblical hermeneutics can be a valuable safeguard, and at times a guideline, in helping the interpreter avoid the problems faced by previous interpreters. The more one understands the proper principles of interpretation, the better qualified he will be to handle the Word of God as an interpreter of the Divine communication.

Since the Fall, man has by nature been spiritually and mentally dull concerning the things of God. The Scriptures attest to this fact: ***Isaiah 6:9-10; Matthew 13:13-17; Jeremiah 5:21; Ezekiel 12:2; II Peter 3:16; Luke 24:45.*** Sin cut off fellowship between God and man, and produced a communication gap which must be bridged. God took the initiative in restoring fellowship by giving His Word. That message must be interpreted for man. The history of hermeneutics shows us man's effort to receive this Divine communication.

The history of hermeneutics has been more fully covered by better qualified men, and the student is referred to these in the Bibliography. The present consideration attempts only to give a brief history of hermeneutics, defining the boundaries of each period, listing the methods most often used, and giving a sketch of the key men and developments of that period.

Throughout the course of these historical sketches the student will come across indented notations. These are interpretative lessons which can be drawn from those particular time periods. This chapter is not designed to catalogue history, rather to interpret it. It will be seen that the prevailing attitude toward the Scriptures during any particular period generally affected the methods by which the Scriptures were interpreted.

I. JEWISH HERMENEUTICS

A. **Period (457 BC - 1975 AD):** The period of Jewish hermeneutics reaches from approximately the time of Ezra to the present day. This is due to the fact that the nation as a whole rejected their Messiah and therefore Jewish hermeneutics is to be distinguished from Christian hermeneutics.

B. **Methods:** In Ancient Jewish hermeneutics the dominant methods of interpretation were the literal and allegorical. In the last few centuries modern Judaism has emphasized rationalistic methods of interpretation.

C. **History**

1. **Ezra, The Father of Hermeneutics:** The weight of opinion considers Ezra to be the first of the notable Jewish interpreters and the founder of the Palestinian literal school of interpretation. With the loss of the temple and its ceremonial function and the cessation of the throne of Judah at Jerusalem, the Jews in Babylonian captivity resorted to the Sacred Writings for comfort and strength. The Law and the Prophets became their refuge when bereft of all the externals of the Mosaic religion. At the close of the 70 years in Babylon, a remnant of the Jews returned to Palestine to rebuild the temple and the city of Jerusalem. Their desire was to restore the glory of their Mosaic heritage. However, the Babylonian Jews had learned to speak Aramaic, not Hebrew. Thus there existed a language gap between them and their Scriptures. Ezra the scribe, and with him a number of Levites, undertook the great task of translating and interpreting the Sacred Writings, concentrating on the Law ***(Nehemiah 8:1-8; 10-18; Ezra 8:15-20).***

   NOTE: This illustrates that in interpretation it is essential to first bridge the linguistic gap. All hermeneutics is based first on translation.

   Ezra the priestly scribe took the Book of the Law and, standing on a pulpit of wood, ***"caused the people to understand the Law . . . So they read in the book of the law of God distinctly, and gave the sense, and caused them to understand the reading" (Nehemiah 8:7, 8).***

So we see in the efforts of Ezra and the Levites the first intimation in Scripture of Jewish interpretation and formal exposition of the Word of God. The books of Ezra and Nehemiah show how the areas of the Law pertaining to mixed marriages, observances of feasts and fasts were interpreted quite literally to the people by this great priest and scribe.

NOTE: Thus we see Ezra using literal and practical methods of interpretation.

2. **The Synagogue — Great and Local:** The word "synagogue" means literally "to lead, bring or gather together." It refers to a place where Jews gather for worship and religious study. The synagogue dates back to the time of the captivity in Babylon. Having no Temple and desirous of gathering together for the reading of the sacred Scriptures, the Jews built synagogues. By means of the synagogue service the Law was kept alive in the hearts of the people. Ezekiel's house was very likely such a gathering place ***(Ezekiel 8:1; 20:1-3).***

The Great Synagogue, in Jewish history, was an assembly or council of 120 members, probably founded and presided over by Ezra after the return from the captivity. Nehemiah referred to the "chief of the fathers of all the people, the priests, and the Levites" under Ezra the Scribe, gathered together to interpret the Law ***(Nehemiah 8:13).*** This verse implies the formation of a council to arrange religious matters; the forerunner of the Sanhedrin, which had its earliest roots in the time of Moses ***(Numbers 11:16, 17)*** and Jehosaphat ***(II Chronicles 19:8-11).*** The Great Synagogue of Ezra's time instituted several post-Mosaic festivals and organized the synagogue ritual, including the systematic reading and exposition of the Scriptures. Their motto was "Set a hedge about the Law."

The Great Synagogue was represented by "the elders" and "they of old time" ***(Matthew 5:21, 27, 33).*** These succeeded the ministry of the prophets and continued through to the days of Christ. By that time it had developed into the Sanhedrin; which consisted of:

a. The High Priest as President
b. The Chief Priests or Heads of the 24 Courses of the Priests
c. The Scribes or Lawyers, interpreters of the Law
d. The Elders, who were representatives of the laity

Because of the need for mass instruction the Jews began to institute local synagogues in various cities, which functioned in allegiance to the Sanhedrin. The local synagogue's services were presided over by a Chief or Rabbi, assisted by a council of elders ***(Mark 5:22, 35; Luke 4:20; John 16:2; Acts 18:8).*** The main object was not public worship, but rather religious instruction from the Law. By New Testament times most cities had a synagogue in which "Moses was preached" ***(Acts 15:21).*** However, these local synagogues could only promulgate the interpretations of the law handed down from the Sanhedrin. Thus, when the Sanhedrin rejected Jesus as their Messiah, so did the local synagogues.

NOTE: Centralized ecclesiastical authority may originate with noble motivation, but it can easily degenerate until it defeats its own purpose. The same walls that lock truth in may also lock further truth out. We should constantly be aware of the dangers involved in any central ecclesiastical body becoming the final authority on the interpretation of Scripture.

3. **The Scribes:** The Hebrew scribe or writer appears to have been at first a court or military official ***(Exodus 5:6; Judges 5:14).*** Later he became a secretary or recorder for kings, priests and prophets ***(II Samuel 8:17; 20:25; II Kings 18:18; I Kings 4:3).*** Finally the scribe was acknowledged as a secretary of state, a doctor or teacher ***(Ezra 7:6).*** As a group, scribes became a class or guild ***(I Chronicles 2:55).*** They were the copyists and authorized expounders of the sacred Scriptures. By the time of Christ they had become known as Lawyers; the official interpreters and expounders of the Law ***(Matthew 22:35; 23:1-33; Luke 5:30; 10:25).*** By failing to maintain the purity of interpretation exemplified by Ezra, they came under the same denunciations of Christ as did the Priests, Pharisees and Sadducees.

NOTE: By missing the spirit of the truth the interpreter will misinterpret the truth and be left only with the letter of it.

4. **Schools of Interpretation:** In the generations succeeding Ezra and Nehemiah, and with the end of the prophetic voice with the prophet Malachi, various schools of interpretation emerged.

a. **The Palestinian Jews**—Ezra was the founder of the Palestinian literalist school of interpretation. Following his example, the Jews accepted totally the inspiration and authority of the Word of God. Their greatest objective was the interpretation of the Law. In dealing with the Scriptures, their order of priority was (1) the Law, (2) the Prophets and (3) the Writings.

However, in seeking to "set a hedge about the law," they desired to formulate an authoritative interpretation. While they guarded the law to the letter, they also accumulated numerous traditions which they placed alongside the law. These traditions grew out of their desire to apply the law to their ever-changing conditions of life. As this body of traditional interpretations grew it became known as the Oral Law, which through the centuries gained equal status with the Written Law in authority. Christ rebuked them for this because the oral traditions made the Word of God "null and void" ***(Mark 7:13.*** Amplified).

In the 2nd Century A.D., Rabbi Judah produced a written compilation of all the oral law then in existence. This Second Law became known as the Mishna, which means "the oral doctrine and the study of it."

In order to further establish the authority of the oral law the Jews originated a false tradition saying that Moses had received it at Mount Sinai. They claimed that he had passed it on to Joshua, who gave it to the elders. The elders passed it on to the prophets, and later it came into the hands of the Rabbis.

NOTE: By adding to the Word of God and canonizing their interpretations, interpreters may cause the Scriptures to be nullified. The interpreter must never exalt his interpretation of Scripture to a place of equal authority with Scripture itself.

In the Mishna, which was an interpretation of the Mosaic Law, there were two kinds of interpretation:

(1) **Halakah** — This refers to legal exegesis which, in the Mishna, was only used in its treatment of the Pentateuch. It was used primarily in dealing with the code of the law. Its aim was to deduce from the Law rules on subjects not specifically dealt with in the Law. This was done by comparing and combining relevant written laws. This type of interpretation could be described as rigid and legalistic.

NOTE: Through this kind of interpretation, much was read into the Law of Moses that was not really there. It also led to the authoritative interpretation by the Pharisees.

(2) **Hagadah** — This refers to homiletic exegesis which, in the Mishna, was used throughout its treatment of the entire Old Testament. It was used primarily in dealing with non-legal portions of Scripture, such as history, prophecy and poetry. Its aim was to stir the Jews to godly living. This was done by using such homiletic devices as wise sayings, parables, allegories, legends, proverbs and mystical interpretations of the Old Testament events. This type of interpretation could be described as devotional and sermonic, with a constant emphasis on the practical.

NOTE: Because this kind of interpretation utilized much non-Biblical material which became authoritative, it weakened the authority of the Scriptures and opened the door to the authoritative use of more legends, secret meanings and allegorical expositions.

With the codification of the Mishna, many Rabbis began to write commentaries on it. These interpretations of the oral law were produced from the 3rd to the 5th Centuries and became known as the

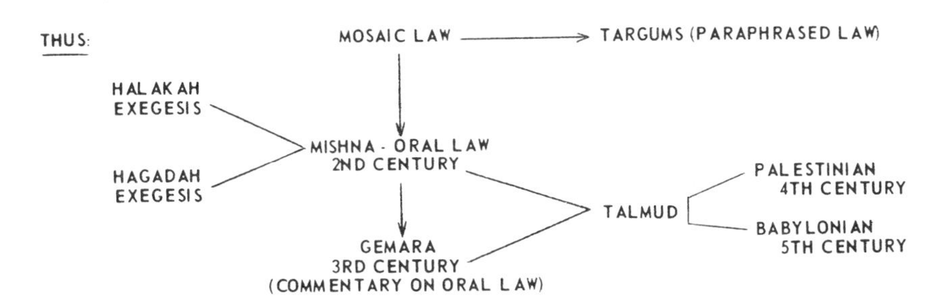

Gemara. Thus, the Gemara was a commentary on a commentary. These two, the Mishna and the Gemara, together constituted the Talmud, of which there were two versions: one produced in Palestine at the close of the 4th Century; one produced in Babylon at the close of the 5th Century. Other writings, known as the Targums, were actually paraphrases of most of the Old Testament.

Since the Hagadic methods of interpretation spread throughout the world of Judaism it is worthwhile to note some of the Hagadic principles. Terry (p. 608) refers to four of the thirty two rules of interpretation collected by Eliezer Ben-Jose as examples of Hagadic hermeneutics.

(1) The use of one of three different particles indicated that there were hidden meanings in the text not evident to the ''literal'' reader. This rule is illustrated by ***Genesis 21:1,*** where it is said, ***''Jehovah visited Sarah''*** (שָׂרָה = Sarah, אֶת = herself). The untranslated particle (אֶת – normally used to identify and emphasize the object of a verb) is supposed to show that the Lord also visited other women besides Sarah.

NOTE: There is no Scriptural basis for this principle. It obviously leads to random exegesis and fanciful interpretations.

(2) A subject will shed light on others while it explains itself. Thus in ***Jeremiah 46:22, ''The voice thereof shall go like a serpent,''*** is a statement which serves, besides describing the loud cry of Egypt, to indicate that the serpent sent up a great cry when the Lord pronounced His curse against it in Eden.

NOTE: This principle detracts from any balanced emphasis of the plain meaning of Scripture.

(3) Great concepts are represented and made plain by small natural things. Thus in ***Deuteronomy 32:2, ''My doctrine shall drop as the rain,''*** the great doctrines of revelation are made understandable by comparison with the rain.

NOTE: This principle is consistent with Scripture and is actually a principle of symbolism demonstrating accommodation.

(4) Explanations are obtained by reducing the letters of a word to their numerical value and substituting another word or phrase having the same value. Thus, the sum of the letters in the name of Eliezer, Abraham's servant, is equivalent to 318, the number of trained men ***(Genesis 14:14).*** Accordingly this shows that Eliezer alone was worth a host of servants.

NOTE: This principle has no foundation in Scripture and turns the Scriptures into putty in the hands of the exegete.

The Palestinian Jews did accept the Bible as the inspired and infallible Word of God, but this belief degenerated into Bibliolatry. With a superstitious reverence for the Word of God, they viewed the very letters of the Law as sacred and even counted them. A prime example of the kind of error that Hagadic hermeneutics led to is seen in Rabbi Akiba. He maintained that every repetition, figure, parallelism, synonym, word, letter, particle, and even the very shape of a letter, had a hidden or secret meaning.

NOTE: The error seen here is letterism, which sees great significance in the minutest details. This arose when men began to worship the Scriptures and forgot their Author.

In reviewing Palestinian Jewish hermeneutics, one ascetic sect worthy of note is the Qumran community. They were a group who had isolated themselves from society in order to live in strict accordance with the Law of Moses. Their exclusivism crept into their hermeneutics, and they tended to interpret Scripture in terms of their own community. This often led them to ignore the context in interpreting a Scripture.

Mickelsen (p. 23) notes that their three main procedures were to interpret the text in terms of (1) Qumran, (2) another contemporary group, and (3) eschatology. His evaluation is that in their haste to apply the Scriptures to themselves and their own times the Qumran interpreters failed to recognize what the writers were trying to convey to those who first read their words.

NOTE: This illustrates one way in which the interpreter can be lead to violate the foundational principle of context. Their exclusivism caused them to be self-centered in their interpretation. Thus, they fell into the pitfall of building their eschatology around their own movement. A "we are the people" attitude will always produce biased and corrupted interpretation.

The Palestinian Jews did develop some sound principles of exegesis that are still valid today. Ramm (p. 46-47) gleans six principles from Hillel, Ishmael and Eliezer, notable Jewish interpreters. He states that they insisted on the following rules:

(1) A word must be understood in terms of its sentence and a sentence in terms of its context.

(2) Scriptures dealing with similar topics should be compared, and in some instances a third Scripture would relieve the apparent contradiction between two Scriptures.

(3) A clear passage is to be given preference over an obscure one if they deal with the same subject matter.

(4) Very close attention is to be paid to spelling, grammar, and figures of speech.

(5) By use of logic we can determine the application of Scripture to those problems in life Scripture has not specifically treated.

(6) The God of Israel spoke in the tongues of men and this asserts that the God of Israel has adapted His revelation to its recipients.

NOTE: These are all valid principles which are discussed in other poritions of this text.

The Palestinian Jews are to be commended for their acceptance of the inspiration and authority of the Scriptures and for their development of some sound principles in relation to literal interpretation. However, a failure to produce sound exegesis was caused by their yielding to traditionalism, letterism and exclusivism.

b. **The Alexandrian Jews**—As the colony of Jews in Alexandria were Hellenized they developed a system of hermeneutics distinct from that of the Jews in Palestine. Their greatest link with Palestinian interpretation was their acceptance of Hagadic principles. This can be seen by the admittance of apocryphal books into the Septuagint. The Jews being saturated with Greek culture, it was only suitable that their Hebrew Scriptures be translated into the modern Greek language. While performing this task, the Jews demonstrated a Hagadic looseness by adding philosophy, fiction and legend to Scripture.

NOTE: Wrong concepts concerning inspiration always constitute a wrong foundation for interpretation. If the foundation is out of line, then the whole structure will be as well.

The interpretation of the Scriptures by the Alexandrian Jews was deeply affected by their Greek cultural environment. The rise of Greek philosophy had caused problems in that it contradicted established Greek religion. To solve the conflict between their philosophy and religion, the Greeks developed the method of interpretation known as allegorization. They taught that the true meaning of a passage was not its literal or plain sense, but was secret, hidden beneath the surface. This allowed them to interpret their religious writings to mean whatever they desired. By allegorizing the religious heritage of their gods, the Greeks were able to bridge the gap which existed between their religion and philosophy.

The Jews in Alexandria, though rejecting Greek religion, began to accept Greek philosophy. Though "Sons of Moses" in religion, the Jews became "Sons of Plato" in philosophy. Consequently they faced a problem very similar to that of the Greeks: how to reconcile their Hebrew faith with their Greek philosophy. The Jews found a ready-made answer in Greek allegorization. It was the "golden calf" that had just come out of the melting pot of Greek religion and philosophy, and the Jews found it convenient to bow down to the same idol. Later on, this method of allegorization filtered into the Christian Church, causing much confusion.

NOTE: Though Scripture often needs to be interpreted culturally, the interpreter must recognize that God's Word is essentially trans-cultural. He must avoid the danger of allowing his own culture to dictate and corrupt his interpretation of Scripture.

Aristobulus (160 BC) is suggested to have been the first Jewish writer who used allegorical methods of interpretation. He said that Greek philosophy borrowed from the Old Testament and especially from the Law of Moses. He also taught that Greek philosophy could be found in the Law by using the allegorical method.

NOTE: Much misinterpretation comes because the interpreter reads into the Scriptures his own ideas or bias. This is called eisegesis (reading into), which is the opposite of exegesis (drawing out what is really there).

The best known of all Jewish interpreters in Alexandria was Philo (20 BC - 54 AD). He was a man of mixture: he possessed a deep reverence for the Scriptures, but also had a great fondness for Greek philosophy. To reconcile these, he counted Greek philosophy as belonging to the Law of Moses. To substantiate this, he developed an elaborate system of allegorization, borrowing some of the Halachic and Hagadic principles from the Palestinian Jews. Though not its originator, he is spoken of as the "fountain-head" of allegorical exegesis. Berkhof (p. 16), briefly defines Philo's principles of interpretation to be the following:

(1) The literal sense must be excluded if it says anything unworthy of God.

(2) The literal sense must be excluded if a contradiction would be involved.

(3) The literal sense must be excluded when the Scripture itself allegorizes.

(4) The Scripture is to be allegorized:

when expressions are doubled
when superfluous words are used
when there is a repetition of facts already known
when an expression is varied
when synonyms are employed
when a play on words is possible in any of its varieties
when words admit of a slight variation
when the expression is unusual
when there is anything abnormal in the number or tense

Philo's principles can be summarized under two main points: he believed that there was a literal sense to Scripture, but that it represented the body of flesh—for the immature; the allegorical or hidden meaning was the important sense, representing the soul—for the mature.

As an example of Philo's exegesis, Ramm (p. 28), points out that Philo interpreted Abraham's journey to Palestine to actually be referring to a Stoic philosopher's moving from sensual understanding (Chaldea), to the enlightenment of Platonism (Palestine), and marrying abstract wisdom (Sarah). Thus Philo missed the mark. As an exegete he was more of an example of what should not be done. He ignored the grammatical, contextual, stylistic and historical factors and opened the door to all types of mininterpretation. By de-emphasizing the historical standpoint of the author, he forced strange and mystic meanings into the text. Through allegorization, he ended up compromising and corrupting the very Scriptures he revered so highly. This could be said as well of the Alexandrian Jews in general.

NOTE: The wrong use of allegorization causes it to become an arbitrary system of interpretation, allowing the interpreter to impose upon Scripture any meaning he desires. He can make the Scriptures say whatever he chooses for them to say. Extreme allegorization does not take into consideration what the writer had in mind when he wrote. It, nevertheless whether theoretically or practically, ignores the literal sense of Scripture.

c. **The Karaites**—A sect of Jews known as the Karaites ("readers") was founded in 800 AD by Anan ben David. They are considered the "Protestants" of Judaism. They rejected the authority of the oral law and the Hagadic method of exegesis. The Karaites were literalists: they accepted as basic the literal rendering of the text unless, by virtue of the nature of the sentence, this was not possible. In rejecting allegorization and the Hagadic method, their exegesis was far more sound that that of the Palestinian or Alexandrian Jews. However, they did accept the Talmud as an aid to understanding the Scriptures. Beginning with the ninth century, the influence of the Karaites became widespread among Judaism.

NOTE: By using the literal sense as the basis for interpretation, sound exegesis will be more readily achieved.

Rabbi Saadia-Gaon (892 AD) became the first Jew to develop the science of grammar.

NOTE: The study of language is one of the first steps toward solid interpretation.

d. **The Cabalists**—This 12th Century movement developed a system of letterism and allegorism through exegetical gymnastics; actually a hyper-literalism. The Massoretic text which had been produced by the Rabbis was looked upon as having supernatural power. The very numbers of the letters, the individual letters, the words, vowel-points, accents, all had special significance. Cabalists also employed the allegorical method of the Alexandrian Jews, resulting in absurd interpretations.

NOTE: Letterism, allegorism and a superstitious reverence for the Scriptures produces utter confusion.

e. **The Spanish Jews**—In Spain, the Jews from the 12th to the 15th Century developed a healthier method of interpretation. The Christian Church was in a general state of darkness, but there were some Spanish Jews who did maintain at least a small lighted lamp. Even in the midst of persecution, certain key men arose and made significant contributions to the science of hermeneutics.

Aben Ezra (1092 AD) was a great rabbinical scholar who favored a thoroughly grammatical interpretation. While refuting the fanciful interpretations of his day, he contended that "if the plain interpretation of a passage be not opposed to reason, why should we seek for any other?" As a matter of balance, he did acknowledge that some phrases contained both a literal and symbolic meaning. His method was to first determine the grammatical sense of a passage, secondly to consult another version, and finally to utilize Jewish tradition.

NOTE: If the literal sense makes sense, seek no other sense.

Moses Maimonides (1135 AD) who, as a youth, was driven from Spain by the Mohammedan persecution, became known among his people as "the Second Moses". His great aims were to harmonize Judaism with science and philosophy, and to harmonize the written and oral laws. His controversial teachings divided Judaism into two bitterly opposed factions.

NOTE: If the interpreter's goal is off center, his efforts will be in vain.

f. **The French Jews**—Among the French Jews there were two men worthy of consideration. One, a scholar of note, was Rashi (1040 AD). His method was to give a literal explanation of the Hebrew text. However, his respect for the Talmud led him to combine Hagadic exegesis with the literal.

NOTE: Holding to a literal method of interpretation will not insure pure doctrine. Mixture can infiltrate any system of hermeneutics through an inconsistency in application.

Another scholar of note was Ralbag (1300 AD). His exegetical, procedure according to Terry (p. 625), was to first explain the words of a section, to then view the passage in the light of its context, and finally to make a practical application.

NOTE: Three prominent principles of interpretation are the linguistic, context, and moral principles.

g. **The Modern Jews**—According to Terry (p. 628), the general trend of the modern Jew is towards rationalism. Their appeal is to reason and conscience in the exposition of the Scriptures. They reject the revelation of God in Christ. They expect no Messiah nor the restoration of the Mosaic economy. Though the Jews were entrusted with the Oracles of God ***(Romans 3:1, 2)***, the veil of unbelief prohibits an understanding of them ***(II Corinthians 3:14-16)***. The Jews will never properly interpret their Scripture until they accept its key, Jesus of Nazareth.

NOTE: The Old Testament cannot be properly interpreted apart from its key, the Lord Jesus Christ.

II. APOSTOLIC HERMENEUTICS

A. **Period (26 AD - 95 AD):** The period of Apostolic Hermeneutics reaches from the ministry of Christ to the death of the Apostle John.

B. **Methods:** In Apostolic Hermeneutics the literal method prevailed. By the inspiration of the Holy Spirit, the New Testament writers infallibly interpreted the Old Testament in their writings.

C. **History**

1. **Jesus Christ, the Perfect Interpreter:** Because Jesus was the Living Word, He could infallibly interpret the written Word. He was the personified interpretation of the Old Testament: the Law, the Psalms and the Prophets ***(John 5:39; Luke 24:27, 44).*** During His ministry He interpreted to His disciples, from the Scriptures, the things concerning Himself. He opened their understanding accordingly. Rules or principles of interpretation were part of His very nature and being, for He was God's Word to man, incarnate; He was the bridge between God and man. The communication gap was bridged in and through Him. Because of the purity of His hermeneutics, Jesus was able to expose all corrupt interpretation. He condemned the Halachic and Hagadic tradition of the elders because they made the Word of God of none effect ***(Matthew 15:1-9; Mark 7:1-7).*** He reproved the Scribes and Pharisees, the authorized interpreters of the Law, for their legalistic interpretations of the Scriptures, which brought the people into total bondage ***(Matthew 23:1-33).*** Christ also rebuked the Sadducees for their ignorance of the power of God and of the Scriptures ***(Matthew 22:29).***

   The religious leaders of His day were blinded by unbelief and false hermeneutics; thus they crucified the very Messiah whose coming their own Scriptures foretold ***(Acts 13:27).***

   The following are examples of some of the principles Jesus used in His interpretation of the Old Testament:

   a. **The Context Principle** ***(Matthew 22:41-46)***—Jesus interpreted ***Psalms 110:1*** in the light of the whole context of the Old Testament, which attests to the Diety of the Messiah.

   b. **The First Mention Principle** ***(Matthew 19:3-9)***—Jesus used the first mention of marriage in ***Genesis 2:24*** to interpret the Mosaic commandments concerning divorce.

   c. **The Election Principle** ***(Matthew 12:15-21)***—On the basis on the election principle, Jesus interpreted ***Isaiah 42:1-4*** to be a reference to His own election as the chosen servant of Jehovah.

   d. **The Covenantal Principle** ***(Matthew 12:1-4)***—When dealing with the violation of the Sabbath Day, Jesus brought in David, a covenant man, as a witness. Because David was involved in a higher covenant, as was Jesus, he was able to transcend the ceremonial law of the Mosaic Covenant.

   e. **The Ethnic Division Principle** ***(Matthew 10:5, 6)***—In commissioning the twelve apostles to go only to ***"the lost sheep of the House of Israel,"*** Jesus used the ethnic division principle to interpret and apply an Old Testament prophetic stream ***(Jeremiah 23:1-4; 50:6, 17; Ezekiel 34:1-19).***

   f. **The Chronometrical Principle** ***(Luke 21:20-24)***—Jesus utilized the chronometrical principle to itnerpret a certain prophetic portion of Daniel ***(Daniel 11:33).***

   g. **The Christo-Centric Principle** ***(Luke 24:27-44)***—On the road to Emmaus, Jesus used the Christo-Centric principle to interpret portions of the Law, the Psalms and the Prophets to the two disciples.

   h. **The Moral Principle** ***(Matthew 24:36-39)***—Jesus used the moral principle to interpret the days of Noah and draw from them a spiritual lesson.

   i. **The Symbolic Principle** ***(Matthew 21:42-44)***—In interpreting two statements from the Old Testament, it seems apparent that Jesus used the symbolic principle to refer to the rock as being symbolic of Himself.

   j. **The Parabolic Principle** ***(Matthew 13:1-9, 18-23)***—With the parabolic principle, Jesus interpreted His own parable of the sower.

   k. **The Typical Principle** ***(Luke 11:29, 30)***—Jesus identified Jonah's experience as typical and then interpreted it using the typical principle.

2. **The Apostles, The Inspired Interpreters:** The Lord Jesus poured out His Spirit upon His Apostles. There is no doubt that great understanding and illumination came to them by the Holy Spirit ***(John 16:9-16; Luke 24:27, 44; II Corinthians 3:14-18).*** They became the infallible interpreters of the Old

Testament writings. This is seen by their use of the Old Testament in the New Testament. The Apostles rejected the allegorical interpretation of the Old Testament as practiced in the Alexandrian school. Paul condemned Jewish fables, Jewish traditions, endless genealogies, false knowledge, Greek philosophy and the Jewish Midrashim. He knew of these things and counted them all refuse for the knowledge of God in Christ ***(Colossians 2:8; I Timothy 1:4; 4:7; 6:20; II Timothy 2:14-16, 23).*** The following are examples of some of the principles the Apostles used in their interpretation of the Old Testament.

a. **The Context Principle** ***(I Peter 2:4-10)***—In verse 6, Peter quotes ***Isaiah 28:16*** and then interprets it by drawing from the context of the Old Testament other relevant statements ***(Psalms 118:22, 23; Isaiah 8:14; Exodus 19:5, 6; Hosea 1:6, 9, 10).***

b. **The First Mention Principle** ***(Hebrews 6:20-7:21)***—In interpreting the statement from ***Psalms 110:4*** concerning the Melchisedec priesthood, the writer to the Hebrews uses the first mention of Melchisedec in Genesis to prove his identity.

c. **The Comparative Mention Principle** ***(Romans 3:1-23)***—In verse 4 Paul quotes ***Psalms 51:4*** and substantiates his interpretation by comparing it with other references from the book of Psalms.

d. **The Progressive Mention Principle** ***(Hebrews 10:37-11:40)***—The writer to the Hebrews quotes a phrase from ***Habakkuk 2:4*** and then draws many examples from the context of the entire Old Testament to develop his interpretation.

e. **The Election Principle** ***(Romans 9:6-13)***—Here Paul uses the election principle to interpret a phrase from ***Genesis 21:12: "In Isaac shall thy seed be called."***

f. **The Covenantal Principle** ***(Hebrews 8-10)***—In ***Hebrews 8:8-12*** a quotation is made from ***Jeremiah 31:31-34.*** The writer then proceeds to use the covenantal principle to expound the meaning of that quotation.

g. **The Ethnic Division Principle** ***(Galatians 3:1-29)***—In verse 8 Paul quotes ***Genesis 12:3: "In thee shall all nations be blessed."*** He then uses the ethnic division principle to show the interpretation and fulfillment of that phrase.

h. **The Chronometrical Principle** ***(II Peter 3:1-13)***—Peter quotes ***Psalms 90:4*** in verse 8 and then interprets it by the chronometrical principle.

i. **The Christo-Centric Principle** ***(Hebrews 10:1-14)***—The writer to the Hebrews utilizes the Christo-Centric principle to interpret ***Psalms 40:6-8.***

j. **The Moral Principle** ***(I Corinthians 9:9-12)***—In dealing with the commandment of Moses concerning oxen, Paul draws out the moral lesson contained in it and applies it to this own situation.

k. **The Symbolic Principle** ***(I Peter 2:4-8)***—In dealing with the symbol of the stone, Peter appeals to several Old Testament passages which interpret its meaning.

l. **The Typical Principle** ***(I Corinthians 10:1-11)***—Here Paul uses the typical principle to interpret the exodus of Israel from Egypt.

m. **The Allegorical Principle** ***(Galatians 4:21-31)***—In This passage, Paul develops and interprets an allegory using people and places from the Old Testament.

In the interpretation of Old Testament quotations found in the New Testament, it is evident that Jesus and the Apostles infallibly used the principles of hermeneutics. Studying the various periods of the history of interpretation is certainly profitable. However, a consideration of the hermeneutics of Jesus and His apostles is of incomparably greater value.

III. PATRISTIC HERMENEUTICS

A. **Period (95 AD - 600 AD):** The period of Patristic exegesis reaches from the close of the New Testament Apostolic period through to the Middle Ages. This period of time may be sectionized into the following:

1. 95-202 AD
   From Clement of Rome to Iranaeus

2. 202-325 AD
   The School of Alexandria
3. 325-600 AD
   The School of Antioch;
   East and West divisions to the close of the 6th century

This period covers the writings of the Ante-Nicene and the Post-Nicene Fathers; from Clement of Rome to Gregory the Great. The New Testament Canon was established during this period. The orthodox doctrines concerning the Person of Christ and the Godhead were formulated out of the controversies over the heresies of this period.

B. **Methods:** In Patristic Hermeneutics the methods of interpretation used were often a mixture of the literal and the allegorical methods. However, the allegorical method was dominant.

C. **History**

1. **95-202 AD from Clement of Rome to Iranaeus:** A brief survey of this period indicates that there was no significant development in the methods of interpreting Scripture. The Fathers, generally speaking, were too busy defending the Christological doctrine against the Ebionite and Gnostic heresies to form any proper system of hermeneutics. They were acting as guardians of the apostle's doctrine in the midst of raging heresies. Consequently, there were many great defenders of the faith but very few expositors of the Word during this time. Though upholding sound doctrine, the Fathers soon lapsed into allegorization in their interpretation.

   NOTE: A doctrinal defensiveness may cause the interpreter to err in his development and application of hermeneutical principles.

   The following is a selection of certain Patristic Fathers from this time period with a brief evaluation of their hermeneutics.

   a. **Clement of Rome (30-100 AD)**—Clement was a man of the Scriptures, quoting at length from them in his writings. He strongly believed that the Old Testament was preparatory for the Christ of the New Testament. Because of this he was generally free from fanciful interpretations of the Word of God.

      NOTE: Laying a heavy emphasis on the use of the Context and Christo-Centric principles will do much to insure sound interpretation.

   b. **Ignatius (30-107 AD)**—Like Clement, Ignatius was Christo-centric in his interpretation of the Scriptures. However, his favorite subject was ecclesiastical order. He exalted the bishop's office and the presbytery as the guardians against heresies. In his interpretation he generally avoided the allegorical method.

      NOTE: A proper emphasis of the Christo-Centric principle may help to preserve the interpreter from the pitfalls of extreme allegorization.

   c. **Barnabas (100 AD)**—His writings are full of mystical allegorizations after the style of Philo. Numerous statements from Scripture are spiritualized and their meanings perverted.

      NOTE: The method of allegorization allows the interpreter to pervert the meaning of Scripture.

   d. **Marcion**—Marcion rejected the God of the Old Testament as the God and Father of our Lord Jesus Christ. Thus, he eliminated the Old Testament because of its irrelevancy to New Testament Christianity. In his extremism he accepted only the parts of the New Testament writings which were non-Jewish in character.

      NOTE: To assent that the Old Testament is irrelevant to New Testament Christianity is to violate, among others, the Context, Christo-Centric, and Ethnic-Division principles.

   e. **Justin Martyr (100-165 AD)**—Justin Martyr wrote the first apologies of the Christian faith. He also made an elaborate attempt to explain how Old Testament Messianic prophecies found their fulfillment in the Christ of the Gospels. However, in his overemphasis on Christology in the Old Testament he failed to recognize what each writer is saying to his own generation. Also, being a philosopher, he tended to mix Plato with Christ. As a result he fell into allegorism and produced many extreme and fanciful interpretations.

NOTE: Balance must be maintained in the use of hermeneutical principles. Emphasizing the Christo-Centric principle to the point of disregarding historical elements is to abuse the Scriptures. Mixing philosophy with Christianity may necessitate allegorization and lead to misinterpretation.

f. **Iranaeus (120-202 AD)**—Iranaeus is known for his battles against the Gnostic heresies. The strength of his interpretation lay in his use of a sound historical perspective.

NOTE: Literal interpretation, with the historical background in plain view, is the foundation for sound doctrine.

2. **202-325 AD The School of Alexandria:** At the beginning of the 3rd Century, Biblical interpretation was greatly influences by the catechetical school of Alexandria. As noted under "Jewish Hermeneutics," Alexandira had become the great melting pot of Greek philosophy and Judaism. Platonic philosophy, Neo-Platonism, Gnosticism and Judaism had all endeavoured to harmonize religion and philosophy by means of the allegorical method. With the spread of Christianity a large population of Hellenized believers developed in Alexandria. The allegorical system of interpretation that had arisen among the pagan Greeks and had been copied by the Alexandrian Jews was readily available to the Christian church. Under the same pressures that were upon the Greeks and the Jews, the Christians chose the same solution: the allegorical method. The terms allegorical, mystical and spiritual became practically synonymous. The allegorical was confused with the typical. By means of allegorization the Old Testament could be used as a Christian document. The Old Testament was looked upon as an obscure book of parables, enigmas and riddles which could only be interpreted through allegorization.

NOTE: Proper motivation in interpretation must be guided by proper principles of interpretation. Attempting to extract New Testament truths from the Old Testament by means of allegorization will lead to misinterpretation.

Two of the most prominent fathers during this period were Clement and Origen. They were the chief representatives of the school of Alexandria. Both regarded the Bible as the inspired Word of God and believed that special rules of hermeneutics had to be applied to interpret it. They admitted the literal sense of Scripture but gave exalted prominence to the allegorical sense.

a. **Clement (153-217 AD)**—Clement of Alexandria, a man of great learning, read widely from the works of Philo. Consequently, he adopted Philo's allegorical method of interpretation. An interest in philosophy also had a great influence on his exegesis. He was the first interpreter to apply the allegorical method to the Old and New Testaments together. He viewed all Scripture as needing allegorical interpretation. He taught that the Bible hides its sense to make its readers inquisitive, and thus to cause them to search for the words of salvation that are hidden therein. According to Ramm (p. 31), Clement taught that Scripture had five possible meanings:

(1) The *historical* sense of Scripture: taking a story in the Old Testament as an actual event in history.

(2) The *doctrinal* sense of Scripture: the obvious moral, religious, and theological teachings of the Bible.

(3) The *prophetic* sense of Scripture: including predictive prophecy and typology.

(4) The *philosophical* sense: follows the Stoics with their cosmic and psychological meaning (which sees meanings in natural objects and historical persons).

(5) The *mystical* sense: deeper moral, spiritual and religious truth symbolized by events or persons.

NOTE: The interpreter's background, good or bad, will greatly influence his system of interpretation. His view of the purpose and nature of Scripture will also affect his view of its interpretation. Mixture will only breed mixture.

b. **Origen (185-254 AD)**—Origen was the disciple and successor of Clement of Alexandria. He surpassed his teacher and became the greatest Biblical critic, theologian and exegete of his era. His methods of interpretation followed those of Philo the Jew and Clement the Christian. Origen regarded the three-fold sense or arrangement of Scripture as being analogous to man's triune being: body (corporeal), soul (psychical), and spirit (spiritual). He believed that the Scripture was literal, moral and mystical (or allegorical). However, in his exegesis, he rarely dealt with the literal or moral, rather majored on the allegorical. Actually, his spiritual interpretation was a mixture of the typological and allegorical methods. His principles of interpretation are briefly outlined here:

(1) The literal meaning of Scripture is its superficial sense; it is to be viewed as "the body" of Scripture rather than the "soul" (moral sense) or the "spirit" (allegorical sense).

(2) The interpreter is dependent upon the enablement of the Spirit of Christ for his understanding of Scripture.

(3) The ultimate meaning of Scripture lies in its Spiritual sense. Therefore, the primary means of interpreting the Scriptures is to spiritualize them. The Bible is essentially a spiritual book; one vast allegory.

(4) The Old Testament is preparatory to the New Testament. "The New is in the Old concealed and the Old is in the New revealed." For this reason the New replaces the Old.

NOTE: An improper concept of Scripture will lead to improper interpretation. The literal sense of Scripture is not to be viewed as the superficial sense but rather as the all-important foundational sense.

3. **325-600 AD The School of Antioch:** Another famous school which notably influences the interpretation of Scripture was the school at Antioch. About the beginning of the 4th Century, a school was established here where the early believers had first been called Christians ***(Acts 11:26).*** This school opposed the Alexandrian school of allegorical exegesis. Their methods of interpreting the Scriptures were more honorable, scientific and profitable. The following is a summary of the hermeneutics of the School of Antioch:

—They recognized the Bible as a *progressive revelation.*
—They believed in the *unity* of the Bible because of its *Christological* emphasis.
—They avoided the *letterism* of the Palestinian Jews.
—They fought and avoided the allegorism of Alexandria, including Origen and Philo.
—They emphasized *literal and historical* exegesis. (For them, "literal" included both plain literal and figurative literal. The significance of figures of speech where included in the literal sense of a passage.)
—They replaced allegory with *typology.*
—They avoided dogmatic exegesis.

NOTE: To avoid allegorical interpretation and to follow literal exegesis is to give proper direction to the hermeneutical process. A proper understanding of the literal sense of Scripture provides a sure foundation upon which the interpreter may build.

The following is an evaluation of three of the Fathers of this period:

a. **Diodorus, of Tarsus (Died 393 AD)**—As a presbyter of Antioch, Diodorus was probably the most influential of that school. He later became the Bishop of Tarsus. Emphasizing historical interpretation, he followed the literal sense of Scripture and made no attempt to explain the mystical. He took a firm stand against allegorical interpretation. He wrote a treatise on his principles of interpretation and instilled them into his pupils.

NOTE: The interpreter must maintain the literal sense of Scripture amidst the pressures of allegorism. He must recognize that developing a sound system of principles is the foundation for the development of doctrine.

b. **Theodore of Mopsuestia (350-428 AD)**—As a disciple of Diodorus, Theodore was first a presbyter of Antioch and later became the Bishop of Mopsuestia. He emphasized grammatico-historical interpretation and had no appreciation for the allegorical method of the Alexandrian school. He repudiated their extreme view of inspiration of certain portions of Scripture. Thus, he was quite liberal in his view of Scripture. Though a great exegete, he tended to be intellectual, rationalistic and dogmatic in his interpretation.

NOTE: The interpreter must not over-react against an extreme lest he fall into the opposite extreme. When faced with an extreme, the good interpreter will maintain balance.

c. **Chrysostom (354-407 AD)**—Though also a disciple of Diodorus, Chrysostom differed greatly with Theodore. As to his view of Scripture, he was much more conservative than Theodore, accepting the infallible inspiration of the Word of God. Though he followed the grammatico-historical method of interpretation, his exegesis was more spiritual and practical in nature. He also rejected the allegorical method.

NOTE: A good interpreter will possess both a proper concept of Scripture as well as proper methods of interpreting it. Sound interpretation goes beyond the intellectual level, and recognizes the spiritual and practical nature of Scripture.

During the 4th and 5th centuries great doctrinal controversies continued to divide the church. The greatest of these was the Nestorian controversy concerning the union and distinction of the human and divine natures in Christ's person. The School of Antioch was accused of unorthodoxy and in time lost its influence. This hastened the Church split, which divided the churches into Eastern and Western Divisions. We will now consider certain church Fathers from the Eastern and Western divisions, noting their contributions to the field of hermeneutics.

d. **The Eastern Division**

(1) **Athanasius of Alexandria (295-373 AD)**—As "the father of Orthodoxy," he was a great defender of the faith against the Arian Heresy. He held generally correct principles of interpretation, though at times he indulged in allegorization.

NOTE: Sound principles of hermeneutics are foundational to sound orthodox doctrine.

(2) **Basil of Caeserea (330-379 AD)**—Basil's background included a thorough knowledge of Origen. He embraced asceticism and became the great propagator of monasticism in Asia Minor. With the death of Athanasius, Basil was one who took up the torch of Orthodoxy. As to hermeneutics, he condemned those who did not accept the obvious sense of Scripture, rather imposed their own fanciful ideas upon it through mystical interpretation. He was basically a sound interpreter.

NOTE: To obtain sound interpretation, the interpreter must avoid the mystical tangent and the tendency to impose his own ideas upon Scripture.

(3) **Theodoret (386-458 AD)**—Trained in a monastery near Antioch, Theodoret was greatly influenced by the teachings of Diodorus, Theodore, and Chrysostom. He followed the literal method of interpretation promulgated by the Antiochian School and produced some of the best specimens of ancient interpretation. Terry (p. 649) quotes Theodoret's preface to the Psalms: "When I happened upon various commentaries, and found some expositors pursuing allegories with great superabundance, other adapting prophecy to certain histories so as to produce an interpretation accommodated to the Jews rather than to the nurselings of the faith, I considered it the part of a wise man to avoid the excess of both, and to connect now with ancient histories whatever belonged to them."

NOTE: In interpreting the relationship of prophecy to history, the interpreter must maintain the delicate balance between the literal and spiritual emphasis.

(4) **Andreas (450- AD)**—As the Bishop of Caesarca in Cappadocia, he wrote a commentary on the book of Revelation. He held to a three-fold sense of Scripture: the literal, the figurative, and the mystical. The mystical sense was the most prominent in his expositions.

e. **The Western Division**

(1) **Tertullian (150-225 AD)**—As "the father of Latin theology" Tertullian wrote mainly in the field of apologetics, battling the Gnostics heresies. To him Christianity was the knowledge of God based on reason and the authority of the orthodox Church. Because of apostolic succession, the Church alone had the right to use the Scriptures to formulate creeds. For Tertullian the orthodox creeds then became an authoritative "rule of faith" by which the Scriptures were

to be interpreted. Though generally sound in his doctrine, he started a trend toward heresy by exalting the authority of the Church in matters of interpretation. He generally maintained the literal sense of Scripture but followed allegorical interpretation in his treatment of prophecy.

NOTE: An inaccurate conception of the fundamental principles of Christianity will lead to a faulty formulation of hermeneutical principles.

(2) **Ambrose (337-397 AD)**—Ambrose, bishop of Milan, was a great violator of sound hermeneutical principles. He treated the historical sense as being irrelevant and proclaimed the glories of the hidden mystical sense of Scripture. He used Paul's statement that "the letter kills but the Spirit gives life" ***(II Corinthians 3:6)*** as a slogan to justify his extremely fanciful allegorical interpretation.

NOTE: In rejecting the laws of literal interpretation, the interpreter is given over to the lawlessness of allegorical interpretation.

(3) **Jerome (340-420 AD)**—Proficient in both Hebrew and Greek, Jerome authored a new translation of the Bible known as the Latin Vulgate. In theory he emphasized the literal and grammatical sense of Scripture, but in practice he often followed the allegorical method, even to the extent of allegorizing the New Testament. He believed that there was no inherent contradiction between the literal and the allegorical. Failing to appreciate the authors viewpoints and purposes, he was unable to enter into the authors' positions and ascertain their main ideas. Though sometimes faulty in his interpretation, he was one of the greatest Biblical scholars of his day.

NOTE: Bridging the language gap alone is insufficient. The interpreter must build a complete bridge between his viewpoint and that of the author.

(4) **Augustine (354-430 AD)**—If Jerome was one of the greatest scholars of this period, Augustine was one of its greatest theologians. Though deficient in the knowledge of the original languages, he did make significant contributions in the fields of theology and hermeneutics. Augustine did accept the allegorical method because it provided him with a means of reconciling his religious background with his Christian faith. However, he did modify allegorism by confining it mainly to the prophetic Scriptures. Following the trend introduced by Jerome he gave prominent place to Church tradition, regarding it as an authority over interpretation. He allowed the Scriptures to be interpreted four ways:

—Historically
—Grammatically
—Comparatively
—Allegorically

According to Ramm (p. 36, 37), Augustine's hermeneutics can be summed up in the following twelve principles:

—A genuine Christian faith is necessary for the understanding of the Scriptures.
—Although the literal and historical are not the end of Scripture, we must hold them in high regard. Not all of the Bible is allegorical by any means, and much of it is both literal and allegorical.
—Scripture has more than one meaning and therefore the allegorical method is proper.
—There is significance in Biblical numbers.
—The Old Testament is a Christian document because it is a Christological document.
—The task of the expositor is to get the meaning out of the Bible, not to bring a meaning into it.
—We must consult the analogy of faith, the true creed, when we interpret. To this must be added love.
—No verse is to be studied as a unit in itself. Therefore we must note the context of the verse.
—If an interpretation is insecure, nothing in the passage can be made a matter of orthodox faith.
—We cannot make the Holy Spirit our substitute for the necessary learning to understand Scripture.

—The obscure passage must yield to the clear passage.
—No Scripture is to be interpreted so as to conflict with any other: the harmony of revelation. But to do this we must distinguish the times: "Distinguish the times and you harmonize the Scriptures." We must take into account progressive revelation.

Though Augustine adhered to basically sound principles of interpretation, in practice he often violated them. As a great theologian with a fondness for allegory, Augustine's influence opened the door for allegorism to become the dominant method of interpretation during the Middle Ages.

NOTE: Failing to bridge the linguistic gap leaves one open to faulty interpretation. Failing to break completely away from a heretical religious background leaves the interpreter open to mixture. When sound principles are adhered to they must also be consistently applied.

(5) **Vincentius (5th Century AD):** According to Terry (p. 659), Vincentius is to be noted for his exaltation of Church tradition in matters of interpretation. In his work *Commonitorium* (434 AD), he attempts to show that the tradition of the Catholic Church, as well as Scripture, are both necessary in order to establish true doctrine. His ecclesiastico-traditional method of interpretation can only be appreciated by those who hold Church tradition and authority above reason and conscience.

NOTE: Using Church tradition as the final authority in matters of doctrine is to violate the supremacy of Scripture and discount the involvement of reason and conscience.

In summarizing the period of Patristic Hermeneutics it is evident that two major streams of interpretation had developed. That which came to a head in the conflict between the School at Antioch and the School at Alexandria had been developing through the previous periods. The first stream was characterized by literal interpretation. It began with Ezra, was preverted by the Palestinian Jews, restored by Jesus and the Apostles, and was proclaimed by the School of Anitoch. The second stream was characterized by allegorical interpretation. It began with the Greek philosophers, was borrowed by the Alexandrian Jews, and was passed on to the School of Alexandria.

IV. MEDIEVAL HERMENEUTICS

A. **Period (600-1517 AD):** The period of Medieval Hermeneutics reaches from the beginning of the 7th century to Martin Luther, The Great Reformer.

B. **Methods:** During this period there were generally four senses attributed to Scripture:

1. The Literal Sense—the plain evident meaning
2. The Allegorical Sense—the hidden theological meaning
3. The Moral Sense—the hidden practical meaning
4. The Eschatological Sense—the futuristic meaning

By far the dominant method of this period was the allegorical.

C. **History:** During the Middle Ages there was a stagnation in the field of Hermeneutics. Originality was superseded by imitation and no new principles of interpretation were formulated. Because of an extreme emphasis on tradition, the writings of this period tended to be merely a rehash of the teachings of the early Church Fathers. This reveals the bondage to Church tradition and authority that existed.

It became an established principle that the interpretation of God's Word had to adapt itself to the tradition and doctrine of the Church. The teachings and expositions of the Fathers became the final explanation of the Bible. The Scriptures were used only to confirm what the Fathers said, and if contradiction existed then the writings of the Fathers were accepted above the authority of the Scriptures. In fact, the teachings of the Fathers were sought for in the Bible.

In Medieval times ignorance and superstition prevailed. Neither the laity nor much of the clery had an understanding of the Scriptures. They had been hidden away for preservation in the monasteries and came to be regarded with superstitious reverence. The Bible was looked on as a book of mysteries and only the scholars of the Church were deemed qualified to unfold its mystical meaning. This mass ignorance resulted in a superstitious consulting of the Scriptures as magic oracles for subjective guidance. Thus, ignorance became the father of superstition and together they blanketed the Middle Ages with spiritual darkness.

We will now briefly consider several men from this period.

1. **Hrabanus Maurus (776-856 AD):** Hrabanus Maurus was a great teacher and a prolific writer. His writings were primarily a compilation of earlier Greek and Latin Fathers. He advocated the four-fold sense of Scripture common to this period: the literal, allegorical, moral, and eschatological senses. As to his method of interpretation he could be classified as a mystical allegorizer.

   NOTE: To emphasize the existence of multiple meanings in Scripture is to allow the interpreter to force his every whim and fancy upon the sacred text of Scripture. It is also to ignore what the writer intended to say, substituting what the interpreter wants to say.

2. **Thomas Aquinas (1225-1274 AD):** Thomas Aquinas, a famous theologian, accepted the four-fold sense of Scripture. In theory he maintained that all the theology was to be soundly based upon the literal sense of Scripture, but he also gave place to the other senses of Scripture, and often emphasized them. In practice he was constantly involved in allegorizing. He viewed the Scriptures, as interpreted by the Church, as the final authority in theological matters.

   NOTE: It is very difficult for the interpreter to adhere to the "multiple sense" view of Scripture without lapsing into allegorization. The one leads to the other.

3. **Bonaventura (1221-1274 AD):** Bonaventura, an associate of Thomas Aquinas, was greatly influenced by the Neo-Platonism of Augustine. Historians have pictured him as a mystic, in contrast to Aquinas who was more of an intellectual. According to Terry (p. 666) he at times assumed a seven-fold sense of Scripture:

   a. The historical sense
   b. The allegorical sense
   c. The mystical sense
   d. The moral sense
   e. The symbolical sense
   f. The synedochical sense
   g. The hyperbolical sense

   NOTE: Violating the literal sense of Scripture breaks down the safeguard against the invention of any number of conjectural senses.

4. **Nicholas of Lyra (1279-1340 AD):** In the field of hermeneutics, Nicholas has been spoken of as the bridge between the Middle Ages and the Reformation. Though he accepted the four-fold sense of Scripture, he emphasized the literal sense and opposed certain allegorical interpretations. It was his work that had a profound influence on Luther and thus he helped to "seed" the Reformation. His interpretation was basically sound.

   NOTE: Exalting the literal sense of Scripture leads to sound exegesis.

5. **John Wycliffe (1328-1384 AD):** Because of his attack on the authority of the Church above Scripture, John Wycliffe has become known as "the morning star of the Reformation." Because of his recognition of Scripture as the final authority in all matters of belief and practice he was compelled to translate the Scriptures into the language of the people.

   NOTE: Before benefit can be derived from Scripture the linguistic gap must be bridged.

In viewing Medieval Hermeneutics one valuable approach is to see what principles emerged in the Catholic Church. The following is condensed from Ramm's discussion of this area (p. 38-45).

— Catholic scholars accept the Latin Vulgate as the authentic version of the Bible. They include the Apocrypha.
— Catholic scholars accept whatever the Church has specifically said about matters of historical criticism.
— Catholic scholars accept the Church's interpretation of all verses it has officially interpreted.
— Catholic scholars accept the literal and historical interpretation of Scripture as the foundation for Bible study.

— Catholic scholars accept the spiritual or mystical meaning as being beyond the literal.
— Catholic scholars accept the Church as the custodian and official interpreter of Scripture.
— Catholic scholars accept the Fathers as aids in interpretation as long as they agree with Church tradition.
— Catholic scholars accept Church tradition as that which fills out what is deficient in the Scriptures.
— Catholic scholars accept the principle of development in understanding the Bible. This gives them license to use implication, deduction, and that which "grows" out of Scripture to formulate doctrine.
— Catholic scholars accept that the true sense of Scriptures in reality is not to be found outside the Catholic Church.

NOTE: Exalting the Church above the Scriptures places fallible men above the authority of God in matters of doctrine and practice. The interpreter must constantly recognize that the only infallible interpreters of Scripture are the Holy Spirit and Scripture itself.

Towards the end of the Middle Ages there came a general revival of learning and a growing interest in the ancient languages. With the invention of printing and the publication of the Bible in Latin, Greek, Hebrew, Chaldee, Syriac and Arabic, the chains of ignorance and superstition were snapped. The Scriptures were appealed to as the final authority above the Church and the binding traditions of the Fathers. All of this began to prepare the way for the Reformation and a new horizon for hermeneutics.

V. REFORMATION HERMENEUTICS

A. **Period (1517-1600 AD):** The period of Reformation Hermeneutics extends from the publication of Martin Luther's ninety-five theses to the end of the 16th Century.

B. **Methods:** There was a gradual breaking away from the four-fold method of the Middle Ages. There was a decided departure from the allegorical method to the grammatico-literal method.

C. **History:** The Renaissance in Europe brought about in the Church a definite loosing from the chains of ignorance and superstition prevalent during Medieval times. It opened the door to a period of intellectual and spiritual enlightenment. A new awareness of "the great gulf" between Divine revelation and human reason paved the way for the battle cry of the Reformation "sola scriptura" (only Scripture). As the Bible was recognized as the only infallible Divine revelation available to man it was exalted above all human reason, including fallible ecclesiastical authority. For this reason the Bible began to be translated into many different languages during the 16th Century. The following is a list of some of the languages into which Scripture was translated during this period:

Danish	1524	Spanish	1543
German-Swiss	1524-1529	Polish	1561
English	1525-1535	Icelandic	
Dutch	1526	Finnish	1500-1600
Italian	1532	Swedish	
German	1534	Hungarian	
French	1535		

NOTE: Bridging the linguistic gap is the first step toward dispelling the darkness of ignorance and breaking the bondage of superstition.

In general, the Reformers contended for the following:

1. The Bible is the inspired Word of God.
2. The Scriptures must be studied in their original languages.
3. The Scriptures alone are infallible; the Church is fallible.
4. The Bible is the highest authority in all matters of theology.
5. The Church is subject to Scripture, not Scripture to the Church. The Church does not determine what the Scriptures teach, rather the Scriptures determine what the Church should teach.
6. Scripture is the interpreter of Scripture.
7. All understanding and exposition of the Bible must conform to the whole of Scriptural revelation.

NOTE: As heresy is fostered by faulty hermeneutics, so sound theology is nourished by proper hermeneutics.

Though there were many great reformers, there were two outstanding exemplary men: Luther and Calvin.

1. **Martin Luther (1483-1546 AD):** Luther's conviction concerning the role of the Church, the authority of the Scriptures, and the needs of the unenlightened masses, motivated him to light the torch of the Reformation. In 1517 he posted his ninety-five theses attacking the authority of the Catholic Church. By 1522 he had translated the New Testament into German and by 1534 he had completed the Bible, thus placing the Bible in the hands of the common people. His theses lit the torch and his translations kept it burning. According to Ramm (p. 53-57) Luther's hermeneutics may be summed up by the following principles:

   a. **The Psychological Principle**—Inspiration demands illumination. The interpreter must depend on the Holy Spirit to quicken his God-given mental abilities.

   b. **The Authority Principle**—The Bible is the supreme and final authority for all theological matters, and is above ecclesiastical authority.

   c. **The Literal Principle**—Allegorism is invalid. The original languages are of primary importance. The interpreter must give attention to grammar and historical setting.

   d. **The Sufficiency Principle**—The meaning of the Scriptures is sufficiently clear so that any believer is capable of interpreting them.

   e. **The Christological Principle**—The function of all interpretation is to find Christ.

   f. **The Law-Gospel Principle**—The Law and the Gospel are to be always kept distinct. The Law is to condemn man and the Gospel is to redeem him.

   NOTE: Accepting the truths of the supremacy of the authority of Scripture and the primacy of the literal method sets the interpreter free from the bondages of ecclesiasticism and allegorism.

2. **John Calvin (1509-1564 AD):** John Calvin, undoubtedly the first scientific interpreter in the history of the Christian Church. He maintained the fundamental principles of Luther but surpassed him in his use of them. He regarded the allegorical method as Satanic but did accept the validity of Old Testament typology. Differing from Luther, he did not force the whole of Scripture into Christological interpretation.

   Calvin's hermeneutics could be summarized in the following statements:

   a. Calvin believed that the Spirit's illumination was vital to the interpreter. He recognized the Spirit's work of inspiration in writing Scripture and the need for the Spirit's work in interpreting Scripture.

   b. Calvin subscribed to the precept that "Scripture interprets Scripture." He exalted the importance of contextual interpretation and felt it necessary to compare all Scriptures treating common subjects.

   c. Calvin insisted upon the literal method of interpretation. He emphasized studies in the areas of grammar, vocabulary, and historical background. He said, "the first business of an interpreter is to let his author say what he does say, instead of attributing to him what we think he ought to say."

   d. Calvin rejected allegorism and its foundation stone: the medieval concept of the multiplicity of meanings in Scripture.

   e. Calvin joined with the other reformers in throwing off the yoke of the Catholic Church in matters of interpretation and theology.

   f. Calvin contended that theology could only be based on entirely proper exegesis. He denounced the use of misinterpretation to support orthodox doctrine.

   NOTE: The proper rules of hermeneutics with a thorough and systematic application of them by a qualified interpreter will produce the highest quality of Biblical interpretation.

From the death of Calvin to the end of the 16th Century both Catholic and Protestant scholars became involved primarily in formulating doctrinal creeds and systematizing their theology. As the battle lines were drawn between Catholicism and Protestantism hermeneutics fell into the realm of polemics. A divided Christendom, with a militant spirit, entered into an age of controversy.

NOTE: When interpretation is forged in the heat of controversy it will always lack that delicate balance produced by an unbiased hermeneutic.

VI. POST-REFORMATION HERMENEUTICS

A. **Period (1600-1800 AD):** The period of Post-Reformation Hermeneutics extends from the beginning of the 17th Century to the close of the 18th Century.

B. **Methods:** During this period most expositors adhered to and developed the hermeneutics of the Reformation: the literal method. This period also saw the rise to prominence of the devotional method of interpretation.

C. **History**

1. **Dogmatism:** As a period of theological dogmatism and controversy, the Post-Reformation stands as a bleak era in Church history. The light of the Reformation was shaded by a spirit of contention and bitterness among theologians. While rejecting the authority of the Catholic Church, they fell into a bondage to the creedal standards of the Protestant Church. In becoming divided amongst themselves, Protestant interpreters used the anvil of Scripture to hammer out their dogmas. They studied the Bible to find proof-texts for their theology and read their creeds into Scripture. However, in spite of the militancy of this period, the Post-Reformation scholars basically followed the guiding principles of the hermeneutics of the Reformers.

   NOTE: In striving to defend purity of doctrine, the careless interpreter may lapse into eisegesis-allowing his theology to control his interpretation. Rather, he should exegete—allowing the interpretation of Scripture to control his theology.

   Johann Cocceius (1603-1669 AD), a Dutch theologian, crossed the current hermeneutical trends in this period, opposing both scholasticism and dogmatic exegesis. His positive contribution was his concept of Scripture. To him Scripture was an organism with various vitally related parts. He believed that each passage must be interpreted by defining its terms, considering its context and relating it to the whole body of truth. On the other hand, by confusing interpretation and application he virtually allowed multiple meanings. He was also guilty of excessive typology in finding Christ and Church history everywhere in the Old Testament, opening again the door to allegorical and mystical methods of interpretation.

   NOTE: The interpreter must recognize the organic nature of Scripture. He must also hold interpretation and application in definite distinction.

2. **Pietism:** Pietism emerged as a reaction against the theological dogmatism of the Post-Reformation. Protestant dogmatism used Scripture as a cold sword and thus destroyed spiritual life. The Pietists beat that sword into a plowshare, desiring to use it to produce life. They studied the Bible for personal edification and spiritual nourishment. The influence of Pietism extended to the Moravians, the Puritans, and the Quakers. The Pietistic principles of interpretation were:

   —The Bible should be studied in its original languages.
   —A thorough knowledge of its historical background must be gained.
   —The Holy Spirit must illuminate and apply the Word to the believer.
   —The Bible should be studied devotionally and applied practically.

   NOTE: The interpreter should combine the grammatical, historical and devotional studies of the Scripture to fulfill their purpose of producing life in the believer.

   Two outstanding Pietists were Spener and Francke.

   a. **Philipp Jakob Spener (1635-1705 AD)**—Philipp Spener is known as the Father of Pietism, in that the name originated with a small devotional meeting in his home. He was greatly influenced by Puritan writings. He believed that purity of heart was much more important than purity of doctrine. As Luther rejected the authority of the Catholic Church, Spener undermined the authority of Protestant creedalism. He encouraged every believer to relate to the Word of God for himself, applying its truths to his practical life.

      NOTE: The interpreter must maintain a balance by emphasizing both purity of heart and doctrine. Devotional interpretation must find its proper place in relation to doctrinal interpretation.

   b. **August Hermann Francke (1663-1727 AD)**—Under Hermann Francke's influence Pietism reached its peak in Germany. As a disciple of Spener, Francke propagated Pietistic principles. He taught that only those who were born again could have insight into the meaning of Scripture. In his lectures he combined exegesis with experience. Grammatical and critical studies were used as the external to bring him to the internal: devotional truth. He displayed strong ascetic tendencies and became legalistic in his attitude toward non-Pietists.

NOTE: Opposing one form of dogmatism may lead to another.

The devotional method of interpretation used by the Pietists did produce a Godly piety and a devout spirituality. However, in an over-reaction against dogmatism the Pietists tended toward mysticism in their interpretation. In their zeal to gain spiritual and practical benefit from Scripture they began to neglect theology.

NOTE: Devotional interpretation is profitable, but it must never be used at the expense of the doctrinal truth of Scripture.

3. **Criticism:** Seeing the weakness and insufficiency of the devotional method, many interpreters turned to a scholastic approach to the study of Scripture. The inadequacy of the dogmatist's ignoring of the historical background of Scripture to find his proof-texts caused many scholars to study the Scriptures analytically. Great strides were made in the field of textual criticism. Manuscripts were scientifically compared and evaluated for the first time. Extensive research in the original languages produced grammars and lexicons. Work was also done to prove the validity of the canon and the genuineness and credibility of its books.

NOTE: The sciences of canonology, textual criticism, and historical criticism are foundational to the proper interpretation of Scripture.

One outstanding scholar of this period and persuasion was, Johann August Ernesti (1707-1781 AD). Ernesti, as a classical scholar, brought to New Testament interpretation the same principles he applied to classical literature. In recognizing the human element in Scripture, he believed that the same basic rules used to interpret secular literature should also be applied to Biblical literature. According to Berkhof (p. 33) Ernesti laid four principles:

a. The manifold sense of Scripture must be rejected and only the literal sense retained.

b. Allegorical and typological interpretations must be disapproved, except in cases where the author indicates that he meant to combine another sense with the literal.

c. Since the Bible has the grammatical sense in common with other books, this should be ascertained similarly in both cases.

d. The literal sense may not be determined by a supposed dogmatical sense.

NOTE: To interpret Scripture, the human element must be recognized and given due consideration. The Bible is both a Divine and a human book.

4. **Rationalism:** Following the tendencies expressed by those involved in criticism, many scholars went a step beyond scholasticism and exalted human reason above the authority of Scriptures. In focusing on the human element of Scripture they so enlarged it as to rule out the Divine. Scholars began to interpret the Bible as they would any other literary work.

Two representatives of this trend of Rationalism were Hobbes (1588-1679 AD) and Spinoza (1632-1677 AD). They taught that man had no need of Divine revelation to be able to discern between the true and the false. Human reason alone was sufficient. They rejected any Scripture that presented things unexplainable by man's intellect.

NOTE: The interpreter must submit his intellect to the divine revelation of Scripture. Failure to do so is to deify the exercise of human reason above the authority of God's Word.

Because of his writings, in which rationalistic concepts are applied to Scripture, Semler (1725-1791 AD) has been called the Father of Rationalism. In his studies in the field of Canonology he became so enraptured with the human and historical elements in the origin of Scripture that he transfered this heavy emphasis into his hermeneutics. He believed that since the Scriptures were written in certain historical settings Divine truth was accommodated to the level of man's experience. Thus, for Semler, the truth of accommodation meant that the Bible was a fallible human production.

NOTE: To the interpreter the truth of accommodation must be submitted to a strict definition of inspiration. The Bible must be regarded as an infallible revelation, the truth of which is applicable to all ages.

VII. MODERN HERMENEUTICS

A. **Period (1800-19— AD):** The period of Modern Hermeneutics reaches from the beginning of the nineteenth century to the present day.

B. **Methods:** All of the methods initiated during previous periods are still in existence today. However, the method which has become most prominent during this period has been the literal method.

C. **History:** Toward the close of the Post-Reformation era two opposing currents began to develop. On the negative side, humanistic rationalism caused interpreters to undermine the value and authority of Scripture by rejecting its Divine inspiration and infallibility. On the positive side, many noble interpreters rushed to the defense of Scripture, and brought to full development the Bible's authority. The rationalism of the Post-Reformation prepared the way for the liberalism of the modern era. On the other hand the Criticism of the Post-Reformation laid the groundwork for the conservatism of the modern age. At the beginning of the Post-Reformation battles raged over the finer points of theology. In modern times the great conflict has been over the foundational elements of the inspiration and authority of Scripture. The following is a brief consideration of these two opposing streams.

1. **Liberalism:** As used here the word "liberalism" is a broad term including all schools of thought that depart from the foundational elements of orthodox Christianity.

   a. **Liberals in General—**According to Ramm (p. 64-69) the religious liberals' approach to Scripture may be listed as follows:

   —Religious liberals believe that "modern mentality" is to govern our approach to Scripture. What is not acceptable to the intellect of modern man is rejected.
   —Religious liberals redefine inspiration. The involvement of the supernatural in the writing of Scripture is denied and inspiration is redefined as the Bible's religious effect on man.
   —The supernatural is redefined. The supernatural is rejected as that which is beyond human knowledge or power, it is redefined to mean an abstract realm of thought.
   —The concept of evolution is applied to the religion of Israel and thereby to its documents. The Scriptures are viewed as being primitive in relation to modern theological thought.
   —The notion of accommodation has been applied to the Bible. The Biblical writers communicated their thoughts cloaked in the real and mythical concepts of their day.
   —The Bible is to be interpreted historically. The historical setting was not the back-drop for the communication of truth, but rather was that which produced the theological concepts of the writer.
   —Philosophy has had an influence on religious liberalism. One result of this has been to exalt the ethical sense of Scripture and reject any theological interpretation of it.

   NOTE: To attack the authority of Scripture is in essence to attack the authority of God, and to leave man without any authoritative standard of truth nor any means of salvation.

   b. **Karl Barth—**In the early part of the twentieth century, Karl Barth endeavoured to part with liberalism, but was unsuccessful in his attempt. Because of his failure to rectify the foundational error of liberalism, he falls under the same classification. The following are his principles of interpretation, as listed by Ramm (p. 70-79):

   —**The Revelation Principle—**The inspiration, infallibility and inerrancy of Scripture is denied. Revelation, in relation to Scripture, means that the Bible merely points man to his own encounter (revelation) with God.
   —**The Christological Principle—**Only that which is directly related to Christ in Scripture is acceptable.
   —**The Totality Principle—**Doctrine cannot be established by specific citations of Scripture. The literal method cannot provide the true meaning of Scripture.
   —**The Mythological Principle—**Biblical events are not necessarily viewed as historical happenings. but rather as mythical stories contrived to communicate truth.
   —**The Existential Principle—**The interpreter must be subjective and experience orientated in his approach to Scripture.

—**The Paradoxical Principle**—The truths of man's religious existence can never be precisely or rationally defined, they are tensions between irreconcilable opposites.

NOTE: Failure to accept the Divine authority of Scripture allows the interpreter to impose upon Scripture faulty principles of interpretation.

2. **Conservativism:** As used here, the word "conservativism" is a broad term including all schools of thought that hold to the foundational elements of orthodox Christianity. In contrast to the principles of liberalism mentioned previously, the following is a summation of the conservatives' approach to Scripture:

   a. Conservatives believe that reason must be submitted to Scripture. There are things in Scripture beyond human reason, yet not contrary to reason. Reason itself is not sufficient to interpret Scripture; illumination is essential.

   b. Conservatives hold to the plenary-verbal inspiration of Scripture, believing the Bible to be an infallible revelation.

   c. Conservatives accept the existence of the supernatural as being beyond human knowledge or power. This is applied not only to the origin of Scripture, but also to its contents.

   d. Conservatives recognize the progressive revelation of truth in Scripture, but view its truth as timeless, applicable to all ages.

   e. Conservatives believe God accommodated truth to man's frame of reference in order to communicate effectively, but this accommodation did not taint the character of the revelation.

   f. Conservatives view the historical settings of Scripture as the backdrops for the communication of truth.

   g. Conservatives support the validity of theological interpretation, believing the Scriptures were given to reveal God to man.

   NOTE: For the interpreter the only proper point of commencement is a complete acceptance of the inspiration, infallibility, and authority of Scripture as God's revelation to man.

In bringing our discussion of the history of Modern Hermeneutics to a close, it must be recognized that during this period the literal method of interpretation has gained wide acceptance. The result has been that the method itself has become highly developed and great strides have been made in its various fields of study.

The following three charts illustrate the progression in the History of Hermeneutics. The first shows the development of hermeneutics through its various periods. The last two will clarify the time element in the chronology of the history of hermeneutics.

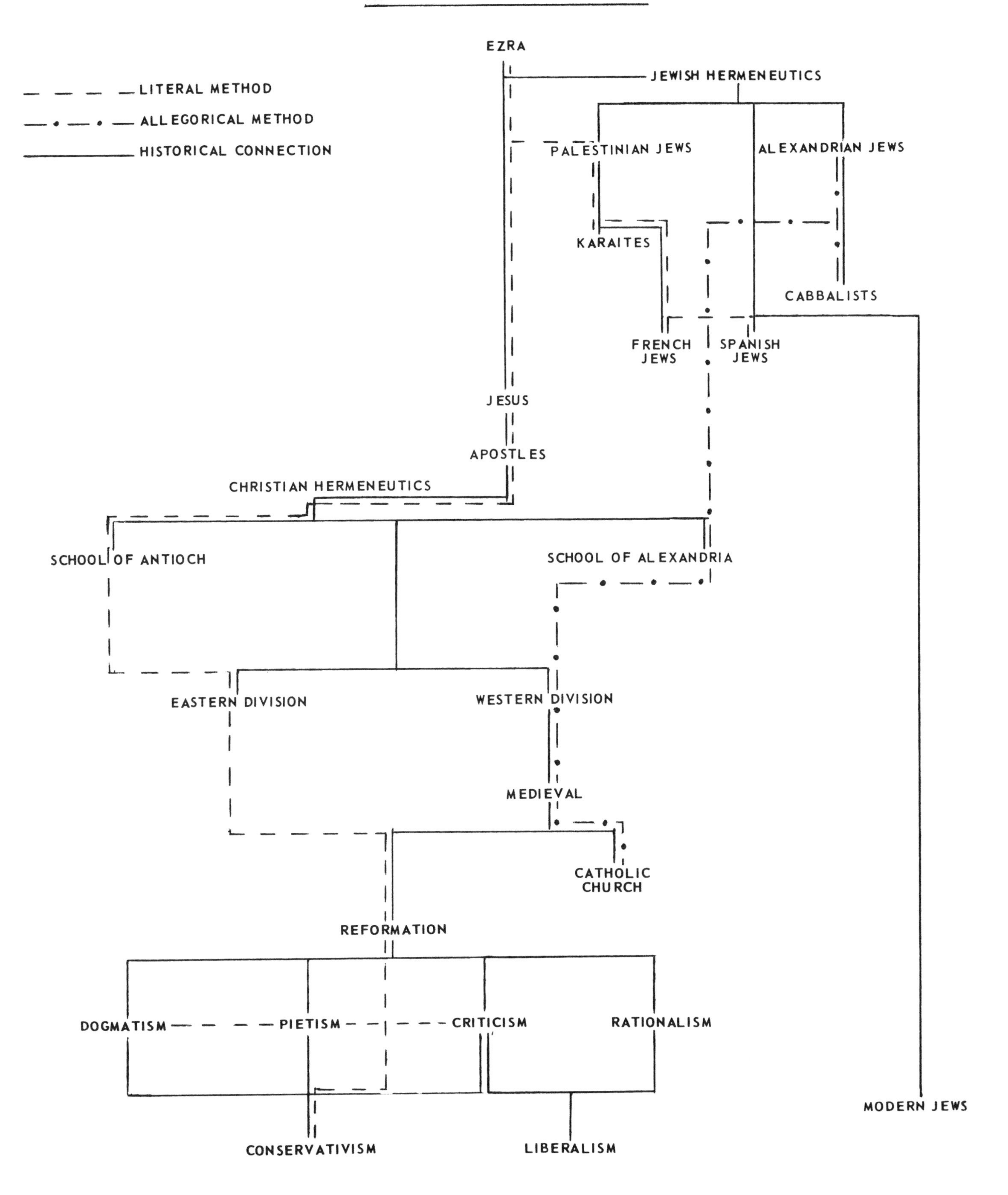
THE PROGRESS OF HERMENEUTICS
LITERAL METHOD
ALLEGORICAL METHOD
HISTORICAL CONNECTION
EZRA
JEWISH HERMENEUTICS
PALESTINIAN JEWS
ALEXANDRIAN JEWS
KARAITES
CABBALISTS
FRENCH JEWS
SPANISH JEWS
JESUS
APOSTLES
CHRISTIAN HERMENEUTICS
SCHOOL OF ANTIOCH
SCHOOL OF ALEXANDRIA
EASTERN DIVISION
WESTERN DIVISION
MEDIEVAL
CATHOLIC CHURCH
REFORMATION
DOGMATISM
PIETISM
CRITICISM
RATIONALISM
MODERN JEWS
CONSERVATIVISM
LIBERALISM

Jesus N.T. Writers	APOSTOLIC HERMENEUTICS 26-95
Clement 30-100 Ignatius 30-107 Barnabas 100 Marcion Justin Martyr 110-165	95-202 Clement to Iranaeus (PATRISTIC HERMENEUTICS 95-595)
Clement 153-217 Origin 185-254	202-325 School of Alexandria (PATRISTIC HERMENEUTICS 95-595)
West - Tertullian 150-225 East - Athanasius 295-373 East - Basil 330-379 West - Ambrose 337-397 West - Jerome 340-420 Theodore 350-428 Chrysostom 354-407 West - Augustine 354-430 Diodorus Died 393 Theodoret 386-458 West - Vincentius 400's East - Andreas 450 -	325-595 School of Antioch East and West Divisions (PATRISTIC HERMENEUTICS 95-595)
Hrabanus Maurus 776-856 Bonaventura 1221-1274 Thomas Aquinas 1225-1274 Nicolas 1279-1340 Wycliffe 1328-1384	MEDIEVAL HERMENEUTICS 600-1517
Luther 1483-1546 Calvin 1509-1564	REFORMATION HERMENEUTICS 1517-1600
Rationalism - Hobbes 1588-1679 Johann Cocceius 1603-1669 Rationalism - Spinoza 1632-1677 Pietism - Spener 1635-1705 Pietism - Francke 1663-1727 Criticism - Ernesti 1707-1781 Rationalism - Semler 1725-1791	POST -REFORMATION HERMENEUTICS 1600-1800
	MODERN HERMENEUTICS 1800-Present

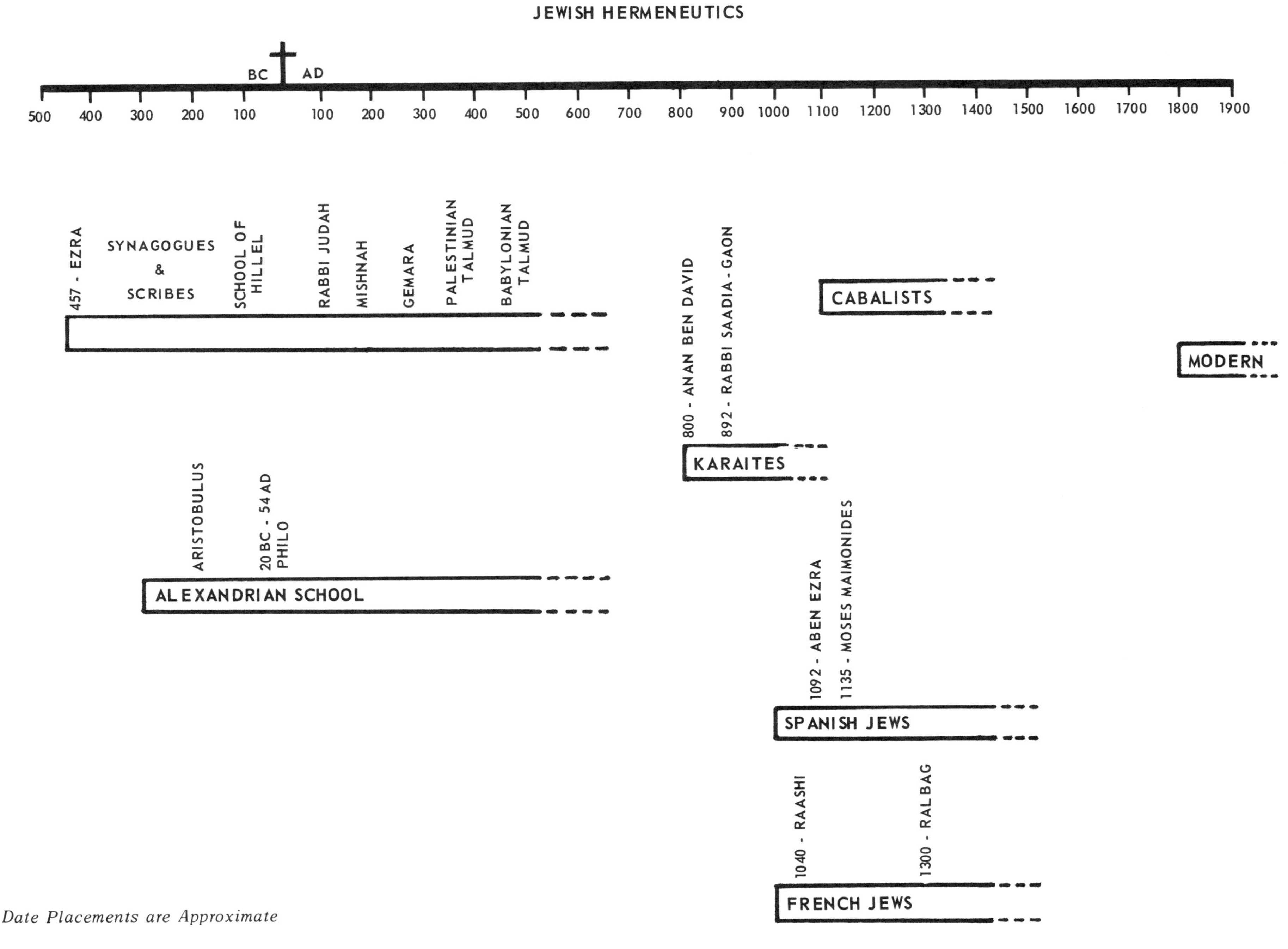

Date Placements are Approximate

Chapter 5
FOUNDATIONS FOR INTERPRETATION

The goal of hermeneutics is to properly determine what God has said in the Scriptures; to determine the meaning of the Word of God. The foundation for reaching this objective is the bridging of the gap between our minds and the minds of the Biblical writers. This bridging of the understanding gap is the foundational *means* for reaching the desired *end:* knowing what God meant by what He said. This gap is basically fourfold: the linguistic gap, the cultural gap, the geographical gap, and the historical gap. Each of these will be considered using a problem/solution approach.

I. THE LINGUISTIC GAP

A. **Problem:** The Bible was written in three languages which are no longer in use. Ancient Hebrew, Ancient Chaldee and Koine Greek have long been extinct as spoken languages.

B. **Solution:** The way to bridge this linguistic gap is to study linguistics. Webster's dictionary defines linguistics as: "The science of languages; the origin, signification, and application of words; also called comparative philology." It is necessary to study Ancient Hebrew, Ancient Chaldee and Koine Greek in order to be able to read and understand the earliest Biblical manuscripts. This involves study in three basic areas: vocabulary, grammar and genre.

1. **Vocabulary:** In order to understand a sentence, it is necessary to understand the words of which that sentence is composed. There are four approaches to accomplishing this task:

   a. The *Etymological* study of a word—attempting to understand a word by examining its origin, derivation, formation and history (e.g., the Greek word for obedience, *HUPAKOE,* comes from two Greek words: *HUPO,* which means "under"; and *AKOUO,* which means "to hear." Thus obedience is a "hearing under").

   b. The *Comparative* study of a word—attempting to understand a word by studying all of its occurrences in Scripture. This can be properly done only by taking a Hebrew or Greek word, not just the English equivalent, and noting every usage of it in Scripture (e.g., the Greek word DIAKRINO is translated in the King James Version: "to discern, to doubt, waver, to be partial, and to make a difference").

   c. The *Cultural* study of a word—attempting to understand a word by ascertaining its original cultural meaning. This involves the literal sense of the word, which is its basic customary and socially designated meaning (e.g., the word "adoption" in modern day culture refers to the transferring of a child from one family to another, but in Hebrew culture it referred to a child coming of age in his own family).

   d. The study of a word in *Cognate Languages*—attempting to understand a word by investigating its equivalents in related languages (e.g., equivalent words in Aramaic may help to clarify the Hebrew, since the two languages are so closely related).

2. **Grammar:** In order to understand a sentence it is not only necessary to have defined its words, but it is also essential to understand the part each word plays in the sentence. This leads to a study of the general principles and particular rules for writing the languages of the Bible. The same methods used to research the meanings of words can also be used to research grammar. The study of vocabulary supplies the parts, while the study of grammar provides the rules for putting the parts together into a whole.

   In studying grammar it soon becomes evident that languages are structurally different. In other words, their sentences and paragraphs are put together in different ways. Languages are structured in one of two basic ways, or in a combination of the two.

   a. **Analytic languages**—These are languages in which the order of the words in a sentence determines the role each word plays in that sentence (e.g., whether a word is a subject, indirect object, or a direct object). Hebrew and English are both analytic languages in that they stress word order.

b. **Synthetic languages**—These are languages in which the ending of a word determines the role it plays in the sentence. Greek is a synthetic language stressing word ending (e.g., *anthropos* = a man [subject]; *anthropo* = to a man [indirect object]; *anthropon* = a man [direct object]).

In summary, we cannot overemphasize the importance of studying *vocabulary and grammar* together in order to arrive at proper exegesis. Word studies alone are insufficient, apart from grammatical considerations, to bring about correct interpretation.

3. **Genre:** In order to understand a writing, its literary genre (kind or style) must first be determined. It is the genre of the passage or book which sets the mood or stance from which the rest of the passage or book is seen. Literary genre can be illustrated by three concentric circles:

   a. **Literary style**—When a book of the Bible is approached, the first step in interpretation is to determine its literary style (e.g., whether it is historical, poetical, apocalytpical or prophetical).

   b. **Literary expression**—Within any literary style there can occur passages utilizing unusual forms of literary expression (e.g., parables, allegories, psalms and riddles).

   c. **Figures of speech**—Within any literary style or expression there may occur a figure of speech; that is, a phrase or a sentence in which the author expresses himself using words in a way differing from their normal use (e.g., metaphors, similes and idioms).

Just as vocabulary should not be considered apart from grammar, neither should vocabulary and grammar be considered apart from literary genre in solving the problem of the linguistic gap. The following is a diagram and illustration of the three circles of genre. It should be recognized that the illustration is partially inadequate in that figures of speech may be found outside of special literary expressions.

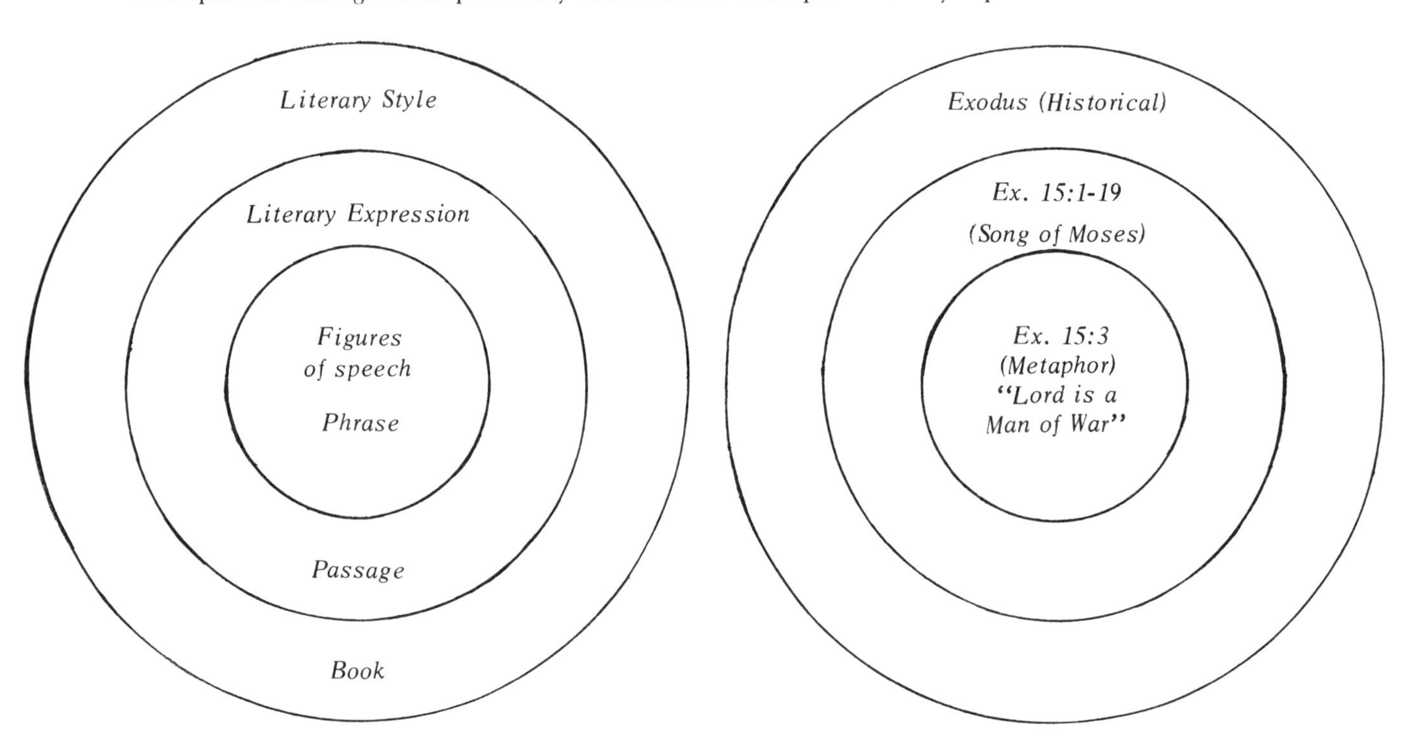

C. **Tools:** The following is only a partial listing of some of the tools that may be used to bridge the linguistic gap.

Concordances

Englishman's Greek Concordance (Zondervan)
Englishman's Hebrew & Chaldee Concordance (Zondervan)

Greek-English Concordance to the New Testament, J.B. Smith (Herald Press)
Strong's Exhaustive Concordance (Abingdon)
Young's Analytical Concordance (Eerdman's)

Lexicons

Analytical Greek Lexicon (Zondervan)
Analytical Hebrew & Chaldee Lexicon, B. Davidson (MacDonald)
Greek English Lexicon, Ardnt & Gingrich (University of Chicago Press)
Greek-English Lexicon, T. S. Green (Zondervan)
Hebrew-English Lexicon, W. Gesenius (Oxford)
Thayer's Greek-English Lexicon (Zondervan)

Lexical Aids

Expository Dictionary of New Testament Words, W. E. Vine (Revell)
Grammatical Insights into the New Testament, N. Turner (T & T Clark)
Lexical Aids for Students of New Testament Greek, B. Metzger (Theological Book Agency, Dist.)
New Testament Words, William Barclay (SCM Press)
New Testament Word Studies, J. A. Bengel (Kregel)
Synonyms of the New Testament, R. C. Trench
Synonyms of the Old Testament, R. B. Girdlestone (Eerdman's)
Syntax of the Moods and Tenses, E. Burton (T & T Clark)
Theological Dictionary of the New Testament, Kittel (Ed. Eerdman's)
Word Pictures in the New Testament, A. T. Robertson (Broadman Press)
Word Studies in the New Testament, M. R. Vincent (Eerdman's)

Grammars

Essentials of New Testament Greek, J. H. Huddilston (Macmillan)
Grammar of the Greek New Testament, A. T. Robertson (Broadman Press)
Greek Grammar of the New Testament, Blass & Debruner (University of Chicago Press)
Hebrew Grammar, Wm. Gesenius (Oxford University)
Introductory Hebrew Grammar, R. L. Harris (Eerdman's)
Manual Grammar of the Greek New Testament, Dana & Mantey (Macmillan)
New Testament Greek for Beginners, J. G. Machen (Macmillan)
Practical Grammar for Classical Hebrew, J. Weingreen (Oxford)
Figures of Speech Used in the Bible, E. W. Bullinger (Baker)

II. THE CULTURAL GAP

A. **Problem:** The cultural contexts of the Biblical writers differ vastly from the cultural context of the modern day reader.

B. **Solution:** This cultural gap may be bridged by studying the cultures in which the writers of Scripture lived. However, the solution to this problem is made more complex by the fact that different writers lived in cultural settings diverse from one another. As the centuries passed, God's people were influenced culturally by the Egyptian, Phoenician, Assyrian, Babylonian, Persian, Grecian and Roman cultures.

By "culture," we mean the ways and means, both material and social, whereby a given people carry on their existence. The cultural gap in its broadest sense would certainly include the linguistic gap, the historical gap, and the geographical gap. But for the purposes of this outline, we are using it in a much narrower sense. The study of Biblical cultures can be divided into two main classifications:

1. **Material Culture:** In order to understand a society it is necessary to study the material features and expressions of that society. This includes a consideration of such things as housing, cooking utensils, food, clothing, agricultural implements, weapons, means of transportation, animals, art forms, and religious articles (e.g., it is impossible to properly interpret ***Jeremiah 2:13*** without an understanding of what a "cistern" represented in that cultural context).

2. **Social Culture:** In order to understand a society it is also necessary to explore the *way* things are done and the *manner* in which the people of that society relate to one another. Considering the way in which a society lives includes such areas as how the people make their living; where they live geographically; how they worship, recreate, make clothing, farm and cook. The *manner* in which the members of a society relate to one another would involve consideration of areas such as family customs, economic practices, civil laws, legal procedures, military tactics; as well as various types of social groupings (e.g., in ***Genesis 29:26*** we find that Jacob would not have been deceived had he been familiar with the marriage customs in the land of Nahor; it is impossible to properly interpret ***I Peter 5:4*** without an understanding of how the ''chief shepherd'' functioned in that day).

The way in which a people live within their environment molds their way of thinking. Therefore to understand the way in which a people think it is necessary to become acquainted with the way they live, bridging the cultural gap.

C. **Tools:** The following is only a partial listing of some of the tools that may be used to bridge the cultural gap.
All the Holy Days and Holidays of the Bible, H. Lockyer (Zondervan)
All the Trades and Occupations of the Bible, H. Lockyer (Zondervan)
Archaeology and the Ancient Testament, J. L. Kelso (Zondervan)
The Bible and Archaeology, J. A. Thomson (Eerdman's)
Biblical Archaeology, G. E. Wright (Westminister Press)
Everyday Life in Bible Times (National Geographic Society)
Insights into Bible Times and Customs, Weiss (Moody)
The Land and the Book, W. M. Thomson (Harper & Brothers)
Life and Times of Jesus the Messiah, A. Edersheim (Eerdmans)
Manners and Customs of the Bible, J. Freeman (Logos International)
Manners and Customs of Bible Lands, F. H. Wight (Moody)
Orientations in Bible Lands, E. W. Rice (American Sunday School Union)

Bible Dictionaries

Bible Dictionary, Smith (Holt, Rinehart & Winston)
Davis Dictionary of the Bible (Revell)
International Standard Bible Encyclopedia (Eerdman's)
The New Bible Dictionary (Eerdman's)
Pictorial Bible Dictionary, M. C. Tenney (Zondervan)
Unger's Bible Dictionary (Moody)

III. THE GEOGRAPHICAL GAP

A. **Problem:** The geographical context of the Biblical writers is foreign to the modern day reader.

B. **Solution:** This geographical gap may be bridged by a study of the geographical setting in which the events and writing of the Bible occurred. The problem is accentuated, however, by the fact that the writers themselves lived in different geographical contexts (e.g., Paul in Rome, Daniel in Babylon, and Moses in the wilderness). The problem is further complicated by the fact that some places mentioned in ancient writings either no longer exist or are no longer called by the same name. The answers to these problems can only be found by using the spade of archaeology. This involves study in three general areas:

1. **Political Geography:** In order to become acquainted with the cities, states and nations mentioned by the Biblical authors, we are dependent upon the research of the archaeologist. We are not necessarily looking to the archaeologist to substantiate the existence of a city or state, rather we are seeking facts concerning that place which will aid us in interpretation (e.g., it would be impossible to understand Elijah's run from Carmel to Jezreel in ***I Kings 18:42-46*** without knowing the location of each and the distance between the two; archaeological evidence has greatly helped in understanding ***Isaiah 44:27-45:2*** relative to the fall of Babylon).

2. **Geological Geography:** In order to understand references to climate, land formations, seas and rivers, we depend in part on archaeological evidences and in part on maps, written descriptions, photography and modern travel. A problem in this area is that, though the physical features of the Middle East have not

changed drastically since Bible days, in some instances the names for them have (e.g., ***Psalms 125:2*** and ***Isaiah 2:2*** will be much more appreciated when the topography of the area around Jerusalem is considered; the significance of ***II Kings 5:10, 12*** will be better understood by a consideration of the rivers mentioned).

3. **Botanical and Zoological Geography:** To understand allusions to plant life and animal life by Bible authors, we are dependent on both archaeology and modern science in order to relate ancient terms to presently known plants and animals, and to study their characteristics and behavioral patterns (e.g., one cannot effectively interpret ***Proverbs 30:19-31,*** or ***Luke 13:32*** without an understanding of the nature, habits and instincts of the creatures mentioned there; a study of Biblical botany will unfold the beauty of ***Song of Solomon 2:1-3).***

Thus research into the political, geological, botanical and zoological divisions of geography enable the interpreter to bridge the geographical gap.

C. **Tools:** The following is only a partial listing of some of the tools that may be used to bridge the geographical gap.

All the Animals of the Bible Lands, G. Cunsdale (Zondervan)
Animals and Birds of the Bible, B. L. Goddard (A P & A)
Baker's Bible Atlas, Pfeiffer (Baker)
Geography of the Bible, D. Baly (Harper & Brothers)
The Macmillan Bible Atlas (Macmillan)
Oxford Bible Atlas (Oxford Press)
The Wycliffe Historical Geography of Bible Lands, Pfeiffer & Vos. (Moody)

See also "Bible Dictionaries" listed under Cultural Tools.

IV. THE HISTORICAL GAP

A. **Problem:** The Historical context of the Biblical writers differs greatly from that of the modern day reader.

B. **Solution:** The way to bridge this historical gap is to become familiar with the historical setting for the events of the Bible and in which the writers lived. But this pursuit is complicated by the fact that the writers lived during a period spanning sixteen centuries, from Moses to John, and in a constantly changing world situation. In each era of history the world situation must be considered from three viewpoints:

1. **Political Background:** In order to understand the significance of events and viewpoints in Scripture, the political background must be taken into account. Succeeding governments have differing effects upon the peoples under their control so that the total lives of individuals are definitely influenced by the political order of which they are a part, whether willingly or unwillingly. In order to interpret the actions of Bible characters and writers, one must do everything possible to mentally place himself within that political environment (e.g., the significance of ***Hosea 12:1*** can only be comprehended in the light of the political relationships between Ephraim, Assyria and Egypt; we cannot understand why the disciples of Jesus misunderstood His statements in ***Matthew 20:21*** and ***Acts 1:6*** without recognizing the political concerns of the day).

2. **Economic Background:** Another factor which must be taken into consideration in order to understand the significance of events and viewpoints in Scripture is the economic background of the period. The economic situation, whether local or universal, exerts great influence on a people's way of life. This is seen by the diversity or uniformity of occupations within a society and the resultant creation of rich and poor classes. The interpreter must imagine himself in the economic situation of the passage he is interpreting (e.g., the economic wealth and need in the Early Church played a major role in fusing the Jewish and Gentile believers; see ***Acts 11:27-29).***

3. **Religious Background:** Finally, in order to properly understand events and viewpoints in Scripture, the religious background must also be considered. Societies have always been greatly influenced by religion; the lives of individuals often revolve around, or are at least affected by their religions. Throughout Scripture God's people are seen in relation to other religious groups as either being influenced by them or in conflict with them. Hence the need for the interpreter to place himself within the religious frame of reference of the writers and characters of Scripture (e.g., the significance of ***Leviticus 18:9-14*** cannot be estimated apart from an evaluation of the Canaanite religions; Paul's conflict in Ephesus can only be brought to life by research into the religious context of Diana worship in Ephesus; ***Acts 19:24-41).***

Thus a study into the political, economic and religious background aids the interpreter in bridging the historical gap.

C. **Tools:** The following is only a partial listing of some of the tools that may be used to bridge the historical gap.

Archaeology & Bible History, J. P. Free (Van Kampen Press)
Archaeology and the Old Testament, Unger (Zondervan)
The Bible and Archaeology, J. A. Thomson (Paternoster Press)
Bible History—Old Testament, A. Edersheim (Eerdman's)
Old Testament Bible History, Edersheim (Eerdman's)
The Life and Times of Jesus the Messiah, A. Edersheim (Eerdman's)
The Works of Flavius Josephus (Kregel)

See also "Bible Dictionaries" listed under Cultural Tools.

THE CONTEXT GROUP OF PRINCIPLES

Ch. 6	The Context Principle
Ch. 7	The First Mention Principle
Ch. 8	The Comparative Mention Principle
Ch. 9	The Progressive Mention Principle
Ch. 10	The Complete Mention Principle

As governing laws and rules of procedure the principles of interpretation listed above may be grouped together because of their inter-relatedness. The relationship between them is that the last four are actually specialized extensions of the Context Principle. When an interpreter begins to use these principles he will realize that they are meant to be used as a group.

Chapter 6
THE CONTEXT PRINCPLE

I. DEFINITION

That principle by which the interpretation of any verse is determined upon a consideration of its context.

II. AMPLIFICATION

The word "context" is composed of two Latin words: "con," meaning "together"; "textus," meaning "woven"; and denotes something that is woven together. In literature it refers to the connection of thought running through a portion or the whole of a writing. In relation to Scripture, it signifies the connection of thought running through either the whole of Scripture, a Testament, a book of the Bible, or a particular passage.

In being used of God to weave the Biblical contexts, the writers of Scripture utilized two methods; writing fresh revelation, and weaving together previous revelation.

Fresh Revelation Context—The writers of Scripture were inspired by the Holy Spirit to write thoughts previously unknown to them. Some examples of this are: Jeremiah's revelation concerning the New Covenant ***(Jeremiah 31:31-34),*** and Paul's revelation of the mystery of the body of Christ ***(Ephesians 2:11-3:21).*** This method of writing context substantiates the need for illumination of the Holy Spirit in interpreting Scripture. That which the Spirit inspires, the Spirit must also interpret.

Woven Revelation Context—Under inspiration, the writers of Scripture at times wove together thoughts already known to them. For example, to establish the universality of guilt in ***Romans 3:9-18*** Paul weaves together five quotations from the Old Testament, and to prove the Son to be greater than the angels the writer to the Hebrews ***(Hebrews 1:4-14)*** weaves together seven quotations from the Psalms. This method of writing context substantiates the need for a context principle of interpreting Scripture. If the Spirit used Scripture to write Scripture then He will also use Scripture to interpret Scripture.

The evaluations of the two methods above lead us to the conclusion that the *method* by which the context was *written* gives rise to the *principle* by which the context may be *interpreted.* The involvement of inspiration in the writing of Scripture necessitates the interpreter receiving illumination. The weaving together of context necessitates the interpreter using the context principle.

These two principles are somewhat implied in ***I Corinthians 2:13,*** where Paul states that ***"we speak, not in the words which man's wisdom teacheth, but which the Holy Ghost teacheth; comparing spiritual things with spiritual."*** The phrase ***"the Holy Ghost teacheth"*** implies the inspiration and illumination of the Holy Spirit. The phrase ***"comparing spiritual things with spiritual"*** implies the use of Scripture in interpreting Scripture, as other translations indicate (***"interpreting spiritual truths with spiritual language"***—Amplified Bible).

One of the oldest and most highly regarded adages of hermeneutics is; "Scripture interprets Scripture." This communicates to us that the Bible, to a large degree, is self-explanatory and that the Holy Spirit will use Scripture to illumine Scripture. This underscores the value of the context principle as the "First Principle of Hermeneutics."

A further amplification of the context principle would be to say that a part can never be understood without the whole. This balances the burden of exegesis which contends that the whole cannot be understood without knowing the meaning of its parts. This paradox has been referred to by interpreters as the "hermeneutical circle" which rotates from part to whole, and from whole to part.

The interpreter must interpret the whole with a knowledge of its parts and interpret each part in the light of the whole.

The context of Scripture falls into four categories:

A. **The Whole of Scripture Context:** The context of any specific verse is the whole of Scripture. No one verse should be used on its own apart from its relationship to the whole body of Scripture. The phrase "Scripture interprets Scripture" means that the best interpreter of a Scripture is the Scripture.

B. **The Testament Context:** Within the whole of Scripture the context of any verse is the Testament in which it is found. Each of the two Testaments has its own distinctive character and emphasis. The general emphasis of the Old Testament is law; the emphasis of the New is grace. That which is the dividing point between the Testaments is the cross. As a general rule, the New is the interpreter of the Old.

"The New is in the Old contained, the Old is in the New explained."

C. **The Book Context:** Within the Scripture and the Testaments, the context of any verse is the specific book in which it is contained. Each of the sixty-six books of the Bible has its own particular purpose, message, and style. (e.g., The general theme of Romans is justification by faith, while the general theme of James is justification by works. Any verse in either book must be interpreted within the context of its respective message).

D. **The Passage Context:** Within the whole of Scripture, the Testaments, and the books of the Bible, the context of any verse is the passage in which it occurs. Each book of the Bible is divided subject-wise into passages, each consisting of a group of consecutive verses pertaining to a particular subject. Any single sentence or verse within a passage must be interpreted in the light of the subject-context of that passage. (e.g., ***Romans 11:26*** must be interpreted in the light of the subject-context of ***Romans 9-11,*** which constitutes the passage.)

These four categories can be illustrated by four concentric rings showing contexts within contexts:

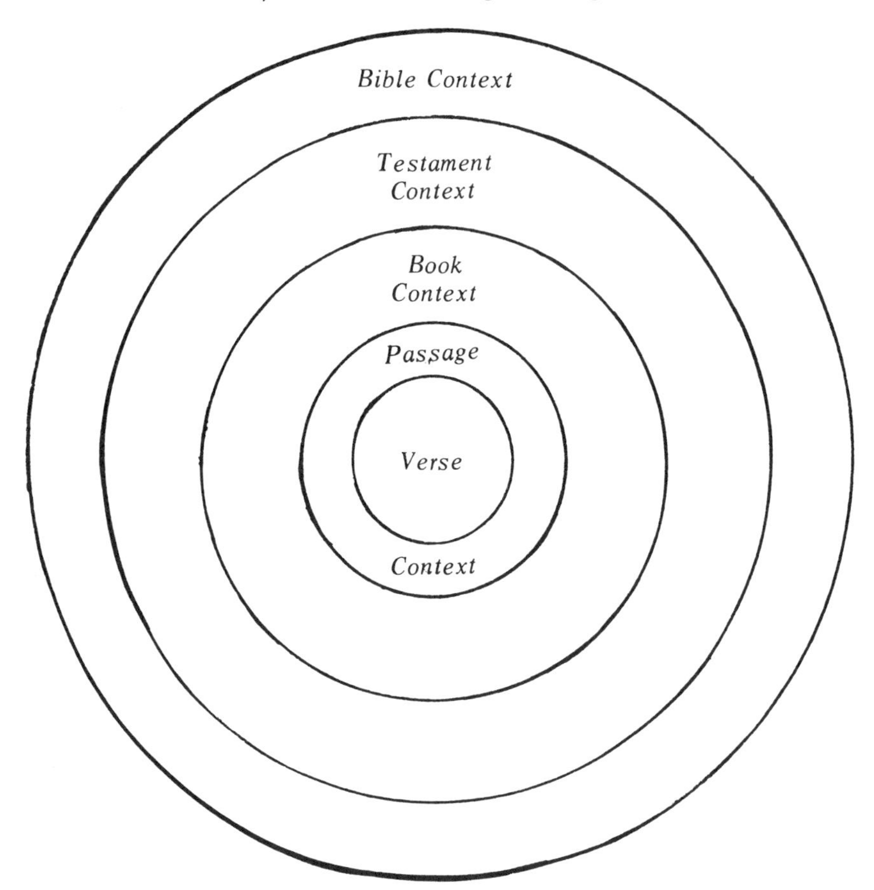

The context of a verse is the passage.
The context of the passage is the book.
The context of the book is the Testament.
The context of the Testament is the whole Bible.

Therefore the old adage "a text out of context is a pretext" must be rephrased to say "a text out of the context of the whole Bible is a pretext." The context of any verse is not only the passage, but also the book, the Testament and the whole Bible.

In conclusion, the literary method of *weaving together context* used in *writing Scripture* gives rise to the *context principle* of *interpreting Scripture.*

III. QUALIFICATION

A. Pervading all interpretation must be a utilization of the context principle.

B. The four-fold aspect of context must constantly be considered and appropriate emphasis should be placed on each of the four. Over-emphasis of any one aspect will produce an imbalance in interpretation, creating the danger of overlooking vast areas of truth.

C. In relation to the context principle, a verse should never be taken out of its setting and given a foreign meaning (a meaning not implied in the passage). Some examples are:

1. ***Matthew 10:9, 10:*** These verses have sometimes been interpreted to mean that a minister must never take any provision with him when traveling. These verses must be interpreted in the light of their context: Jesus was specifically commanding the twelve apostles for a specific mission. If they are interpreted to refer to all Christian ministry, we would have to assume also that ministry to the Gentiles and the Samaritans is forbidden, and only ministry to the house of Israel is permitted.

2. ***Luke 24:49:*** This verse has at times been interpreted to mean that the Church should have "tarrying meetings" for the reception of the Baptism of the Holy Spirit. But the New Testament context of the book of Acts shows that tarrying was not necessary after the initial outpouring of the Holy Spirit at Pentecost. Had this verse been given to show us how to receive this enduement, then the context would also necessitate that we go to Jerusalem and there do our "tarrying."

D. In using the context principle, we must always allow the clear statements of Scripture to interpret the obscure. To reverse this order will cause confusion. For example:

1. ***Psalms 115:17; Ecclesiastes 9:5:*** These obscure verses concerning the state of the dead must be interpreted in the light of Jesus' clear teachings in ***Luke 16:19-31.***

2. ***Isaiah 53:*** This entire passage remains obscure to the reader unless viewed in light of the clear account of the Messiah's sufferings in the Gospels. (Note in ***Acts 8:26-35*** that Philip had to explain ***Isaiah 53*** to the eunuch.)

E. The context principle can be used to solve problems and apparent discrepancies in Scripture:

1. ***Genesis 35:2*** raises the question as to whether Jacob and his house were worshipping idols. The answer is to be found in the context of ***Genesis 31:25-35*** and ***Genesis 34:26-29,*** where we find that the idols had been kept as family heirlooms rather than as objects of worship.

2. ***Genesis 37:25, 28, 36; 39:1*** presents an apparent discrepancy in confusing the Ishmaelites with the Midianites. The solution to this is to be found in the context of ***Genesis 16: 11, 12*** and ***25:1, 2,*** where we find that Ishmael and Midian were half-brothers and settled in the same country.

3. ***Jeremiah 32:4*** and ***34:3*** seem to contradict ***Ezekiel 12:13.*** How could Zedekiah go to Babylon, see the king of Babylon, yet not see Babylon? The answer is to be found in the context of ***II Kings 25:6, 7*** where the fulfillment of these prophecies is reconciled. Zedekiah saw the king of Babylon in Jerusalem, had his eyes put out, and then was taken captive to Babylon.

F. To a certain extent, the use of the context principle enables us to determine the application of Scripture to those specifics of life that Scripture has not specifically treated.

IV. DEMONSTRATION

Hebrews 10:38 — "Now the just shall live by faith:" Let us consider this verse in the light of its four-fold context.

A. **The Passage Context *(Hebrews 10:19-12:2):*** The subject matter of this passage is "faith." This is the key word in the passage, used twenty-seven times. The subject is introduced in ***10:19-22*** with an exhortation to draw near to God with full assurance of faith in the blood of Jesus, our High Priest, who made the way for our entrance.

Then verses ***23-29*** follow with an exhortation to maintain this profession of faith, and with a warning against wavering or drawing back in unbelief. Chapter 10 flows into the phrase under consideration while Chapter 11 flows out from it, the latter providing illustrations from antiquity of how the just did live by faith. The subject is concluded in Chapter 12:2 by pointing to Jesus, who is the author and finisher of the faith of the just.

B. **The Book Context:** The purpose of the book of Hebrews is to show the superiority of Christ to all previous revelations. Christ is seen to be better than the prophets, the angels, Moses, and Joshua. The primary message is that the priesthood of Christ after the order of Melchisedec, with its perfect sacrifice and heavenly sanctuary found in the New Covenant, is far superior to the Aaronic priesthood with its animal sacrifices and earthly sanctuary within the Old Covenant. The goal of the book is faith in Christ as the mediator between God and man. The theme of faith in Chapters 10 and 12 must be viewed in contradistinction with the theme of unbelief in Chapters 3 and 4.

C. **The Testament Context:** Because Christ has come, He to whom the whole of the Old Testament pointed, the theme of the New Testament is faith in Him. The phrase being considered is unusual in that three New Testament epistles are built upon it: the use of the phrase in ***Romans 1:17*** emphasizes justification by faith in contrast to works; in ***Galatians 3:11*** it emphasizes life by faith in contrast to death by law; in ***Hebrews 10:38*** the nature of faith is contrasted with unbelief.

Romans 1:17	***"The JUST shall live by faith."***
Galatians 3:11	***"The just shall LIVE by faith."***
Hebrews 10:38	***"The just shall live by FAITH."***

D. **The Whole of Scripture Context:** The Bible as a whole reveals that it is the sin of unbelief that severs man's relationship with God and that only through the righteousness which is by faith can man be justified in His sight. Whether under the law of the Old Covenant or the grace of the New Covenant the just can live only by faith. It is in ***Habakkuk 2:4*** that we find this phrase first used. The relevance of this phrase to the whole of the Scriptural Context is confirmed by both the Old and New Testament writers' use of it, and by the list of the heroes of faith in ***Hebrews 11.***

It should be noted that the writer to the Hebrews himself utilized the context principle by interpreting ***Habakkuk 2:4*** in the light of the lives of Old Testament saints recorded in the Old Testament historical books. Thus, he used Old Testament history to interpret a verse out of Old Testament prophecy.

Chapter 7
THE FIRST MENTION PRINCIPLE

I. DEFINITION

The First Mention Principle is that principle by which the interpretation of any verse is aided by considering the first time its subject appears in Scripture.

II. AMPLIFICATION

In general, the first time a thing is mentioned in Scripture it carries with it a meaning which will be consistent throughout the entire Bible.

The first mention is:

—*A key* which unlocks the door into the full truth
—*A gateway* into the path of truth
—*A guide* to discovering the truth in its progressive unfolding
—*The first link* in a long chain of revelation
—*A seed* which has within it the full truth that is to be developed in all subsequent mentions

This presupposes that the Bible is viewed as a complete Book, rather than merely a compilation of books. Though it has many human authors, in the ultimate sense there is really only one author—God. ***Hebrews 1:1*** tells us: ***"God . . . spake in time past unto the fathers by the prophets";*** in ***Jeremiah 15:19*** God said to the prophet ***"thou shalt be as my mouth."*** Though the Bible writers were like many mouthpieces, there is only one Divine speaker throughout Scripture; the Bible is the Word of God. Since God knows the end from the beginning, as an author He was able to formulate in the first mention of a thing that which characterizes it in its progressive unfolding.

In writing Scripture, God used the literary method of first mention in that He indicated by the first mention of Scriptural subjects the truths, in His mind, that were to be connected with those subjects in subsequent mentions. This can be illustrated in six major areas which involve the use of first mention: (a) Principles, (b) Events, (c) Symbols, (D) Persons, (E) Places and (F) Prophecy.

A. **Principles:** God utilized the method of first mention in introducing a wide array of principles in Scripture. Generally, the first mention of a principle is to be seen in its demonstration rather than in its being represented in a word. In referring to the first mention of a principle we are not referring to the first mention of the *word* embodying the principle, but we are referring to the first *demonstration* of the principle. For example, though ***Genesis 15:6*** is the first use of the word "believe," the principle of faith is demonstrated in ***Genesis 3:20, 21.*** So the first mention of faith should be considered in ***Genesis 3*** rather than ***Genesis 15.***

God's use of first mention in relation to Scriptural principles is by demonstration rather than by signification. In Scripture God demonstrated the principle before He labelled it. Therefore God, in the first mention (demonstration) of a Scriptural principle, gave the full truth in seed form.

Genesis 1:1-3:	First mention of the principle of the agreement of the Spirit and the Word. ***"The Spirit of God moved . . . and God said . . . ."***
Genesis 1:27, 28:	First mention of the principle of kingship and dominion.
Genesis 3:21:	First mention of the principle of substitutionary sacrifice.

B. **Events:** God made use of the method of first mention in dealing with events in Scripture. In the first mention of Scriptural events the full truth was given in seed form.

Genesis 1:1:	First mention of the event of Creation.
Genesis 3:1-7:	First mention of the event of the fall of man.
Genesis 6-8:	First mention of the event of the flood.

C. **Symbols:** God utilized the method of first mention in introducing that which would become a symbol in Scripture. The link between that which becomes a symbol and what it symbolized was the characteristics common to both.

Things used as symbol	Common Characteristics	Things symbolized

In the first mention of that which becomes a symbol, the full truth is in seed form.

Genesis 1:9, 10: First mention of seas, which become a symbol.
Genesis 1:11, 12: First mention of seed and fruit, which become symbols.
Genesis 1:14-18: First mention of sun, moon and stars, which become symbols.

D. **Persons:** God utilized the method of first mention in presenting personalities in Scripture. In the first mention of persons in the Bible, the full truth of their characteristics is given in seed form.

Genesis 1:1: First mention of the person of God.
Genesis 1:26, 27: First mention of Adam and Eve.
Genesis 4:1, 2: First mention of Cain and Abel.

E. **Places:** God utilized the method of first mention in dealing with places in Scripture. Thus, in the first mention of places in the Bible, the full truth of their character and significance is given in seed form.

Genesis 2:8: First mention of Eden.
Genesis 10:10: First mention of Babylon.
Genesis 22:2: First mention of Mt. Moriah.

F. **Prophecy:** God utilized the method of first mention in prophetic themes in Scripture. Thus, in the first mention of prophetic subjects, the full truth is given in seed form.

Genesis 3:15: First Messianic prophecy mentioned.
Genesis 12:2, 3: First Abrahamic Covenant prophecy mentioned.
Genesis 25:23: First Esau/Edom Prophecy mentioned.

These illustrations shows that the *literary method of first mention* in writing Scripture gives rise to the *first mention principle* of interpreting Scripture.

III. QUALIFICATION

A. The first step in using the first mention principle is to accurately locate the first mention.

B. Never refer only to the first mention of a *word* in the Bible, rather try to discover if the *principle of that word* has been demonstrated previous to its use.

C. No subsequent mention of a subject should be used to contradict or violate that which is in the first mention.

D. The first mention principle may be used in relation to all subjects but its limitations should always be kept in full view. It must not be overemphasized, rather kept in its proper perspective.

E. The first mention principle should never be used alone to interpret a verse, as it is insufficient for a full interpretation. This principle must be used in conjunction with others.

IV. DEMONSTRATION

A. **Principles**

1. ***Romans 3:24, 25: "Being justified freely by His grace through the redemption that is in Christ Jesus: whom God hath set forth to be a propitiation through faith in His blood . . . ."***

The subject of these verses is justification by grace through faith in the blood of Jesus. The interpretation of these verses is greatly aided by considering the first demonstration of the principle in ***Genesis 3:21.*** With the fall of man, God came in grace and executed the death penalty upon a substitutionary victim. This verse implies bloodshed by the fact that Adam and Eve were clothed with coats of skin provided by the death of an animal. Adam and Eve were thus justified by grace through faith in the blood; they were clothed in the death of another. The first mention of this principle is a seed embodying within it the full truth of the doctrine of justification by grace through faith in the blood.

2. ***Zechariah 4:6: "Not by might, nor by power, but by My Spirit, saith the Lord of Hosts."***

This word was given to Zerubbabel by the Lord as a word of encouragement to not depend on natural strength, but to depend rather on the power of the Spirit. By referring to the first demonstration of the principle of the Spirit's operations in ***Genesis 1:2,*** light is shed upon the subject. We discover the Spirit moving in a way which would be impossible for man in his natural strength. The significance of ***Genesis 1:2*** in relation to this principle is that it points out that it was by the power of the Spirit that the strength of the natural realm was created. And so why should Zerubbabel want to depend on the lesser natural strength when he could depend on the greater Spiritual power that created the lesser?

B. **Events**

1. ***Luke 17:26, 27: "And as it was in the days of Noe, so shall it be also in the days of the Son of man. They did eat, they drank, they married wives, they were given in marriage, until the day that Noe entered into the ark, and the flood came, and destroyed them all."***

The subject of these verses is the corruption of mankind in the days of Noah which brought about the event of the flood. The first mention of this event is found in ***Genesis 6-8.*** In ***Genesis 6:1-13,*** the background of the event is seen to be the corruption of mankind. Then ***Genesis 7:11-24*** gives the account of God's judgment upon all the earth by water. God preserved a faithful remnant, Noah and his family, from destruction by the flood. Thus, our understanding of the verses in Luke is based on the first mention of this event found in Genesis.

2. ***Romans 5:12: "Wherefore, as by one man sin entered into the world, and death by sin; and so death passed upon all men, for that all have sinned:"***

The subject of this verse is the entrance of sin and death into the world by one man. This verse is a subsequent mention of an event first mentioned in ***Genesis 3:1-7***, These verses record the fall of man; in which the first sin occurred, resulting in the entrance of death. In viewing ***Genesis 2:17,*** we find that death came as a result of sin. The one man by whom sin entered was Adam. The initial sin was eating of fruit of the tree of the knowledge of good and evil. This act made Adam and his seed subject to death. Thus, the first mention of this event in Genesis gives us the historical details necessary to understand the doctrinal statement of Romans.

C. **Symbols**

1. ***Daniel 7:2, 3: "The four winds of the heaven strove upon the great sea. And four great beasts came up from the sea . . ."***

In these verses, the sea is used as a symbol. The first mention of the sea is found in ***Genesis 1:9, 10.*** Though the first mention of the sea does not interpret the symbol, it does reveal certain characteristics of that which later becomes a symbol. The characteristics of the sea seen in Genesis are vastness and complexity of motion. This information aids in interpreting the verses in Daniel.

2. ***I Corinthians 15:41, 42: "There is one glory of the sun, and another glory of the moon, and another glory of the stars: for one star differeth from another star in glory. So also is the resurrection of the dead . . . ."***

The subject here is the differing glories of the celestial bodies. The first mention of the sun, moon and stars is found in ***Genesis 1:14-18.*** In this passage, the sun is referred to as the greaterlight ruling the day, the moon is the lesser light ruling the night, and the stars are referred to as having a part in the night. They were given to divide the light from the darkness, to give light upon the earth, and to be for signs, seasons, days and years. These heavenly bodies are characterized by rulership and varying glories in light bearing, which aids us in understanding the significance of the statements in ***I Corinthians 15:41, 42.***

D. **Persons**

1. ***Revelation 20:2: "And he laid hold on the dragon, that old serpent, which is the Devil, and Satan, and bound him a thousand years."***

The subject of this verse is the person of Satan. He is referred to as that old serpent and judgment is pronounced on him. The first mention of him is found in ***Genesis 3:1-15.*** Satan is here presented as a serpent manifesting subtilty and deception. He is seen challenging the Word of God, deceiving Eve, bringing about the fall of man by causing him to disobey the Word of God, and coming under Divine judgment. Thus the first mention in Genesis provides the background for understanding the full significance of the verse in Revelation.

2. ***Luke 1:17: "And he shall go before Him in the spirit and power of Elias, to turn the hearts of the fathers to the children, and the disobedient to the wisdom of the just; to make ready a people prepared for the Lord."***

This verse pertains to Elijah. He is first mentioned in ***I Kings 17:1-7,*** where we see him pronouncing judgment by the Word of the Lord. The ultimate purpose of his ministry was to bring about repentance in the nation of Israel. This first mention aids us in understanding how John the Baptist was to come in the spirit and power of Elijah, calling the nation to repentance.

E. **Places**

1. ***Jude 7: "Even as Sodom and Gomorrha, and the cities about them in like manner, giving themselves over to fornication . . . are set forth for an example, suffering the vengeance of eternal fire."***

The subject of this verse centers around the cities of Sodom and Gomorrha. The first mention of these cities is in ***Genesis 13:10-13*** and it points out their great wickedness before the Lord, which became the cause for their great judgment. The first mention in Genesis provides the background for understanding the verse in Jude.

2. ***Zechariah 9:9: "Rejoice greatly, O daughter of Zion; shout, O daughter of Jerusalem: behold thy King cometh unto thee: He is just, and having salvation; lowly, and riding upon an ass, and upon a colt, the foal of an ass."***

The subject of this verse involves the holy hill of Zion. The first mention of Zion is found in ***II Samuel 5:6-9,*** which shows us that Zion was a stronghold and became the city of King David. Thus, the first mention of Zion in ***II Samuel*** aids us in realizing the full significance of the statement in ***Zechariah.***

F. **Prophecy.**

1. ***Luke 1:32, 33: "He shall be great, and shall be called the Son of the Highest: and the Lord God shall give unto Him the throne of His father David: And He shall reign over the house of Jacob forever; and of His kingdom there shall be no end."***

The subject of these verses is the prophecy of the everlasting throne and kingdom of David. The first mention of this prophetic stream is in the Davidic Covenant recorded in ***II Samuel 7:12-17.*** The clauses of the Covenant point out that God would set up David's seed upon his throne forever. Thus, the first mention of this prophetic theme provides help in understanding the reference in Luke.

2. ***Isaiah 7:14: "Therefore the Lord Himself shall give you a sign; Behold, a virgin shall conceive and bear a Son, and shall call His name Immanuel."***

The subject of this verse is a prophecy of the incarnation. The first mention of this prophetic stream is in ***Genesis 3:15,*** where the seed of the woman is referred to. This prophecy actually implies the virgin birth. The first mention in Genesis thus aids in interpreting the prophecy in Isaiah.

Chapter 8
THE COMPARATIVE MENTION PRINCIPLE

I. DEFINITION

The Comparative Mention Principle is that principle by which a certain verse or group of verses may be interpreted by comparing and/or contrasting it with another verse or group of verses.

II. AMPLIFICATION

To *"compare"* means to bring things together in order to examine the relationships they bear to each other, especially with the view of ascertaining their agreement or disagreement; points of resemblance or difference. To *"contrast"* means to place together in view things widely differing from each other, though of the same category or class, in order to make the difference more vividly marked. In the comparative mention principle these words denote a bringing together of Scriptures which deal with a certain subject area in order to clarify the interpretation of each by comparison or contrast. This principle can then be seen to be an integral part of the context principle in that Scripture is used to interpret Scripture: ***"Comparing spiritual things with spiritual"* (I Corinthians 2:13).** The Bible writers themselves used the literary method of comparison and contrast in their writing of Scripture. This can be illustrated in seven major areas that involve comparison and contrast: (A) Principles, (B) Events, (C) Symbols, (D) Persons, (E) Places, (F) Prophecy and (G) Parables.

A. **Principles:** Bible writers used comparison and contrast in dealing with a wide array of principles. In ***Deuteronomy 28:1-6, 15-19*** there is a contrasting of the blessing of obedience with the curse of disobedience:

Blessing		Cursing
vs. 1, 2	Obedience	— vs. 15 Disobedience
vs. 3	Blessed city, field	— vs. 16 Cursed in city, field
vs. 4	Blessed fruit, land, man	— vs. 18 Cursed fruit, land, man
vs. 5	Blessed basket, store	— vs. 17 Cursed basket, store
vs. 6	Blessed coming in, going out	— vs. 19 Cursed coming in, going out

B. **Events:** Bible writers used comparison and contrast in dealing with historical events. In ***John 3:14, 15*** Jesus said, ***"As Moses lifted up the serpent in the wilderness, even so must the Son of man be lifted up."*** In ***Luke 17:26*** He proclaimed, ***"As it was in the days of Noe, so shall it be also in the days of the Son of man."***

C. **Symbols:** Comparison and contrast are used in relation to symbolic things. In ***Hebrews 8:2, 5, 8-12,*** the contrast between the earthly and heavenly Tabernacle is set forth. ***II Corinthians 3:1-18*** contrasts the Tables of Stone and the Tables of the Heart:

Tables of Stone	Tables of Heart
Tablets of stone	—Tablets of the heart
Written with finger of God	—Written with the Spirit of God
Ministration of death	—Ministration of life
The letter killeth	—The Spirit giveth life
Glory to be done away	—Glory which is greater to remain
The Old Testament	—The New Testament
Ministration of condemnation	—Ministration of Righteousness
Veil on the face of Moses	—No veil; may behold His face; be changed
Done away, abolished	—That which remaineth

D. **Persons:** Bible writers used comparison and contrast in dealing with persons. ***I Corinthians 15:45-49*** contrasts the First Adam with the Last Adam:

First Adam	Last Adam
The Natural	—The Spiritual
Living soul	—The quickening spirit
Of the earth, earthly	—The Lord from heaven
Image of the earthly	—Image of the heavenly
The first man	—The second man

Romans 5:12-21 does likewise:

One man's disobedience	—One man's obedience
Many made sinners	—Many made righteous
Death unto condemnation	—Life unto justification

Hebrews 5:1-5 contrasts the Priesthood of Aaron with the Priesthood of Jesus.

E. **Places:** Bible writers used comparison and contrast in dealing with places. ***Hebrews 12:18-21, 22-29*** contrasts Mt. Sinai with Mt. Sion:

Mt. Sinai	Mt. Sion
Mount that might be touched	—Spiritual mount
Mt. Sinai, Law Covenant	—Mt. Sion, Grace Covenant
Trumpet, Voice of words	—Voice of Jesus
Moses, Old Covenant Mediator	—Jesus, New Covenant Mediator
Blood of animals	—Blood of Jesus
Voice shook the mount	—Voice will shake all things
Angels involved in giving of the Law	—Innumerable company of angels
The Nation of Israel, God's General Assembly, Firstborn	—General Assembly and Church of the Firstborn
Quaking, smoke, fire	—God is a consuming fire

Revelation 11:8 compares Jerusalem with Sodom and Egypt: "*. . . the great City, which spiritually is called Sodom and Egypt, where also our Lord was crucified.*"

F. **Prophecy:** Bible writers used comparison and contrast in dealing with prophecy and fulfillment. ***Acts 2:14-36*** compares Joel's and David's prophecies with the events of the Day of Pentecost and the Lord Jesus Christ in His enthronement. ***Acts 15:1-20*** compares the prophecies of Amos and the other prophets with the salvation of the Gentiles. ***Matthew 1:18-25*** compares Isaiah's prophecy with the virgin birth of Jesus.

G. **Parables:** Bible writers recorded the use of comparison and contrast in dealing with parables. ***Matthew 13:3-9, 18-23***—The Parable of the Sower:

Parable	The Interpretation
A sower soweth the seed	—The seed is the Word
Wayside ground	—Hearer of Word, understands not
Stony ground	—Hears Word, no depth, stony heart
Thorny ground	—Thorns of riches, cares of this life
Good ground	—Good, honest heart, fruitfulness

Compare ***Mark 4:26-29; Luke 8:4-15,*** with ***Matthew 13:3-9, 18-23*** in order to gain a full interpretation by the comparative mention principle. ***Matthew 13:24-30, 36-43***—The Parable of the Wheat and Tares:

Parable	The Interpretation
A man who sowed seed	—The Son of Man
The good seed	—The children of the Kingdom of God
The enemy	—The Devil
The field	—The world
The tares, corrupt seed	—The children of the Wicked One
The time of the harvest	—The harvest is the end of the age

Tares gathered into bundles first and cast into the fire	—The wicked gathered together and into the fire
The wheat gathered into the garner	—The good gathered into the heavenly kingdom

These illustrations show that the writers used comparison and contrast in writing Scripture, which gives rise to the comparative mention principle of interpreting Scripture. Once again, a means of the writing of Scripture leads us to a principle by which it is interpreted.

The *literary method of comparison and contrast* used in writing Scripture gives rise to the *comparative mention principle* of interpreting Scripture.

III. QUALIFICATION

A. This principle should be used whenever there is more than one verse or passage in Scripture which deals with the same subject. In other words, when studying a subject in the Bible, all that the Bible has to say on that subject must be taken into consideration.

B. No doctrine should be formulated on the basis of one verse or passage of Scripture. For example:

1. ***I Corinthians 15:29:*** This verse has been used as the basis for the doctrine of ''baptism for the dead.'' However, this is nowhere else mentioned in Scripture and a cultural understanding of this passage shows that it was a non-Christian ceremony.

2. ***Mark 16:16:*** The doctrine of baptism would be left quite incomplete if it were based on this one verse alone. By itself, this verse could lead to error if it were not compared with other Scriptures on baptism in the Gospels, Acts and the Epistles.

C. Passages can be compared only when, by reason of internal evidence, they are shown to deal with the same subject.

D. Passages should not be compared when, by so doing, interpretation is derived that conflicts with other clear statements of Scripture. Discretion must be used in comparing Scripture with Scripture.

E. When comparing verses or passages, first determine the meaning of the clearer passages and then proceed to interpret the more obscure ones in the light of these.

F. The comparative mention principle may be used to solve problems and apparent discrepancies in Scripture. Sometimes two apparently contradictory verses may be reconciled by considering an appropriate third verse. For example:

Romans 4:2, 3:	Justified by faith	***James 2:17, 18, 20, 26***
James 2:21, 24:	Justified by works	Faith and Works reconciled

Two apparently contradictory verses are reconciled by bringing in a third in the comparative mention principle.

IV. DEMONSTRATION

A. **Principles: *Ephesians 4:22-24; Colossians 3:5-14***—both of these passages deal with the contrast between the old man and the new man. We will consider these two together by dealing with their contrastive elements. In doing so we can use the Colossians passage to interpret the Ephesians passage, since Colossians lists both the characteristic sins of the old man and the characteristic virtues of the new man. Thus, by comparison and contrast, these passages are interpreted.

Ephesians 4:22-24	***Colossians 3:5-14***
Put off	—Put off
The old man	—All these (list of sins)
Be renewed	—Renewed in knowledge
Spirit of your mind	—Image of Him
Put on	—Put on
The new man	—(List of virtues)

B. **Events:** ***Matthew 9:20-22; Mark 5:25-34; Luke 8:43-48***—Each of these passages record the healing of the woman having an issue of blood. Only by harmonizing the details given in these three accounts can there be a full interpretation; each supplies information not supplied by others. Thus, only by comparison can the event be interpreted.

Matthew 9:20-22	*Mark 5:25-34*	*Luke 8:43-48*
Woman diseased 12 years Touched hem of Faith made her whole	—Suffered physicians —Spent all she had —Nothing bettered —Grew worse —Touched garment Virtue gone out of Him Disciples reaction She fell down, told truth Whole of plague. Peace	—Spent all living on doctors —Incurable —Touched border of garment —All denied touching Him —Peter the spokesman here also Faith made whole, go in peace

C. **Symbols:** ***Genesis 22:7, 8; Exodus 12:1-4; 29:38-41; Isaiah 53:7; John 1:29, 36; Acts 8:32; I Peter 1:19, 20; Revelation 5:6, 8, 12, 13; 12:11; 13:8; 22:1-3.*** To interpret the symbol of the lamb in Scripture, it is necessary to gather and compare the verses pertaining to this symbol. In this way symbols are interpreted by the comparative mention principle.

Genesis 22:7, 8:	***"Where is the lamb for a burnt offering?" ". . . God will provide Himself a lamb . . ."***
Exodus 12:1-4:	The Passover Lamb.
Exodus 29:38-41:	The lamb for the morning and evening sacrifice.
Isaiah 53:7:	***"He is brought as a lamb to the slaughter, and as a sheep before her shearers is dumb, so He openeth not His mouth."***
John 1:29, 36:	***"Behold, the lamb of God which taketh away the sin of the world."***
Acts 8:32:	***"He was led as a sheep to the slaughter; and like a lamb dumb before His shearer, so opened He not His mouth."***
I Peter 1:19, 20:	***"But with the precious blood of Christ, as of a lamb without blemish and without spot: who verily was foreordained before the foundation of the world, but was manifest in these last times for you."***
Revelation 5:6, 8, 12, 13:	The worthy slain Lamb.
Revelation 12:11:	Satan overcome by the blood of the Lamb.
Revelation 13:8:	The Lamb's Book of Life.
Revelation 22:1, 3:	The Throne of God and of the Lamb.

D. **Persons:** ***Genesis 5:21-24; Hebrews 11:5, 6; Jude 14, 15.*** In order to arrive at a complete Biblical character study of Enoch each of these three passages must be compared. To gain a clear understanding of persons in the Bible the Scriptures that mention them must be brought together and compared.

Genesis 5:21-24:	Enoch's translation.
Hebrews 11:5, 6:	Enoch's faith.
Jude 14, 15:	Enoch's prophecy.

E. **Places:** ***Genesis 10, 11; Daniel 1-5; Isaiah 13, 14, 47, 48; Jeremiah 50, 51; Revelation 17, 18.*** In order to gain a clear understanding of the City of Babylon in Scripture, all of these chapters must be considered and compared. To understand places in the Bible, the Scriptures that mention them must be brought together and compared.

Genesis 10, 11:	The origin of Babylon.
Daniel 1-5:	The glory of Babylon.
Isaiah 13, 14:	The king of Babylon.
Isaiah 47, 48:	The prophecy against the wise men of Babylon.
Jeremiah 50, 51:	Prophecies of the fall of Babylon.
Revelation 17, 18:	Judgment on Babylon.

F. **Prophecy:** ***Revelation 17, 18; Jeremiah 51.*** These prophetic chapters are concerned with the fall of Babylon. In viewing the prophecy of the fall of Old Testament Babylon, we find that they are comparable. In interpreting prophecy, prophetic passages relating to the same matter must be brought together and compared.

Rev. 17, 18	***Jer. 51***	
17:1, 15 —	***51:13***	The great whore
17:4 —	***51:7***	The cup
17:2	— ***51:7***	Drunken Babylon
17:4	— ***51:13***	Her raiment
17:6	— ***51:49***	Killing the saints
18:2, 21	— ***51:8***	Fall of Babylon
18:21	— ***51:63***	The millstone judgment
18:2, 3	— ***51:37***	Evil and corrupt birds
18:20	— ***51:48***	Rejoicing over downfall

G. **Parables:** ***Matthew 21:33-41; Mark 12:1-9; Luke 20:9-16.*** These passages record Christ's parable of the vineyard. They must first be compared with each other to obtain all the details; then other Scriptures should be brought to bear upon the interpretation of the parable. The comparative mention principle plays a vital role in the interpretation of parables.

The following is a comparison of the Gospel accounts of this parable:

Mark 12:1-9

1 And he began to speak unto them in parables. A man planted a vineyard, and set a hedge about it, and digged a pit for the winepress, and built a tower, and let it out to husbandmen, and went into another country.
2 And at the season he sent to the husbandmen a servant, that he might receive from the husbandmen of the fruits of the vineyard.
3 And they took him and beat him, and sent him away
4 empty. And again he sent unto them another servant: and him they wounded in the head, and handled shamefully.
5 And he sent another; and him they killed: and many others; beating some, and killing
6 some. He had yet one, a beloved son: he sent him last unto them, saying, they will rever-
7 ence my son. But those husbandmen said among themselves This is the heir; come, let us kill him, and the inheritance shall be ours.
8 And they took him, and killed him, and cast him forth out of the vineyard.
9 What therefore will the lord of the vineyard do? He will come and destroy the husbandmen, and will give the vineyard unto others.

Matthew 21:33-41

33 Hear another parable; There was a man that was a householder, which planted a vineyard, and set a hedge about it, and digged a winepress in it, and built a tower, and let it out to husbandmen, and went into another country.
34 And when the season of the fruits drew near, he sent his servants to the husbandmen, to receive his fruits.
35 And the husbandmen took his servants, and beat one, and killed another, and stoned another.
36 Again, he sent other servants more than the first: and they did unto them in like manner.
37 But afterward he sent unto them his son, saying, They will reverence my son.
38 But the husbandmen, when they saw the son, said among themselves, This is the heir; come let us kill him and take his inheritance.
39 And they took him, and cast him forth out of the vineyard, and killed him.
40 When therefore the lord of the vineyard shall come, what will he do unto those husbandmen?
41 They say unto him, He will miserably destroy those miserable men, and will let out the vineyard unto other husbandmen, which shall render him the fruits in their seasons.

Luke 20:9-16

9 And he began to speak unto the people this parable [*see Isaiah 5:1-2]* : A man planted a vineyard, and let it out to husbandmen, and went into another country for a long time.
10 And at the season he sent unto the husbandmen a servant, that they should give him of the fruit of the vineyard: but the husbandmen beat him, and sent him away empty.
11 And he sent yet another servant: and him also they beat, and handled him shamefully, and sent him away empty.
12 And he sent yet a third: and him also they wounded, and
13 cast him forth. And the Lord of the vineyard said, What shall I do? I will send my beloved son: it may be they will reverence him.
14 But when the husbandmen saw him, they reasoned one with another, saying, This is the heir: let us kill him, that the inheritance may be ours.
15 And they cast him forth out of the vineyard, and killed him. What therefore will the lord of the vineyard do unto them?
16 He will come and destroy these husbandmen, and will give the vineyard unto others. And when they heard it, they said, God forbid.

The following is an interpretation of the parable using the comparative mention principle in relation to symbols:

Parable Symbols	**Interpretation by Comparative Scriptures**
A certain householder	—God the Father
Planted vineyard, hedged it	—Israel Nation ***Isaiah 5:1; Psalms 80:9***
Digged winepress, built tower	—Winepress ***Isaiah 5:1-7***
Let out to husbandmen	—Rulers, Kings, Priests, Elders of Israel
Far country	—Heavenly country ***Hebrews 11:11-16***
Time of the fruit drew near	—
Sent His servants	—The prophets sent ***Hebrews 1:1; Jeremiah 35:15***
Husbandmen evilly treated them	—Killed and rejected the prophets ***II Chronicles 24:21; 36:16; Matthew 23:35, 37; Acts 7:52***
More servants sent	—More prophets sent, Major and Minor Prophets
Treated them likewise	—***Jeremiah 37:15; II Kings 17:13***
Last of all He sent His Son	—***John 3:16; Hebrews 1:1-12; Mark 12:6***
Husbandmen killed the Heir	—Heir of all things ***Psalms 2:8; Hebrews 1:2***
They caught Him	—In Gethsemane ***Matthew 26:47-56***
Cast Him out of vineyard	—Outside the City ***Hebrews 13:11-13; John 19:7***
Slew Him	—Slew, hanged on a tree ***Acts 10:39-43***
Lord of husbandmen miserably destroy those husbandmen	—Jerusalem destroyed in AD 70 ***Luke 19:41-44***
Let out vineyard to other husbandmen to get fruits	—Kingdom taken from Jewry, given to a Nation (Church, ***I Peter 2:5-9)*** who renders fruits ***Matthew 21:43***

By comparing the accounts of this parable in the Gospels and the parable symbols with other Scriptures pertaining to the same subject, we gain a fuller and clearer interpretation of this parable.

SPECIAL NOTE:** In considering ***Luke 24:25-27, 44-46, it seems evident that Jesus himself used the comparative mention principle by bringing together Scriptures from the Law, the Psalms and the Prophets and interpreting them as being fulfilled in Himself. Also, in ***Acts 17:1-3*** it seems that Paul used this principle as he reasoned from the Scriptures that Jesus of Nazareth was indeed the Christ.

Chapter 9
THE PROGRESSIVE MENTION PRINCIPLE

I. DEFINITION

That principle by which the interpretation of any verse is aided by a consideration of the progressive mentions of its subject in Scripture.

II. AMPLIFICATION

It is important to realize that the Word of God is a progressive revelation given, over the centuries, by God to man. The method of progressive revelation is implied in ***Isaiah 28:13,*** within the context of God's dealings with Israel: ***"But the Word of the Lord was unto them precept upon precept, precept upon precept; line upon line, line upon line; here a little, there a little . . . ."*** By ***"progressive revelation"*** we mean the successive unfolding of a continuous theme to its consummation. God, as the virtual author of Scripture, was able to progressively reveal His person and purpose. These themes in Scripture can be symbolized as "rivers of truth" that begin in Genesis and run through the books of the Bible into the "sea" of Revelation. God did not give the full truth at once, rather He unfolded it progressively to man step by step, detail by detail, each portion giving further amplification and clarification. Thus, God spoke ***"in many separate revelations, each of which set forth a portion of the truth" (Hebrews 1:1*** Amplified***).***

In writing Scripture, God utilized the literary method of progressive mention such that in each successive mention of a Biblical subject He gave further light as to its significance and a clearer understanding of its meaning. This can be illustrated in six major areas which involve the use of progressive mention: (A) Principles, (B) Events, (C) Symbols, (D) Persons, (E) Places and (F) Prophecy.

A. **Principles:** God utilized the method of progressive mention in developing a wide array of principles in Scripture.

The Principle of the Agreement of the Spirit and the Word

Genesis 1:1-3:	*"The Spirit of God moved . . . and God said . . ."*
II Samuel 23:2:	*"The Spirit of the Lord spake by me, and His word was in my tongue."*
II Chronicles 20:14, 15:	*". . . came the Spirit . . . and he said . . . thus saith the Lord . . ."*
Isaiah 61:1:	*"The Spirit of the Lord God is upon me; because the Lord hath anointed me to preach good tidings . . ."*
John 1:14, 32:	*"And the Word was made flesh . . . the Spirit descending . . . abode upon Him."*
Acts 10:44:	*"While Peter yet spake these words, the Holy Ghost fell on all them which heard the word."*
Ephesians 6:17:	*". . . the sword of the Spirit, which is the Word of God."*

These verses are only samples to point out how this principle is unfolded progressively in Scripture.

B. **Events:** God utilized the method of progressive mention in dealing with events in Scripture and their significance.

The Event of the Fall of Man

Genesis 3:1-7:	Man sins by partaking of the Tree of the Knowledge of Good and Evil.
Job 31:33:	*"If I covered my transgressions as Adam . . ."*
Romans 5:12-21:	*"By one man sin entered into the world . . ."*
I Corinthians 15:22:	*"As in Adam all die . . ."*
I Timothy 2:13, 14:	*"Adam was not deceived . . ."*

These passages reveal progressively the significance of this event.

C. **Symbols:** God utilized the method of progressive mention in developing the truths connected with that which He used as symbols in Scripture.

The Symbols of the Sun, Moon, and Stars

Genesis 1:14-18:	The sun, moon and stars set in the heavens as signs.
Genesis 37:9, 10:	Joseph's dream of the sun, moon and stars used as a symbol of the family.
Psalms 148:3:	"Praise ye Him, sun and moon: praise Him, all ye stars of light."
Ezekiel 32:7:	The sun, moon and stars darkened
Luke 21:25:	Signs in the sun, moon and stars
I Corinthians 15:41, 42:	The glory of the sun, moon and stars
Revelation 6:12, 13:	The sun, moon darkened, stars fell
Revelation 12:1:	A woman clothed with the sun, moon and stars

These Scriptures, as well as many others, show a progression of thought concerning the literal and symbolic significance of these heavenly bodies.

D. **Persons:** God utilized the method of progressive mention in presenting the name, character, office and function of persons in Scripture.

The Person of God—His Redemptive Names

Genesis 2:4:	The Lord, the Creator
Genesis 14:22:	The Lord, the Most High God
Genesis 22:14:	The Lord, the Provider
Exodus 15:26:	The Lord, the Healer
Exodus 17:15:	The Lord, the Banner
Judges 6:24:	The Lord, our Peace
Psalms 23:1:	The Lord, the Shepherd
Jeremiah 23:6:	The Lord, our Righteousness
Acts 2:36:	The Lord Jesus Christ
Revelation 22:21:	The Lord Jesus Christ

The verses, together with others, unfold the progressive revelation of the glories of the compound redemptive names of God.

E. **Places:** God utilized the method of progressive mention in dealing with places in Scripture and their significance.

The Place of Babylon

Genesis 10:	The Origin of Babylon
Joshua 7:21:	A garment from Babylon
Isaiah 13, 14:	The burden of Babylon
Isaiah 46, 47:	Prophecies of the fall of Babylon
Jeremiah 50, 51:	Prophecies of the fall of Babylon
Zechariah 5:	Two women going to Babylon
I Peter 5:13:	The church at Babylon
Revelation 17:	Babylon, the woman
Revelation 18:	Babylon, the city

In these chapters a definite progressive development of God's estimate of Babylon can be seen.

F. **Prophecy:** God utilized the method of progressive mention in developing prophetic themes in Scripture.

Messianic Prophecy

Genesis 3:15:	The seed of the woman
Genesis 12:3:	The seed of Abraham
Genesis 49:10:	From the tribe of Judah
Numbers 24:7:	The star of Jacob
Deuteronomy 18:15:	The Prophet
Psalms 22:	The sufferings
Psalms 110:4:	The Melchizedek Priesthood

Isaiah 7:14:	Born of a virgin
Isaiah 53:	The sufferings
Zechariah 12:	Sold for silver

These Scriptures, with many others, illustrate God's progressive revelation of the prophetic theme concerning the Messiah.

These illustrations show that the *literary method of progressive mention* used in writing Scripture gives rise to the *progressive mention principle* of interpreting Scripture.

III. QUALIFICATION

A. The progressive mention principle is to be seen as:

1. An extension of the first mention principle, and
2. A part of the complete mention principle.

Therefore, it must be used in connection with these two principles especially.

B. It must be recognized that because truth is progressively unfolded in Scripture, no one verse contains the whole truth on any given theme. Each verse is a part of the whole and cannot be interpreted apart from the whole. No doctrine can be built on one verse, but rather must rest upon the whole of relevant Scripture.

C. No mention of a theme in Scripture should be used to contradict or violate any other mention of it.

D. Caution must be used in linking Scriptures together in a continuous chain. Only internal evidence showing an intrinsic link qualifies a group of verses to be a chain of progressive revelation in Scripture.

IV. DEMONSTRATION

A. **Principles:** ***Hebrews 9:22—"without shedding of blood is no remission."*** The subject of this verse is the forgiveness of sins through the shedding of blood. This verse can be properly interpreted only upon a consideration of the principle of bloodshed as it is progressively revealed through the Word. (Because of the vastness of this subject in Scripture, we will only consider some of the most vital references.)

Genesis 4:10, 11:	The shed blood speaks to God of death
Genesis 9:4:	Blood is the life of man
Exodus 12:	The blood is a sign with which God identifies
Exodus 24:8:	The covenant founded on sacrificial blood
Leviticus 17:10-14:	The life of the flesh is in the blood, the blood is an atonement for the soul
Luke 22:20:	The New Testament established with the blood of Jesus
Romans 5:9:	Justification by His blood
Ephesians 1:7:	Redemption through His blood
Hebrews 13:20:	Sanctification through His blood
Revelation 12:11:	Satan overcome through the blood of the Lamb

These Scriptures reveal the principle of bloodshed as being that shed blood is the evidence of death; shed blood is life poured forth. Because the penalty of sin is death and the shedding of blood represents death, it is only the shedding of blood that can atone for sin. In relation to the blood of Christ, all its benefits come to the believer through the shedding of His blood; that is, His death. God can only remit sin that has been judged by death.

B. **Events:** ***Matthew 10:15—"It shall be more tolerable for the land of Sodom and Gomorrha in the day of judgment . . ."*** The subject of this verse involves the event of the destruction of Sodom and Gomorrha. The progressive mentions of this event in Scripture shed light on the impact of this statement by Jesus.

Genesis 13:10-13:	Sodom and Gomorrha as the garden of Eden before its destruction
Genesis 18, 19:	Sodom and Gomorrha destroyed by fire, brimstone from heaven for its great wickedness
Deuteronomy 29:23:	Sodom and Gomorrha overthrown in the Lord's wrath
Isaiah 13:19:	Babylon to be utterly desolated as Sodom and Gomorrha

Amos 5:11:	Israel overthrown as Sodom and Gomorrha
Luke 17:28-30:	Cities of the world to be judged unexpectedly (as Sodom) at the Second Coming of Christ
II Peter 2:6-9:	Sodom and Gomorrha set forth as God's example judgment upon wicked cities
Jude 7:	Sodom and Gomorrha an example suffering the vengeance of eternal fire
Revelation 11:8:	The spiritual condition of Jerusalem is as Sodom

These Scriptures together reveal that the event of the destruction of Sodom and Gomorrha was by far the most devastating and conclusive judgment of God upon wicked cities prior to the final judgment upon the wicked cities of the world. It is seen as a supernatural cataclysm, a complete desolation, an unexpected judgment, and an example of eternal vengeance. In the verse under consideration, Jesus was saying that the final judgment upon some cities was to be even greater than the terrible end of Sodom and Gomorrha.

C. **Symbols:** ***I Peter 2:4—"To whom coming, as unto a living stone . . ."*** The subject of this verse involves the symbol of a stone (or rock), the significance of which is progressively revealed in Scripture. (Because of the vastness of this subject in Scripture, we will only consider some of the most vital references.)

Genesis 28:16-22:	The rock anointed to be Bethel, the House of God
Genesis 49:24:	The shepherd, the stone of Israel
Exodus 17:1-17:	The smitten rock provides living waters
Deuteronomy 32:4, 15:	God, the rock of our salvation
Deuteronomy 32:18:	The rock that begat thee
Psalms 31 :2:	The strong rock
Psalms 62:7:	The rock of strength and refuge
Psalms 95:1:	The rock of defense
Isaiah 42:11:	The inhabitants of the rock
Daniel 2:34, 35:	The stone-kingdom smashing the world kingdoms
Matthew 16:18:	The foundation rock of the church
I Peter 2:6, 8:	The chief cornerstone, the stone of stumbling, rock of offense

These verses and others interpret the living stone of ***I Peter 2:4*** to be none other than God Himself. The truths that are unfolded progressively in relation to this symbol find their consummation in the person and work of Christ.

D. **Persons:** ***Galatians 3:29—"If ye be Christ's, then are ye Abraham's seed, and heirs according to the promise."*** The subject of this verse involves the person of Abraham. His role in God's redemptive plan is progressively revealed in Scripture. (Because of the many references to Abraham in Scripture, we will only consider some of the most vital ones.)

Genesis 12:1-3:	Abraham obeys the call of the Lord
Genesis 15:6:	Abraham believed God's promise of an innumerable seed
Genesis 22:1-5, 18:	Abraham's seed to bless all nations
Exodus 3:6:	The God of Abraham speaks to Moses
Psalms 105:8-11:	God's covenant with Abraham
Isaiah 51:2:	***"Look unto Abraham your father . . ."***
Matthew 1:1:	Jesus: the son of Abraham
Romans 4:	Abraham justified by faith; the father of all who believe
Galatians 3:16:	Abraham's seed is Christ
Hebrews 11:8:	***"By faith Abraham . . . obeyed . . ."***

These passages of Scripture, with their progressive unfolding of truth, aid us in interpreting ***Galatians 3:29.*** Because Abraham believed and obeyed the Word of God, he was justified by faith and was thus chosen to be the father of a seed; namely, Christ and His Church. Abraham's seed is seen as being all those who believe in Christ.

E. **Places:** ***Isaiah 2:3—". . . out of Zion shall go forth the law . . ."*** The subject of this phrase involves the city of Zion, the significance of which is revealed progressively in Scripture. (Because of the many references to Zion in Scripture, we will consider some of the most vital ones.)

II Samuel 5:6-9:	The stronghold of Zion becomes the city of David
II Samuel 6:12-19:	The Ark of the Covenant brought into the Tabernacle of David in Zion

Psalms 2:6:	Zion is God's holy mount where He sets His King
Psalms 48:2:	Zion is the city of the great King
Psalms 50:2:	Zion is the perfection of beauty
Psalms 87:2:	God loves Zion more than all Jacob's dwellings
Isaiah 28:16:	A foundation stone laid in Zion
Zechariah 2:10:	God dwelling in the midst of a rejoicing Zion
Zechariah 8:3:	Zion called a city of truth
Matthew 21:4, 5:	The King comes to Zion
Romans 9:33:	A stumbling stone and rock of offense in Zion
Hebrews 12:22:	Mount Zion and the heavenly Jerusalem; the true place of worship
I Peter 2:6-8:	The chief cornerstone in Zion
Revelation 14:1:	The Lamb standing with the redeemed on Mount Zion

Together, these verses reveal Zion to be the city of the King, where the Ark containing the law resided. Thus, in Zion there was a foundation and chief cornerstone which pointed to the Lord Jesus Christ in His church as our King and Lawgiver. The church becomes the Zion, from whence God's law goes forth into all the earth.

F. **Prophecy:** ***Galatians 3:8—"And the Scripture, foreseeing that God would justify the heathen through faith, preached before the gospel unto Abraham, saying, "In thee shall all nations be blessed."*** The subject of this verse involves the prophecy of the heathen nations coming into the blessings of the Gospel. (There are many references involved, since this prophetic theme is progressively developed through the Old and New Testaments. We will consider only a few of these here.)

Genesis 12:1-3:	To Abraham: ***"In thee shall all families of the earth be blessed."***
Genesis 22:18:	To Abraham: ***"In thy seed shall all the nations of the earth be blessed."***
Genesis 26:2-4:	To Isaac: ***"In thy seed shall all the nations of the earth be blessed."***
Genesis 28:13, 14:	To Jacob: ***"In thee and in thy seed shall all the families of the earth be blessed."***
Psalms 22:27-31:	Kindreds and nations to worship the Lord
Psalms 72:17:	All nations shall call Him blessed
Isaiah 52:15:	Messiah shall sprinkle many nations with His blood
Micah 4:1, 2:	Nations to come to the house of the Lord
Zechariah 2:11:	Many nations shall be joined to the Lord in that day
Malachi 1:11:	God's name to be great among the Gentiles
Matthew 12:21:	Gentiles shall trust in His name
Luke 24:47:	Repentance and remission of sins preached to all nations
Romans 11:	The Gentiles grafted into the good olive tree by faith in Christ
Revelation 5:9, 10:	The redeemed out of every kindred, and tongue, and people, and nation worship the Lamb

These sample Scriptures show the progression of thought pertaining to the blessing of the gospel of Christ that was to come to all nations. This promise was first made to Abraham, who became the father of all them that believe, because through him Christ, the promised seed, came. Christ is the gospel personified and it is only through Him that all nations can be blessed.

Chapter 10
THE COMPLETE MENTION PRINCIPLE

I. DEFINITION

That principle by which the interpretation of any verse is determined upon a consideration of the complete mention of its subject in Scripture.

II. AMPLIFICATION

The Word of God contains countless subjects to which there are more than a single reference. In order to understand these subjects every reference to them must be gathered and considered as a whole. The term "complete mention" is used here to refer to the total aggregate of references to any individual subject in Scripture.

God, who had in mind as a whole the full truth of that which he desired to reveal to man, nevertheless communicated it to man in a very fragmentary fashion. He gave to each author certain fragments to record, thus making it necessary for an interpreter to assemble these fragments. Only as these parts are pieced together can the full truth be seen as a whole.

This can be illustrated in six major areas which involve the use of complete mention: (A) Principles, (B) Events, (C) Symbols, (D) Persons, (E) Places and (F) Prophecy.

NOTE: Because of the similarity between this principle and the progressive mention principle, we will illustrate only one of the six areas.

C. **Symbols:** God used the method of complete mention in presenting a vast assortment of symbols in Scripture.

The Symbol of Leaven

Exodus 12:15	*"Put away leaven out of your house: for whosoever eateth leavened bread . . . shall be cut off"*
Exodus 12:19	*"Whosoever eateth that which is leavened . . . cut off"*
Exodus 12:20	*"Ye shall eat nothing leavened"*
Exodus 12:34	*"Took their dough before it was leavened"*
Exodus 12:39	*"For it was not leavened"*
Exodus 13:3	*"No leavened bread be eaten"*
Exodus 13:7	*"No leavened bread be seen with thee"*
	"Neither shall there be leaven seen with thee"
Exodus 23:18:	*"Not offer the blood of my sacrifice with leavened bread"*
Exodus 34:25:	*"Not offer the blood of my sacrifice with leaven"*
Leviticus 2:11:	*"No meat offering . . . shall be made with leaven"*
Leviticus 2:11:	*"Burn no leaven"*
Leviticus 6:17:	*"It shall not be baked with leaven"*
Leviticus 7:13:	*"Offer for his offering leavened bread"*
Leviticus 10:12:	*"Eat it without leaven beside the altar"*
Leviticus 23:17:	*"They shall be baken with leaven"*
Deuteronomy 16:3:	*"Thou shalt eat no leavened bread"*
Deuteronomy 16:4:	*"No leavened bread seen with thee"*
Hosea 7:4:	*"Kneaded the dough until it be leavened"*
Amos 4:5:	*"Sacrifice of thanksgiving with leaven"*
Matthew 13:33:	*"The kingdom of heaven is like unto leaven"*
	"Till the whole was leavened"
Matthew 16:6, 11:	*"Beware of the leaven of the Pharisees"*
Matthew 16:12:	*"Not beware of the leaven of bread"*
Mark 8:15:	*"Beware of the leaven of the Pharisees"*
	"And of the leaven of Herod"

Luke 12:1:	***"Beware ye of the leaven of the Pharisees"***
Luke 13:21:	***"It is like leaven, which a woman took . . . till the whole was leavened"***
I Corinthians 5:6:	***"A little leaven leaveneth the whole lump"***
I Corinthians 5:7:	***"Purge out therefore the old leaven"***
I Corinthians 5:8:	***"Not with old leaven"***
	"Neither with the leaven of malice and wickedness"
Galatians 5:9:	***"A little leaven leaveneth the whole lump"***

These verses comprise the complete body of references to leaven in Scripture. Together, these Scriptures give us the full truth of that which God desired to communicate concerning leaven.

Thus, the literary *method of complete mention* (communicating the whole in fragments) used in writing Scripture gives rise to the *complete mention principle* (assembling the fragments) of interpreting Scripture.

III. QUALIFICATION

A. The complete mention principle is to be seen as the ultimate end of (1) the first mention principle, and (2) the progressive mention principle, and will logically be used in connection with both.

The three principles working together may be illustrated as:

"first the blade,	First Mention Principle
then the ear,	Progressive Mention Principle
then the full corn."	Complete Mention Principle

B. This principle requires that no single verse relevant to any specific subject be left out in formulating the doctrinal teaching on that subject. Each relevant verse is an integral part of the whole, supplementing, adding to, clarifying and illuminating the others. The full truth of a subject can only be realized by a consideration of its complete mention in Scripture.

C. No one reference can be used to contradict another, rather only to qualify it.

D. Care must be used when applying this principle so as not to violate the distinctive aspects of a subject in Scripture. Any given subject in Scripture may have various facets or applications and these must not be confused. For example, "The glory of the Lord" is a subject which may refer to God's being, to an expression of His character, to a manifestation of His presence, or to blessing and judgment in relation to His people and the world.

IV. DEMONSTRATION

NOTE: Because of the similarity between this principle and the progressive mention principle, we will demonstrate this principle in only one of the six areas.

C. **Symbols:** ***Revelation 3:7—"These things saith He that is holy, He that is true, He that hath the key of David, He that openeth, and no man shutteth; and shutteth, and no man openeth . . ."*** The subject of this verse involves the symbol of the key, the significance of which can be determined only upon a consideration of its complete mention in Scripture.

Judges 3:25:	A key used to open the doors of the king's parlor
Isaiah 22:22:	The key of the House of David laid upon the shoulder of Eliakim giving him the authority to open and shut doors
Matthew 16:19:	The keys of the kingdom of heaven used in binding and loosing
Luke 11:15:	The key of knowledge
Revelation 1:18:	The keys of death and hell
Revelation 9:1:	The key of the bottomless pit
Revelation 20:1:	The key of the bottomless pit

The complete mention listed above of the symbol of the key is interpreted by Scripture as being the authority to open and shut doors. It reveals that the one who holds the key has the power and authority to bind or loose; to release or hold that with which the key is associated; thus able to exercise control. A consideration of ***Revelation 3:7*** in the light of the use of the complete mention principle shows that Christ, the Son of David, has the authority of the kingdom and throne of David. He is the one who is in control and exercises all power and authority in heaven and in earth.

THE DIVINE PROGRAM GROUP OF PRINCIPLES

Ch. 11 The Election Principle
Ch. 12 The Covenantal Principle
Ch. 13 The Ethnic Division Principle
Ch. 14 The Chronometrical Principle
Ch. 15 The Dispensations Redefined
Ch. 16 The Breach Principle

These theological principles may be grouped together because they each arise out of the interpretation of the purposes of God as revealed in Scripture. These principles all assume the practice of allowing the whole of God's revealed purpose to affect the interpretation of the parts of His revelation. Thus in using these principles, the interpreter will be causing the interpreted whole to affect the interpretation of its individual parts. The student should note that Chapter 15 is not a principle of interpretation but rather a redefinition of the Dispensations as they relate to the Chronometrical Principle.

Chapter 11
THE ELECTION PRINCIPLE

I. DEFINITION

That principle by which the interpretation of any verse or group of verses is determined by considering its relation to the election involved in the purposes of God.

II. AMPLIFICATION

A. **Definition of Election:** According to Webster's Dictionary, the word "election" means "to choose out; a choosing or choice." In theology it refers to the selection of, or giving preference to, certain persons or nations relative to the purposes of God pertaining to time or eternity. The following is a consideration of the relevant Hebrew and Greek words:

Old Testament Hebrew:
BAWKHEER = "to select, choose, the person chosen"
Translated:
- choose — ***II Samuel 21:6***
- chosen one — ***I Chronicles 16:13; Psalms 89:3; 105:6, 43; 106:5, 23; Isaiah 43:20; 65:15***
- elect — ***Isaiah 42:1; 45:4; 65:9, 22***

New Testament Greek:
EKLOGE = "selection, choice, the act of picking out, the person chosen"
Translated:
- chosen — ***Acts 9:15***
- election — ***Romans 9:11; 11:5, 7, 28; I Thessalonians 1:4; II Peter 1:10***

EKLECTOS = "picked out, chosen (by God)"
Translated:
- chosen — ***Matthew 20:16; 22:14; Luke 23:35; Romans 16:13; I Peter 2:4, 9; Revelation 17:14***
- elect — ***Matthew 24:22, 24, 31; Mark 13:20, 27; Luke 18:7; Romans 8:33; Colossians 3:12; I Timothy 5:21; II Timothy 2:10; Titus 1:1; I Peter 1:2, 2:6; II John 1:13***

The word "election" in its simplest meaning refers to the intention, process, and result of making a choice. It refers to an act of the will, but more specifically in the Scriptures refers to an act of the Divine will.

B. **Distinctions in Election:** There are two major aspects of God's election that must be distinguished:

1. **Election of Time:** This refers to God's choosing of individuals or nations to fulfill His purposes in relation to time. It pertains to a temporal purpose, whether positive or negative. Such was the case with Pharoah, Moses, Cyrus, Paul, Israel, Assyria, and Babylon.
2. **Election of Eternity:** This refers to the destiny of all freewill moral agents in relation to eternity.

C. **Election in Redemption:** In relation to the plan of redemption, election may be defined as the sovereign act of God in grace whereby he chose in Christ Jesus all those whom He foreknew would accept Him.

1. Election is a *sovereign act of God,* whereby certain are chosen among mankind for Himself ***(John 15:19).*** (God was under no obligation to elect anyone, since all had lost their standing before Him.)
2. Election is wholly of *grace,* apart from human merit ***(Romans 9:11; 11:5, 6).*** He chose those who were utterly unworthy of salvation. Man deserved the exact opposite; but in His grace God chose to save some.

3. Election is only applicable to those who are "in Christ." God could not choose man in himself because of his sinfulness and ill-deserving state; God could only choose man in the merits of another.

4. Election is according to and soundly *based on God's foreknowledge* ***(I Peter 1:1, 2).*** God chose only those whom He foreknew would accept Christ.

D. **Election in Revelation:** God, being the virtual author of Scripture, was able to reveal His elective purposes in the unfolding drama of creation and redemption throughout the Book He was writing. Though the Bible had various human writers, there was but one Divine Author, moving behind the scenes to guide and direct the inclusion of content relative to election in this Book of Books.

Thus, the literary method of *elective revelation* used in writing Scripture gives rise to the *election* principle of interpreting Scripture.

III. QUALIFICATION

A. The first step in using this principle is to determine whether the verse or passage under consideration has any relationship to God's elective purposes. This principle will not necessarily aid in the interpretation of every verse of Scripture, rather applies only where the truth of election is involved.

B. The distinction between the election of time and the election of eternity must be constantly kept in mind.

C. The election principle is vitally linked to the covenantal principle and should therefore be used in conjunction with it, whether relative to time or eternity.

D. A balanced concept of the doctrine of election is absolutely essential to the effective use of this principle.

IV. DEMONSTRATION

Malachi 1:2, 3—". . . Was not Esau Jacob's brother? saith the Lord: yet I loved Jacob, and I hated Esau, . . ."

The subject of this verse is God's hatred for Esau and His love for Jacob. The problems presented by this verse can only be solved by viewing it in the light of God's purposes in election. In ***Genesis 25:19-34,*** we have the account of these twin sons of Isaac and Rebecca. Even before their birth God spoke to Rebecca concerning these two sons, saying, ***"Two nations are in thy womb, and two manner of people shall be separated from thy bowels; and the one people shall be stronger than the other people; and the elder shall serve the younger."*** This shows God's preference and choice of Jacob above Esau before their birth, even though Esau was born first. The characteristics manifested in Esau and Jacob and the subsequent history of the nations proceeding from them only serve to confirm God's choice.

The New Testament offers more specific aid in helping us to understand this Divine choice. In ***Romans 9:6-24*** Paul writes concerning Esau and Jacob, quoting from Malachi: ***"For the children being not yet born, neither having done any good or evil, that the purpose of God according to election might stand, not of works, but of Him that calleth; It was said unto her, The elder shall serve the younger. As it is written, Jacob have I loved, but Esau have I hated."*** The reason for God's election of Jacob for His purpose, and His rejection of Esau, is to be found in His sovereign will, grace and foreknowledge. God could love Jacob and hate Esau before their birth because He foreknew their characters and the history of their nations.

Chapter 12
THE COVENANTAL PRINCIPLE

I. DEFINITION

That principle by which the interpretation of a verse or group of verses is determined by a consideration of its Covenantal setting.

II. AMPLIFICATION

A. **Definition of "Covenant":** In English the word "covenant" signifies a mutual understanding between two or more parties, each binding himself to fulfill obligations. In Scripture, the Hebrew and Greek words denote a somewhat different meaning:

Old Testament Hebrew:

BERIYTH	=	"to cut, to contract" (because of being made by passing between pieces of flesh—***Genesis 15:17; Jeremiah 34:18***).	
		Translated:	
		confederacy	***Genesis 14:13; Obadiah 7***
		covenant	***Genesis 6:18; Exodus 2:24; 24:7, 8; 34:28; Leviticus 2:13; Joshua 3:3; Psalms 89:3, 4, 34; Daniel 9:27***
		league	***Joshua 9:6, 7, 11, 15, 16; Judges 2:2***

New Testament Greek:

DIATHEKE	=	"a disposition, arrangement, testament, will"	
		Translated:	
		testament	***Matthew 26:28; Hebrews 7:22; 9:15-17, 20; Revelation 11:19***
		covenant	***Luke 1:72; Romans 9:4; Ephesians 2:12; Hebrews 12:24; 13:20***
SUNTITHEMAI	=	"to put together, place together, to make arrangement"	
		Translated:	
		covenanted	***Luke 22:5***
		agreed	***John 9:22; Acts 23:20***
		assented	***Acts 24:9***

The word "covenant" in Scripture refers to an agreement or a contract between men, or between God and man. In Scripture, we find that men often made covenants with men in relation to various matters (e.g., ***Genesis 21:27, 31, 32***—covenant between Abraham and Abimelech concerning the well of Beersheba; ***Luke 22:5***—covenant between the chief priests and Judas concerning the price of betrayal).

The covenantal principle under consideration here pertains only to the covenants between God and man. In every case in Scripture when a covenant was instituted between God and man, God is seen as the initiator. Man did not come to God with a proposal seeking God's approval, rather God came to man declaring His will and seeking man's adherence. It is a contract between God and man drawn up by God and presented to man. Man can either accept it or reject it, but he cannot change it. However, the usage of "covenant" in Scripture does not always contain the idea of joint obligation, but usually signifies an obligation undertaken by a single person: God. In these instances, the aspect of covenant is emphasized in "the promise" ***(Galatians 3:17; Romans 15:8).***

B. **Kinds of Covenants:** There are two kinds of Divine Covenants seen in Scripture:

1. **Unconditional Covenant:** A covenant in which God obligates Himself to fulfill the promises of the covenant regardless of man's response; a covenant whose fulfillment is *not* dependent upon man's fulfilling certain conditions. Formula: "I will" ***(Exodus 6:3-8; Genesis 9:11).***

2. **Conditional Covenant:** A covenant in which God obligates himself to fulfill the promises of the covenant only upon man's obedience to the conditions set forth by God. A covenant whose fulfillment *is* dependent upon man's fulfilling certain conditions. Formula: "If . . . then . . ." ***(Exodus 19:5; Deuteronomy 28:58, 59).***

C. **Classification of Covenants:** God has revealed Himself as a covenant making and covenant keeping God ***(Psalms 111:9; Hebrews 6:12-17).*** The source of the covenants is the grace of God and the purpose of the covenants is to make man in the image of God and to bring man to full fellowship with Him. There are nine specific Divine covenants revealed in Scripture, eight of which are progressive expressions of the first. The covenants are:

1. The Everlasting Covenant
2. The Edenic Covenant
3. The Adamic Covenant
4. The Noahic Covenant
5. The Abrahamic Covenant
6. The Mosaic Covenant
7. The Palestinian Covenant
8. The Davidic Covenant
9. The New Covenant

These covenants involve eternity and time. The Everlasting Covenant, made in the counsels of the Godhead in eternity is an all-encompassing covenant. It includes in itself the other eight covenants, each of which constitute a progressively unfolding expression of it in time, as related to man. All nine covenants are involved in God's creative and redemptive nature and plan. The Everlasting and Edenic Covenants involve primarily creation's plan, while the Adamic, Noahic, Abrahamic, Mosaic, Palestinian, Davidic and New Covenants involve more specifically the outworking of redemption's plan.

D. **Elements of the Covenants:** There are basically three parts to each of the Divine covenants. Any covenant is incomplete and, therefore, invalid without the testimony of these three things. These three parts are:

1. The *Words* or Promises of the Covenant
2. The *Blood* of the Covenant
3. The *Seal* of the Covenant

These three elements which constitute a covenant will be noted in the following outline.

E. **Outline of the Covenants**

1. **The Everlasting Covenant—*Hebrews 13:20, 21***

   a. **The Words or Promises of the Covenant**—This covenant was made in eternity in the counsels of the eternal Godhead; Father, Son and Holy Spirit. It was made according to God's eternal purpose which He purposed in Christ before the world began ***(Ephesians 1:4, 2:10; 3:11; John 17:5).*** It was founded upon God's foreknowledge, election and predestined purpose.

   b. **The Blood of the Covenant**—The blood of the Everlasting Covenant is seen in the fact that the Lamb of God was slain from the foundation of the world ***(Hebrews 13:20, 21; Acts 20:28).*** This plan was *before* the foundation of the world ***(Ephesians 1:4; I Corinthians 2:7; Ephesians 2:10; Matthew 25:34; John 17:5).*** This plan was also *from* the foundation of the world ***(I Peter 1:19, 20; Revelation 13:8; 17:8).***

   c. **The Seal of the Covenant**—The Divine seal involved ***"eternal life which God promised before the world began" (Titus 1:2*** with ***II Timothy 1:9).*** It is consummated in the glorified body of Christ, and ultimately the Church ***(Philippians 3:21).***

2. **The Edenic Covenant—*Genesis 1:26-30***

   a. **The Words of Promises of the Covenant**—Though the word "covenant" is not specifically used in relation to Eden, covenantal language is evident. (Refer to First Mention Principle.) The Edenic Covenant involved the creation of man in the image of God. It was made before the entrance of sin.

Adam had only one commandment given to him. The promises of dominion depended upon obedience. Hence, this covenant was a conditional covenant ***(Genesis 2:16, 17).***

b. **The Blood of the Covenant**—Adam was made a living soul. The soul life of man is in the blood ***(Leviticus 17:11-14).*** Adam originally had sinless blood. It has been suggested that sinless blood was shed for Adam's bride to come forth from his side. This shadowed forth the truth that the Last Adam shed sinless covenant blood to provide His bride. Adam was indeed a type of Him who was to come ***(Romans 5:14*** with ***Ephesians 5:23-32).***

c. **The Seal of the Covenant—*Genesis 2:8-17; 3:22-24***—The tree of eternal life was the sign or seal of the Edenic Covenant. It was forfeited through sin and man was cast out of the Paradise of God. The tree of life is restored in and through Christ ***(Revelation 2:7; 22:2, 14).***

3. **The Adamic Covenant—*Genesis 3:1-24***

a. **The Words or Promises of the Covenant**—Though the word "covenant" is not specifically mentioned here, covenantal language is evident. The Adamic Covenant was made after the entrance of sin. It is the most comprehensive covenant of all. It is an unconditional covenant. It was founded on the grace of God and involved the promises of redemption for man and the ultimate bruising of the head of Satan ***(Genesis 3:15).***

b. **The Blood of the Covenant—*Genesis 3:21***—Adam and Eve witnessed the first substitutionary death and the shedding of sacrificial animal blood. God was the first one to shed blood. The innocent died for the guilty. It foreshadowed the plan of redemption and the broken body and shed blood of the Lamb of God. It was covenant blood.

c. **The Seal of the Adamic Covenant—*Genesis 3:21***—The seal of the covenant to Adam and Eve were the coats of skin. They discarded the fig leaf covering and accepted the coats of skin; a covering acceptable to God and provided through the death of a victim. These coats of skin shadowed forth the seal of a faith-righteousness that would come through Christ ***(John 1:29; Romans 4).***

4. **The Noahic Covenant—*Genesis 8-9***

a. **The Words or Promises of the Covenant—*Genesis 9:1-17***—It is here that we have the first specific mention of the word "covenant." This covenant was made with Noah and every living creature after the flood. The language of the covenant is very similar to the language of the covenant made with Adam ***(Genesis 9:1-12*** with ***Genesis 1:26-30).*** This also is an unconditional covenant. The promises of God concerning the earth never being destroyed with a flood again were made to all generations.

b. **The Blood of the Covenant—*Genesis 8:20-21***—Noah sacrificed to the Lord burnt offerings of every clean beast and fowl. Here faith in substitutionary blood is evidenced ***(Hebrews 11:6, 7).*** Life is forfeited and covenant blood becomes the evidence of death.

c. **The Seal of the Covenant—*Genesis 9:12-17***—The sign or seal or token of the Noahic Covenant was the rainbow. It is still the seal of that covenant to all the world. Any reference to the rainbow in Scripture attests to the fact that God is a covenant keeping God ***(Revelation 4:3; 10:1-2).***

5. **The Abrahamic Covenant—*Genesis 12:1-3; 15; 17; 22***

a. **The Words or Promises of the Covenant**—Abraham is the father of all who believe ***(Romans 4:16).*** The promises of God involved in the Abrahamic Covenant touch the natural and the spiritual, the temporal and the eternal. The major promise was the promise of salvation through Christ, the seed of Abraham ***(Matthew 1:1; Galatians 3:16).*** It was to be through Christ that all the nations would be blessed. This covenant was confirmed to Isaac ***(Genesis 26:2-4)*** and to Jacob ***(Genesis 28:3-14).*** It was an unconditional covenant.

b. **The Blood of the Covenant—*Genesis 15***—The covenant blood was shed in the offering of the God-appointed five sacrifices mentioned in ***Genesis 15.*** God passed between the pieces of those sacrifices as He covenanted with Abraham.

c. **The Seal of the Covenant—*Genesis 17***—The sign, seal or token of the covenant was circumcision. It is distinctly called the seal of the covenant ***(Romans 4:11*** with ***Acts 7:8).*** This point to circumcision of the heart, that of the Spirit; not of the letter or of the flesh ***(Romans 2:28-29).***

6. **The Mosaic Covenant—*Exodus 20-40***

   a. **The Words or Promises of the Covenant**—This covenant was expressly made with the chosen nation, Israel ***(Deuteronomy 4:10-13; 5:1-33).*** It held promises out to Israel specifically and this also was a conditional covenant. The words were summarized in the ten commandments and amplified in the civil laws. This covenant involved distinction of meats, keeping of Sabbaths, and festival days.

   b. **The Blood of the Covenant—*Exodus 24:3-8; Hebrews 9:18-20***—The Mosaic Covenant was established upon sacrificial blood. It was called the blood of the covenant, and it was sprinkled on the people and the book of the covenant.

   c. **The Seal of the Covenant—*Exodus 31:12-18***—The Mosaic Covenant had the seal of the Sabbath day upon it. This seal was distinctly the seal of this covenant; not any other. It pointed to the true Sabbath rest which would be found in Christ ***(Matthew 12:28-30; Hebrews 3-4).***

7. **The Palestinian Covenant—*Deuteronomy 27-28-29-30***

   a. **The Words or Promises of the Covenant**—This covenant is vitally linked with the Mosaic Covenant. Because of this it is not often recognized as a covenant. However, ***Deuteronomy 29:1*** clarifies this matter for us. It states, ***"These are the words of the covenant which the Lord commanded Moses to make with the children of Israel in the land of Moab, beside the covenant which He made with them in Horeb."*** It was made with the generation who were about to enter the land. It was a conditional covenant. Its promises concerned the blessings and/or cursings upon Palestine, the promised land. Israel's dwelling in the land was conditional. If these conditions were not met they would be expelled ***(Leviticus 26*** along with ***Deuteronomy 28-29).***

   b. **The Blood of the Covenant—*Deuteronomy 27:1-8***—The day the new generation of Israel entered Canaan land, an altar of stones was built to the Lord and sacrificial offerings were made. It signified the cleansing of the land by atoning covenant blood.

   c. **The Seal of the Covenant—*Deuteronomy 11; 28; 29***—The seal of God upon the land was to be evidenced in the early and latter rains. Blessing and fruitfulness by the rains was God's seal to Israel upon their obedience to the laws of His land. When God withheld the rains it was the evidence of His withholding the seal of His blessing. This seal foreshadowed the coming of the early and latter rains in the outpouring of the Holy Spirit ***(James 5:7*** with ***Joel 2:23-32).***

8. **The Davidic Covenant—*II Samuel 7:4-29; Psalms 89***

   a. **The Words or Promises of the Covenant**—The covenant that God made with David was an unconditional covenant. It was by implication an integral part of the Abrahamic Covenant. The major promise of the Davidic Covenant was that which involved the coming of Jesus Christ, who was of the seed of David as well as the seed of Abraham ***(Matthew 1:1).*** He would take the throne of David and rule and reign upon it as a righteous king forever ***(Genesis 49:8-12; Psalms 89:3-4, 34, 35; Psalms 132:11-12; I Kings 8:20-25; Jeremiah 33:20-21; Isaiah 9:6-9; Luke 1:30-33).***

   b. **The Blood of the Covenant—*II Samuel 6:17-18; 7:1-3***—As in all previous covenants, sacrificial blood was shed, so it was for the Davidic Covenant. David offered sacrifices to the Lord at the return of the Ark of the Covenant. It was at this time that the Everlasting Covenant was made with David concerning his seed, Jesus Christ.

   c. **The Seal of the Covenant—*Psalms 89:27-37***—As God took the rainbow to be the token of the Noahic Covenant, God here used the sun and the moon to be the token or seal of the Davidic Covenant. God promised David that as long as the sun and the moon existed, the seed of David would sit upon his throne. This seal finds it ultimate fulfillment in Jesus Christ, the King of Kings and Lord of Lords, the ruler of this world.

9. **The New Covenant—*Matthew 26:26-29; Hebrews 8-9; Jeremiah 31:31-34***

   a. **The Words or Promises of the Covenant**—Jesus Christ is the New Covenant personified ***(Isaiah 42:6; 49:8).*** He is the mediator of the New Covenant. The New Covenant is the covenant of grace and it is everlasting. This covenant is the consummation of all previous covenants, and it is the covenant which brings redeemed mankind into the Everlasting Covenant—the eternal purposes of God. It will never be superceded by another covenant, because it fulfills all others in itself.

b. **The Blood of the Covenant—*Matthew 26:26; John 19:34, 35; I John 1:7*—**The precious and incorruptible blood of Jesus is the blood of the New Covanent ***(Revelation 12:11; Hebrews 9).*** All previous covenantal sacrificial blood pointed to His blood. The blood of Jesus fulfills and abolishes all typical animal blood. It is the blood of the Everlasting Covenant ***(Hebrews 13:20);*** the blood of the Lamb slain from the foundation of the world ***(I Peter 1:19, 20).*** It is the blood of God ***(Acts 20:28).*** God will never return to animal blood now that He has the blood of His beloved Son.

c. **The Seal of the Covenant—*II Corinthians 1:21, 22; Revelation 7:1-4, 14:1-2*—**The sign and seal of the New Covenant is the infilling or baptism in the Holy Spirit. The Lord Jesus had the seal of God upon Him ***(John 3:33, 34),*** and the believer in Christ is also to receive the seal of God ***(Ephesians 1:13, 14; 4:30; II Corinthians 1:21, 22; Acts 2:4).*** This seal fulfills in itself all previous seals. It is worthy of note that God never took the seal of any other covenant and placed it upon another. Each covenant had its own distinctive seal. However, all previous seals pointed to the New Covenant seal.

F. **Summary of Covenantal Revelation:** In the light of the all-embracing revelation of God's covenants, the Bible is not to be viewed merely as a compilation of sixty-six books, but is rather to be seen as ONE BOOK having ONE AUTHOR, with a progression of thought throughout. God Himself was the Mastermind of Scripture, utilizing various literary methods in presenting His thoughts in an integrated and harmonious manner. God, being the author of all Scripture, wove throughout the books of the Bible the progressive revelation of His covenantal dealings with man.

The literary method of *progressive covenantal revelation* used in writing Scripture gives rise to the *Covenantal Principle* of interpreting Scripture.

III. QUALIFICATION

A. The first step in using the Covenantal Principle is determining which covenant or covenants are being referred to in the verse or passage under consideration. This is done by noting covenantal language.

B. It is only practical to use the Covenantal Principle when the verse or passage at hand involves covenantal elements or covenantal language.

C. In using the Covenantal Principle, the interpreter must recognize that he is working from whole to part and from part to whole. He must have an understanding of the covenants as a whole to interpret the part, but he must interpret the parts in order to realize the whole.

D. In using this principle, there must be a recognition of the interrelatedness of the covenants and their ultimate fulfillment in the New Covenant.

E. The interpreter must recognize that he is under the New Covenant and must view the other covenants from that standpoint. Thus he interprets all covenants in the light of the New Covenant.

IV. DEMONSTRATION

A. **The Edenic Covenant:** ***Revelation 2:7—"To him that overcometh will I give to eat of the tree of life, which is in the midst of the Paradise of God." Revelation 22:14—"Blessed are they that do His commandments, that they may have the right to the tree of life."***

In order to arrive at a proper interpretation of these verses, the Edenic Covenant must be referred to because it is under this covenant that the tree of life is first mentioned. Adam and Eve forfeited their right to eat of the tree of life when they failed to fulfill the condition of the Edenic Covenant by eating of the forbidden fruit of the Tree of Knowledge of Good and Evil. Thus they did not "overcome" because they did not ***"do His commandments"*** and lost the ***"right to the tree of life," "which is in the midst of the Paradise of God" (Genesis 2:8-17; 3:22-24).***

B. **The Adamic Covenant:** ***Romans 16:20—"And the God of peace shall bruise Satan under your feet shortly."***

In order to understand the full implication of this verse it must be considered in the light of the Adamic

Covenant. After the entrance of sin into the human race, God said to the serpent, ***"And I will put enmity between thee and the woman, and between thy seed and her seed; it shall bruise thy head, and thou shalt bruise his heel" (Genesis 3:15).*** The verse in Romans points toward the fulfillment of the prophetic word of the Adamic Covenant. Thus, this verse draws its significance from the fact that it is a reiteration of the first Messianic promise of redemption.

C. **The Noahic Covenant:** ***Revelation 4:3—"And there was a rainbow round about the throne, in sight like unto an emerald."***

This verse must be interpreted in connection with the Noahic Covenant. The rainbow was the seal of the Noahic Covenant. It was placed in the heavens to be a reminder to God and man that God would never again destroy the whole earth with a flood ***(Genesis 9:8-17).*** The rainbow around the throne in Revelation shows that God is keeping the seal of the Noahic Covenant constantly before Him, proving His faithfulness to His promise.

D. **The Abrahamic Covenant:** ***Galatians 3:29—"And if ye be Christ's, then are ye Abraham's seed, and heirs according to the promise."***

It is impossible to properly interpret this verse without a recognition of that which is involved in the Abrahamic Covenant. As previously noted, from Abraham was to come two seed lines: natural and spiritual ***(Genesis 13:16; 15:5).*** To these two seed lines there were two sets of promises: natural and spiritual. The natural promises pertained to land, seed, and possessions ***(Genesis 12:1-3; 22:16-18).*** The spiritual promises pertained to the Messiah and His ministry to all the nations of the earth. These promises included justification by faith and the reception of the Spirit ***(Galatians 3:8, 14).*** Thus, this verse is stating that the person who belongs to Christ is Abraham's seed and is in covenant relationship with God, being an heir of the promise of the Abrahamic Covenant through Christ.

E. **The Mosaic Covenant:** ***Galatians 4:10—"Ye observe days, and months, and times, and years."***

The subject matter of this verse can only be understood by relating it to the Mosaic Covenant. Under this covenant, Israel was commanded to observe Sabbath days, Festival months, times of convocation, and Sabbath and Jubilee years ***(Leviticus 23, 25).*** In Galatians, Paul is referring back to these observances belonging to the Law Covenant. For the Galatian believers under the New Covenant to keep these observances is to place themselves back under the Mosaic Covenant.

F. **The Palestinian Covenant:** ***Jeremiah 25:11—"And this whole land shall be a desolation, and an astonishment; and these nations shall serve the king of Babylon seventy years."***

The reason for this judgment upon the promised land can only be ascertained by referring back to the Palestinian Covenant. Under this covenant God threatened to remove Israel out of the land by captivity to another nation if they ever broke the conditions of the covenant ***(Deuteronomy 29:1-29).*** The verse in Jeremiah transforms this threat into a prophecy, about to be executed because of Judah's idolatry.

G. **The Davidic Covenant:** ***Luke 1:32, 33—". . . and the Lord God shall give unto Him the throne of His father David; and He shall reign over the house of Jacob forever; and of His kingdom there shall be no end."***

This verse must be interpreted with respect to the promise of the Davidic Covenant. This promise is basically four-fold, relating to:

1. A Seed
2. A House
3. A Throne
4. A Kingdom

The verses in Luke prophesied that this four-fold promise would find its fulfillment in the Lord Jesus Christ, the son of David.

H. **The New Covenant:** ***Jeremiah 31:31—"Behold, the days come, saith the Lord, that I will make a new covenant with the house of Israel, and with the house of Judah . . ."***

This prophecy can only be understood by linking it with its fulfillment when Messiah established the New Covenant. At the last supper, just prior to the crucifixion, Jesus said, ***"This is My Blood of the NEW Testament (covenant) which is shed for many for the remission of sins" (Matthew 26:28).*** Therefore, the days that Jeremiah prophesied of are shown to be the days of Messiah, in which He established the New Covenant.

I. **The Everlasting Covenant:** ***Titus 1:2, 3—"In hope of eternal life, which God, that cannot lie, promised before the world began; but hath in due times manifested His word through preaching . . ."***

A proper understanding of this verse can only be reached by relating its contents to the Everlasting Covenant. The Everlasting Covenant was made before time began, in the eternal counsel of the Godhead, in the event of the entrance of sin and death into the human race. It is the Creative and Redemptive strains of the eternal purpose of God and the heavenly foundation of all the covenants expressed in time. The main promise of the Everlasting Covenant is eternal life ***(I John 2:25).*** By eternal life is meant conformity to the image of God and full fellowship with Him. Thus these verses in Titus speak of our hope in this promise made in the Everlasting Covenant.

SPECIAL NOTE: It is worthy of note to recognize that a number of passages or chapters in the Bible involve several of the covenants, and only by a study of the language of the context can it be determined which covenants are referred to. Examples of this are seen in the following references.

1. ***Ezekiel 16:59-62:*** The Abrahamic, Mosaic and Everlasting Covenants are all involved in these verses.
2. ***Hosea 1:6-10; 2:18-23:*** The Mosaic, Abrahamic and New Covenants are involved in the language in these passages of Hosea.
3. ***Galatians 3:1-29:*** The Abrahamic, Mosaic and New Covenants are seen in their principles in this chapter.
4. ***Romans 9, 10, 11:*** These chapters dealing with the blindness and cutting off of natural Israel and their grafting in again by faith involve the three great covenants: The Abrahamic, Mosaic and New Covenants.

Chapter 13
THE ETHNIC DIVISION PRINCIPLE

I. DEFINITION

That principle by which the interpretation of any verse or passage of Scripture is determined upon a consideration of God's appointed ethnic divisions.

II. AMPLIFICATION

A. **Definition:** The word "ethnic" has to do with the basic divisions of mankind distinguished by culture. The following are the main words used in Scripture relative to the ethnic divisions of mankind:

Old Testament Hebrew:

UMMAH = "a collection; i.e., community of persons"
Translated:
nations — ***Ezra 4:10; Daniel 3:4, 7, 29***
people — ***Numbers 25:15; Psalms 117:1***

GOY = "a massing; a foreign nation; hence a Gentile"
Translated:
Gentiles — ***Genesis 10:5; Isaiah 11:10; 42:1, 6; 49:22; 54:3; 60:3, 5, 11, 16***
heathen — ***Psalms 2:1, 8; 102:15; Jeremiah 10:2; Ezekiel 11:12, 16; 39:21; Malachi 1:11***
nation(s) — ***Genesis 10:31, 32; Deuteronomy 9:1, 4, 5; I Chronicles 16:20; Psalms 22:27, 28; Isaiah 2:2, 4; 52:15; Malachi 3:12***
people — ***Joshua 10:13; II Kings 6:18; Daniel 11:23***

LEOM = "to gather; a community"
Translated:
nation — ***Genesis 27:29; Psalms 47:3; 57:9***
people — ***Genesis 25:23; Psalms 148:11; Isaiah 55:4***
folk — ***Jeremiah 51:58***

AM = "a people (as a congregated unit); specially, a tribe"
Translated:
folk — ***Genesis 33:15; Proverbs 30:26***
nation(s) — ***Exodus 21:8; Deuteronomy 30:3; I Chronicles 16:24; Psalms 108:3***
people — ***Psalms 29:11; 102:18, 22; Habakkuk 3:13; Zechariah 8:22; Malachi 1:4***

New Testament Greek:

ETHNOS = "a race (as of the same habit); i.e., a tribe; specially a foreign (non-Jewish) one"
Translated:
Gentile — ***Matthew 10:5, 18; Mark 10:42; Acts 4:27; Romans 9:24, 30***
heathen — ***II Corinthians 11:26; Galatians 1:16; 3:8***
nation(s) — ***Mark 11:17; John 11:50-52; Acts 14:16; Romans 4:17, 18***
people — ***Romans 10:19***

GENOS = "offspring, family, nation, the aggregate of many individuals of the same nature, kind, sort, species"

Translated:

born	***Acts 18:2, 24***
country (man)	***Acts 4:36; II Corinthians 11:26***
diversity	***I Corinthians 12:28***
generation	***I Peter 2:9***
kind (red)	***Matthew 13:47; Acts 7:13, 19***
nation	***Mark 7:26***
offspring	***Acts 17:28, 29; Revelation 22:16***
stock	***Acts 13:26; Philippians 3:5***

The above words indicate that an ethnic group is to be viewed as a community of persons sharing the same ancestry and participating in the culture. These words are applied to Israel/Judah, Gentile nations, and the Church.

B. **Classification:** The apostle Paul recognized that while God is no respecter of persons, He has instituted certain ethnic distinctions. Paul noted the three basic ethnic divisions in the human race in ***I Corinthians 10:32: "Give none offense,***

neither to the Jews,
nor to the Gentiles,
nor to the church of God:"

Thus, in God's mind, the three main divisions of the human race are the Jews, the Gentiles, and the Church. The Word of God must be rightly divided in relation to these three classes of people.

C. **Origination:** From the creation of Adam to the tower of Babel ***(Genesis 1:1; 11:9),*** mankind was one race, speaking one language. The event recorded in ***Genesis 11*** gives us the background of the reason for the division of mankind into diverse nations. The origin of the nations is described in this chapter. Out of these nations God chose a nation for Himself and for His own purposes. In the Old Testament there are two major ethnic divisions: the chosen nation (Israel), and the Gentile nations. The New Testament introduces the third major ethnic division, which is the Church, composed of both Jew and Gentile.

1. **The Chosen Nation**

a. **The Choice—**Scripture reveals that Israel was the nation which God chose to fulfill His own purposes. God took Israel as a nation from the midst of the nations and made a great nation out of them by His statutes, laws, and judgments ***(Deuteronomy 4:6-8, 34).*** In the covenant with Abraham God said that He would make of him a great nation ***(Genesis 12:2, 3).*** God also promised Abraham that He would make him the father of many nations ***(Genesis 17:1-7).***

b. **The Reason—**God chose Israel to be a special people to Himself above all the people on the earth because of His love and the covenant He made with Israel's fathers: Abraham, Isaac, and Jacob ***(Deuteronomy 7:6-9; 9:1-6).*** There were a number of things involved in the purpose for this Divine choice:

(1) Chosen to *bless* all nations ***(Genesis 9:27; 12:2, 3; 17:4-7; 18:18; 22:16-18).***
(2) Chosen to receive the *oracles* of God ***(Romans 3:2).***
(3) Chosen to receive the *blessings of God* ***(Romans 9:4, 5).***

—**The Adoption**—Adopted as God's son from among the nations ***(Exodus 4:22-23).***
—**The Skekinah Glory of God**—The visible manifestation of the presence of God in the glory-cloud.
—**The Covenants**—The Abrahamic, the Mosaic, the Palestinian, the David, and the New Covenants.
—**The Giving of the Law**—The moral, civil, and cermonial laws.
—**The Service of God**—The Tabernacle of Moses, the Tabernacle of David, and the Temple of Solomon with their respective orders of worship.
—**The Promises**—Particularly as they relate to the seed (as the sand and as the stars) and the land.

—**The Fathers**—Abraham, Isaac, and Jacob being particularly the three fathers of Israel ***(Exodus 3:6; Genesis 48:15, 16).***
—**The Messiah**—As pertaining to His human nature ***(Romans 1:3).***

The summation of these shows the choice of Israel as a nation to receive and be the guardians of the written Word; and to be the progenitors of the Living Word through which all nations would be blessed.

c. **The Division**—Israel was a united nation from the time of the exodus under Moses through the reigns of Saul, David, and Solomon—under whom the nation reached its highest glory. After the death of Solomon the nation was divided into two houses; two kingdoms; two nations; known as Israel and Judah ***(I Kings 11, 12).*** God permitted this division in order to fulfill His distinctive purpose for each nation. It must be recognized that from that time on there were two dynasties, two kingdoms, and two destinies. These two nations went into two different captivities, to two different places, at two different times, under two different world kingdoms. Israel went into captivity to Assyria and Judah to Babylon. This the prophets of each nation clearly foretold beforehand.

Therefore, in interpreting the prophets, the distinction between these kingdoms to which they were prophesying must constantly be kept in mind. Some prophecies were distinctly given to Israel and others to Judah; these should not be confused. The Lord foretold through the prophet Jeremiah that He would make a New Covenant with the House of Israel and with the House of Judah ***(Jeremiah 31:31-34; Hebrews 8:8-13).*** The prophet Ezekiel foretold that God would make Israel and Judah (two sticks) one in the hand of the Son of man ***(Ezekiel 37:15-19).*** ***"And I will make them one nation in the land upon the mountains of Israel; and one king shall be king to them all: and they shall be no more two nations, neither shall they be divided into two kingdoms any more at all" (Ezekiel 37:22).*** This union can come about only through the New Covenant in the Lord Jesus Christ.

2. **The Gentile Nations**

a. **Their Condition**—In Scripture the term "Gentiles" is used to refer to all nations besides Israel/ Judah. It denotes all peoples not in Covenant relationship with God, as was Israel. Paul aptly describes the condition of the Gentiles in ***Ephesians 2:11, 12:***

—Gentiles in the flesh—as to natural and national birth.
—Uncircumcision in the flesh—not in Abrahamic Covenant relationship with God.
—Without Christ—having no Saviour; no anointed one.
—Aliens from the commonwealth of Israel—estranged and outlawed from the rights of Israel as a nation.
—Strangers from the Covenants of promise—the Abrahamic, Mosaic, Palestinian, and Davidic Covenants and the promises, privileges, and blessings therein.
—Having no hope—no Messianic expectation.
—Without God in the world—having general, but no special revelation of God.
—Afar off—no nearness of relationship to God.

Paul, later on in the same epistle, summarized the spiritual condition of the Gentiles as ***"having the understanding darkened, being alienated from the life of God through the ignorance that is in them, because of the blindness of their heart" (Ephesians 4:18).*** (Read also ***Romans 1:18-32).***

b. **Their Salvation**—The writers of the Old Testament Scriptures were concerned primarily with the chosen nation and only dealt with the Gentile nations as they related to it ***(Deuteronomy 32:8; Acts 17:26).*** However, the Scriptures also plainly declare that God is no respecter of persons ***(Acts 10:34, 35).*** As already noted, Israel was chosen as a nation to eventually bless all other nations. The following Scriptures attest to this fact:

—All nations to be blessed through the seed of Abraham ***(Genesis 22:18).***
—All families of the earth to be blessed ***(Genesis 26:4).***
—All kindreds of the nations to worship God ***(Psalms 22:27, 28).***
—All nations to flow to the house of the Lord ***(Isaiah 2:2, 3).***

—Gentiles to seek the Root of Jesse ***(Isaiah 11:10).***
—Messiah to sprinkle many nations with blood ***(Isaiah 52:15).***

—Many nations shall be joined to the Lord in that day ***(Zechariah 2:11).***
—The name of the Lord to be great among the Gentiles ***(Malachi 1:11).***
—The Gentiles shall trust in His name ***(Matthew 12:21).***

The great commission involves the taking of the Gospel of Christ to every creature, making disciples of *all nations* ***(Matthew 28:19; Mark 16:15; Luke 24:47; Acts 1:8).*** The book of Acts shows God's turning from the chosen nation to the Gentile nations in order to take out of them a people for His name ***(Acts 9:15; 13:44-49; 14:1, 2; 15:14-18; 28:23-31).***

The Scriptures clearly show that the Gentile nations would be blessed through the chosen nation by "the Seed"—Messiah. ***"And the Scripture, forseeing that God would justify the heathen through faith, preached before the gospel unto Abraham, saying In thee shall all nations be blessed" (Galatians 3:8).***

3. **The Church**

a. **Definition of the Church**—The third group mentioned by Paul in ***I Corinthians 10:32*** is ***"the church of God."*** The word Church is a translation of the Greek word EKKLESIA, which is made up of two other words: EK, which means "out of" and KALEO, which means "to call." Thus the work EKKLESIA means literally "the called out ones." It is used in Scripture to refer to the nation of Israel and to the Christian community of believers, whether in heaven or on earth:

(1) Israel—the Church in the wilderness ***(Acts 7:38)***
(2) Saints in Heaven ***(Hebrews 12:23)***
(3) Saints on Earth ***(Revelation 1:11)***

In these three the word Church is used in its two basic senses: universal and local. We understand the universal Church to include the redeemed of all ages both in heaven and earth, and the local Church to be a visible expression of it.

b. **Calling of the Church**—God has always had a people for Himself; a company of called out ones. Being a "called out one" involves:

—Being called out of darkness into light ***(I Peter 2:9).***
—Being called to a vocation ***(Ephesians 4:1).***
—Being called to a calling of hope ***(Ephesians 4:4).***
—Being called with a holy calling ***(II Timothy 1:9).***
—Being called to a high calling ***(Philippians 3:14).***
—Being called to a heavenly calling ***(Hebrews 3:2).***
—Being called unto eternal glory by Christ Jesus ***(I Peter 5:10).***
—Being called to His Kingdom and glory ***(I Thessalonians 2:12).***

c. **Composition of the Church**—The Church, as it is revealed in the New Testament, is composed of both Jew and Gentile. As God called Israel as a nation from the midst of the nations and constituted them as His Church in the Old Testament, so God now calls people unto Himself out of every nation, whether Jew or Gentile, and constitutes them as His Church in the New Testament. The New Testament Church is revealed as the body of Christ composed of Jew and Gentile:

—Christ is the builder of His Church ***(Matthew 16:18).***
—The Lord adds to His Church ***(Acts 2:47).***
—Christ is the head of the body—the Church ***(Colossians 2:19).***
—The Church is Christ's body ***(Ephesians 1:22, 23).***
—Jew and Gentile all baptized into one body ***(I Corinthians 12:13).***
—Jew and Gentile are one new man in Christ ***(Ephesians 2:15, 16).***
—Jew and Gentile are fellow-heirs in the same body ***(Ephesians 3:6).***

Thus the Church, being the third major ethnic division, is a called out company, consisting of Jew and Gentile, circumcision and uncircumcision, chosen nation and Gentile nations in the one body of Christ. National divisions are determined by natural birth, but by spiritual birth all national distinctions cease to exist, for ***"there is neither Jew nor Greek, there is neither bond nor free, there is neither male nor female: for ye are all one in Christ Jesus" (Galatians 3:28). "For in Christ Jesus neither circumcision avails anything, nor uncircumcision, but a new creature" (Galatians 6:15).***

d. **Significance of the Church**—This Church taken out of every kindred, tongue, people, and nation ***(Revelation 5:9)*** now constitutes God's nation. It is the true Israel of God entitled to the spiritual promises in the Abrahamic Covenant:

—Those in Christ are ***"an holy nation" (I Peter 2:9).***
—The kingdom was taken from Judah and given to a nation that would bring forth the fruits thereof ***(Matthew 21:43).***
—The prophets foretold of a righteous nation that would keep the truths ***(Isaiah 26:2).***
—Salvation was offered to a nation not yet called by His name ***(Isaiah 65:1;*** also ***Romans 10:20, 21).***
—All those who are new creatures in Christ Jesus constitute the Israel of God ***(Galatians 6:15, 16).***
—The Gentile by faith in Christ is brought into the commonwealth of Israel ***(Ephesians 2:12).***
—The believing Gentile is grafted into the olive tree of Israel ***(Romans 11).***
—The Israel after the flesh are not necessarily the Israel after the Spirit ***(Romans 9:6-8).***
—The true Jew and true circumcision is of the heart and in the spirit, and not of the flesh or the letter ***(Romans 2:28, 29).***
—The believers in Christ are Abraham's seed and heirs according to the promise ***(Galatians 3:16, 29).***

These Scriptures attest to the fact that the Church, composed of Jew and Gentile, is God's holy nation, the true Israel of God, the seed of Abraham, and the called out company. This is the "mystery" revealed to Paul: that Jew and Gentile would become one body in Christ ***(Ephesians 3:1-9).***

D. **Conclusion:** In conclusion it can be seen that the three main ethnic divisions mentioned by Paul in ***I Corinthians 10:32*** are supported by the testimony of Scripture. (Note: For further study, trace these three distinctions through the book of Acts.)

Thus the literary method of *progressive ethnic division revelation* used in writing Scripture gives rise to the *Ethnic Division Principle* of interpreting Scripture.

III. QUALIFICATION

A. The first step in using this principle is to determine whether the verse or passage under consideration is relevant to any of the three main ethnic divisions. To facilitate this one may ask the following questions:

1. Does this verse refer to the united nation, the *whole* House of Israel?
2. Does it refer to the ten-tribed House of Israel, the Northern Kingdom?
3. Does it refer to the two-tribed (plus the Levites) House of Judah, the Southern Kingdom?
4. Does it refer to the Gentile nations?
5. Does it refer to the Church, chosen out of every nation?

B. In interpretation, extreme caution must be used in order to avoid confusing these ethnic divisions. That which is said of one division must not be interpreted as referring to another.

1. The same is also true of certain divisions within these main divisions. This becomes especially important in interpreting the prophets. Some of the prophets ministered distinctly to the House of Israel and others to the House of Judah. However, even though the prophets generally were sent to one specific House, sometimes they prophesied concerning both Houses (e.g., Isaiah and Jeremiah were sent to the House of Judah. Hosea was sent to the House of Israel. Micah was sent to both Houses. Yet all these prophets at times gave utterances involving both Houses. See ***Isaiah 1:1, 2; Jeremiah 1:3; Micah 1:1, 2; Hosea 1:1-3; Jeremiah 31:31-34; Isaiah 8:14; Hosea 1:4-7).*** Unless this distinction is maintained the prophets may seem to contradict each other.

2. The interpreter must realize that the name "Israel" is used in Scripture to refer to:

   a. The patriarch Jacob ***(Genesis 49:1, 2).***
   b. The twelve tribes of "Israel" ***(Exodus 19:3).***
   c. The ten-tribed Hosue of Israel, the northern kingdom ***(I Kings 12:21).***
   d. The two-tribed House of Judah, the southern kingdom ***(Ezra 6:21***—spoken of here as the children of Israel).
   e. The Church, the spiritual Israel of God ***(Galatians 6:16; Romans 9:6).***

Israel is used as a collective name and thus may involve both Houses. Judah, however, is never used in a collective sense of the whole twelve-tribed nation.

3. Some interpreters have haphazardly interpreted prophecies given concerning Israel and Judah to be relevant primarily to the Church. Some Bibles, with their marginal headings, have brought much confusion to Bible students by randomly assigning the blessings and promises in the prophets to the New Testament Church, leaving all the curses and judgments to Israel and Judah. Great care should be taken in looking for the Church in the prophets.

4. Other interpreters fail completely to see the Church at all in the Old Testament, thus missing a vital link in the purposes of God. There is an interpretive danger of exalting the chosen nation and natural birth above the Church and spiritual birth.

5. Generally, the key to finding the Church in the Old Testament prophets is found in the prophecies concerning the coming of the Gentiles into Messianic blessings through the New Covenant in Christ.

   The term "Gentile" has a two-fold significance in the Old Testament:

   a. It is used as a collective term, referring to the heathen nations surrounding Israel ***(Jeremiah 46:1).***
   b. It is used to designate those out of all nations who would come to Christ ***(Romans 15:8-12).***

C. This principle should be used in connection with the Covenantal Principle and the Election Principle.

IV. DEMONSTRATION

A. **The Chosen Nation:** ***Jeremiah 31:31-34—"Behold, the days come, saith the Lord, that I will make a new covenant with the house of Israel, and with the house of Judah . . ."***

The burden of this passage involves God making a new covenant with the ethnic division of the human race known as Israel/Judah. The prophet speaks of the time when God took the nation of Israel out of Egypt and brought them to Mt. Sinai, where He made a covenant with them. This was the Mosaic Covenant and is referred to specifically in Scripture as the Old Covenant ***(Hebrews 8:8-13).*** Jeremiah points out that they broke this covenant, divorcing themselves from Jehovah, their husband ***(Jeremiah 3:6-8; Isaiah 50:1).*** The purpose of this New Covenant was to allow Israel to come back into relationship with God. The New Covenant was to be made with Israel/Judah and not with the Gentiles or the Church. However, when Jesus fulfilled this prophecy and established the New Covenant ***(Matthew 26:26-29)*** with His disciples, who were of the House of Judah, He spoke of His sacrifice at Calvary, which would in due time involve the Church, composed of Jew and Gentile. Both Jew and Gentile were to come into relationship with God through faith in Christ on the basis of the New Covenant. This New Covenant was made with Israel/Judah, but it also involved the Church. Thus, our interpretation of ***Jeremiah 31:31*** includes these main points:

1. God, in Christ, was to make this New Covenant.
2. Christ made this covenant at His first coming through the work of the cross.
3. This covenant was to be a completely new arrangement between God and man.
4. The covenant was to be made distinctly with the chosen nation.
5. The covenant would eventually include those out of every nation who would believe in the blood of the Lamb and accept the terms of the New Covenant.

B. **The Gentile Nations:** ***Matthew 12:17-21—"Behold My Servant, whom I have chosen; My Beloved, in whom My soul is well pleased: I will put My Spirit upon Him, and He shall show judgment to the Gentiles . . . And in His name shall the Gentiles trust."***

This passage is quoted from ***Isaiah 42:1-4*** and deals with Messiah's ministry to the Gentiles. This prophecy is spoken concerning the ethnic division of the Gentiles, not the chosen nation. The Gentiles were not in covenant relationship with God, were outside the commonwealth of Israel, and therefore were not entitled to the blessings of God. The prophet refers to a time when the Gentiles would come into blessing and trust in Messiah's name. There are two main streams of prophecies in the Old Testament pertaining to the Gentiles: prophecies of judgment ***(Isaiah 15-21; Jeremiah 46-51; Ezekiel 25-32),*** and prophecies of blessing ***(Isaiah 11:10; 42:1-4, 6; 49:6; 52:15; 55:5; 60:1-5; Zechariah 2:11; Malachi 1:11).*** The prophecies of blessing could only be fulfilled in Christ. Outside of Christ they could only have judgment. Thus, this passage in Matthew is Christ's confirmation that through Him the Gentiles would be blessed.

C. **The Church:** ***Matthew 16:18—". . . upon this rock I will build My church . . ."***

The subject of this verse involves the Church. The word Church means "the called out ones." In using this term Jesus was not referring to the ethnic divisions of the chosen nation, nor to the Gentile nations. Rather He was referring to those who would be called out of every kindred, tongue, tribe and nation. These, the redeemed through faith in His blood, would constitute the third ethnic division, the New Testament Church. In Matthew and Acts the redeemed are spoken of corporately as the Church ***(Matthew 18:17; Acts 2:47).*** In the epistles the progression of this thought is that the Church is the body of Christ ***(Colossians 1:18; Ephesians 1:22, 23).*** Paul states that ***"by one Spirit are we all baptized into one body, whether we be Jews or Gentiles . . ." (I Corinthians 12:13),*** and that in Christ ***"there is neither Jew nor Greek . . ." (Galatians 3:28).*** Therefore, this Church of which Christ spoke was to be composed of the redeemed of every nation, but these national distinctions were to cease in the Church, the body of Christ, the one new man ***(Ephesians 2:14-16).***

Chapter 14
THE CHRONOMETRICAL PRINCIPLE

I. DEFINITION

That principle by which the interpretation of a verse or passage is determined upon a consideration of its chronometrical setting.

II. AMPLIFICATION

A. **Definition:** The word "chronometrical" is taken from two Greek words; CHRONOS meaning "time", and METRON meaning "measure". Note the following relevant words as defined by the dictionary:

chronometry:	"The art of measuring time; the measuring of time by periods or divisions."
chronometer:	"An instrument that measures time; specifically, a compact timekeeper of the highest possible accuracy."
chronographer:	"One who writes concerning time or the events of time."

The Scriptures clearly reveal that God is the great chronographer of the ages. God Himself is eternal; He is not limited to time or by time. Well did Moses say, ***"from everlasting to everlasting, Thou art God . . . For a thousand years in Thy sight are but as yesterday when it is past, and as a watch in the night" (Psalms 90:2, 4).***

Man is subject to time, but God is the guardian of time and the designer of its ages. The writer to the Hebrews tells us that ***"through faith we understand that the worlds*** *(Greek; ages-translations vary in their handling of the word AION)* ***were framed by the word of God . . ." (Hebrews 11:3).*** Time is but a fragment of eternity in which God is working out His eternal purposes pertaining to creation and redemption.

The Scriptural basis upon which this principle is built is the usage of these words: age(s), time(s), and season(s).

Old Testament Hebrew

MOWADAH	=	"an appointment; i.e., a fixed time or season; specifically a festival" Translated:	
		feasts	***Leviticus 23:2, 4, 37, 44; Numbers 15:3; 29:39; Lamentations 2:6; Zechariah 8:19***
		season(s)	***Genesis 1:14; Exodus 13:10; Leviticus 23:4; Numbers 9:2, 3, 7; 28:2***
		time(s)	***Genesis 17:21; 18:14; Exodus 23:15; 34:18; Psalms 102:13; Daniel 8:19; 11:27, 29, 35; Habakkuk 2:3***
ETH	=	"time" Translated:	
		season(s)	***Exodus 18:22, 26; Leviticus 26:4; Deuteronomy 11:14; 28:12; Psalms 1:3; 145:15; Jeremiah 5:24***
		time(s)	***Judges 10:14; I Chronicles 12:22; 29:30; Esther 1:13; 4:14; Job 24:1; Psalms 31:15; Ecclesiastes 3:1-17; Daniel 11:35, 40; 12:1, 4, 9, 11; Zechariah 10:1***
YOWM	=	"a day literally or figuratively (a space of time)" Translated:	
		day(s)	***Genesis 1:5; 5:1-8, Job 24:1; Isaiah 2:2; 13:6, 9; Jeremiah 23:20; Hosea 9:7; Joel 2:29, 31; Malachi 4:5***
		time(s)	***Genesis 4:3; Numbers 13:20; Deuteronomy 10:10; 20:19; Joshua 3:15; 11:18; I Samuel 14:18; II Kings 19:25; Psalms 27:5***

New Testament Greek

AION = "an age; by extension, perpetuity of time; by implication, the world; an unbroken age, a segment of time, an era, a period of time viewed in relation to what takes place in it"
Translated:

age(s)	***Ephesians 2:7; Colossians 1:26***
course	***Ephesians 2:2***
eternal	***Ephesians 3:11; I Timothy 1:17***
forever	***Philippians 4:20; I Timothy 1:17; Hebrews 1:8; Revelation 20:10***
world(s)	***Matthew 13:39, 40, 49; 24:3; I Corinthians 10:11; Hebrews 1:2; 11:3***

GENEA = "a generation; by implication, an age, a period of time (of limited duration)"
Translated:

age(s)	***Ephesians 3:5, 21***
generation(s)	***Luke 1:48, 50; Colossians 1:26***
nation	***Philippians 2:15***
time(s)	***Acts 14:16; 15:21***

KAIROS = "an occasion; i.e., set or proper time; a measure of time; a fixed and definite time; a seasonable time; the right time; a period of time; a limited portion of time"
Translated:

season(s)	***Luke 4:13; 12:42; Acts 1:7; 14:17; I Thessalonians 5:1***
time(s)	***Mark 1:15; Luke 19:44; 21:24; Acts 3:19; Romans 5:6; 13:11; II Corinthians 6:2; Ephesians 1:10; I Thessalonians 2:17; II Thessalonians 2:6; I Timothy 4:1; II Timothy 3:1; Hebrews 9:10; I Peter 1:5, 11; Revelation 1:3; 11:18; 22:10***

KRONOS = "a space of time (in general); a period of time; by implying delay"
Translated:

season(s)	***Acts 19:22; 20:18; Revelation 6:11; 20:3***
space	***Acts 15:33; Revelation 2:21***
time(s)	***Acts 1:6, 7; 3:21; 7:17; 17:30; Galatians 4:4; I Thessalonians 5:1; I Peter 1:20; Jude 18; Revelation 10:6***

Together these words support the concept that God has divided and arranged time into a series of successive ages, times and seasons.

B. **Classification:** These ages can be divided as follows:

Past Ages	—The Eternal Ages Past
	—Age of Creation
	—Re-creation
	—Age of the Patriarchs-Promise; Adam-Abraham
	—Age of the Chosen Nation-Law: Isaac-Christ
Present Age	—The Messianic Age-first coming to second coming
Future Ages	—The Age to Come
	—The Eternal Ages Future

Each of these ages will now be considered separately but briefly:

1. **The Past Ages:** This is an all-inclusive term referring to all the ages of time prior to New Testament times. It can also be used in a more limited sense to indicate any one of the ages prior to the cross.

Hebrews 1:1 ***"God, who at sundry times and in divers manners spake in time past unto the fathers by the prophets."***

Colossians 1:26 ***"Even the mystery which hath been hid from ages and from generations, but now is made manifest to his saints."***

a. **The Eternal Ages Past**—God Himself is eternal; unlimited as to time. He is the I AM, having no beginning nor ending.

Psalms 90:2 ***". . . from everlasting to everlasting, thou art God."***

Revelation 1:8 ***"I am Alpha and Omega, the beginning and the ending, saith the Lord, which is, and which was, and which is to come, the Almighty."*** (See also ***Revelation 1:4; Isaiah 41:4.)***

These verses encompass time past, time present, and time future—eternity. The expressions "from everlasting" and "which was" both refer to God's existence in eternity past.

b. **The Age of Creation**—Though Scripture is somewhat silent concerning the creation of the angelic hosts and the universe of worlds, it does imply an age prior to the creation of the earth as we know it, in which these were created.

Genesis 1:1 ***"In the beginning God created the heaven and the earth."***

Colossians 1:16, 17 ***"For by Him were all things created, that are in heaven, and that are in earth, visible and invisible, whether they be thrones, or dominions, or principalities, or powers: all things were created by Him, and for Him: and He is before all things, and by Him all things consist."*** (See also ***Revelation 4:11.)***

c. **The Age of Re-creation**—Many Bible scholars assume that between verses 1 and 2 of ***Genesis 1,*** the fall of Satan took place, bringing about the chaotic condition spoken of in verse 2. ***Isaiah 45:18*** implies that when God created the heavens and the earth He did not create the earth "without form and void," nor in a state of darkness. ***"For thus says the Lord Who created the heavens, God Himself Who formed the earth and made it, Who established it and created it not a worthless waste; He formed it to be inhabited: I am the Lord, and there is no one else" (Isaiah 45:18*** Amp.). In connection with this it is suggested that there was an indefinite period of time between the chaotic condition described in verse 2 and the events of the rest of the chapter.

The remainder of ***Genesis 1*** is actually a description of a period of re-creation. By "re-creation" we mean "to create or form anew; to re-make." Thus God brings light out of darkness, order out of chaos, fruitfulness out of barrenness, and life out of death, crowning this period with the creation of man, God's masterpiece. This age included the refashioning of the earth and the creation of man, a new creature, in the image of God.

d. **The Age of the Patriarchs: Promise**—From Adam to Abraham there was a period of about 2,000 years. This "Age of the Fathers" was bounded by Adam, the father of the human race ***(Genesis 5:1)*** and Abraham, the father of all them that believe ***(Romans 4:16, 17).*** This time period is substantiated by the genealogies given in ***Genesis 5, 10 and 11*** concerning the Godly patriarchs. As noted in the Covenantal Principle Adam, Noah, and Abraham each received special covenantal promises, thus distinguishing this period as the Age of Promise.

e. **The Age of the Chosen Nation: Law**—From Isaac to Jesus there was another period of about 2,000 years. This "Age of the Sons" was bounded by Isaac, the only begotten son of the Old Testament ***(Hebrews 11:17),*** and Jesus, the only begotten son of the New Testament ***(John 3:16).*** God's promise to Abraham was centered in Isaac in that God said, ***". . . in Isaac shall thy seed be called" (Hebrews 11:18).*** It was to be through the only begotten son that the chosen nation would come into existence. This nation, in its infancy, was spoken of as God's son: ***"Israel is my son, even my firstborn" (Exodus 4:22, 23).*** ***"When Israel was a child, then I loved him, and called My son out of Egypt" (Hosea 11:1).*** To this many-membered son was given the Law Covenant with its Tabernacle, Priesthood, Sacrifices, Feasts and Statutes, which were as "tutors and governors" to bring this son to maturity. With the failure of this son to fulfill the purposes of God, the Father brought in His only begotten Son, ***"made under the law, to redeem them that were under the law" (Galatians 4:4, 5).*** This closed the Age of Law.

2. **The Present Age:** This term is used to refer to the New Testament Era. It is referred to in Scripture as:

—This world (age) ***(Matthew 13:22, 40; Luke 16:8; 20:34; Galatians 1:4; Titus 2:12)***
—The time of reformation ***(Hebrews 9:10)***
—The times of restitution ***(Acts 3:21)***
—The last days ***(Acts 2:17; Hebrews 1:2)***

This period is also known as the Messianic Age.

a. **The Messianic Age: Spirit**—From the first coming of Christ to His second coming is a period of approximately 2,000 years. This is the age in which the Lord Jesus is performing His Messianic work. This work, though one, involves two distinct phases: the first and second comings; the second being the ultimate completion of that which was begun in the first. This period is also referred to as the Age of the Holy Spirit, and is bounded by two great outpourings of the Spirit.

The New Testament clearly teaches that Christ came as the fulfillment of the promises, and the fulfiller and abolisher of the law. This He did when, by grace, He instituted the New Covenant in His blood, thus making provision for the outpouring of the Spirit and the formation of the Church as His body. Christ came at the end of the past ages and introduced the present Messianic Age.

I Corinthians 10:11 "Upon whom the ends of the world (Greek; ages) are come."

Hebrews 9:26 "Now once in the end of the world (Greek; ages) hath He appeared to put away sin by the sacrifice of Himself."

It is during this Messianic Age that the mystery of the one body of Christ, composed of Jew and Gentile, is being revealed.

Ephesians 3:4-6 "The mystery of Christ which in other ages was not made known unto the sons of men, as it is now revealed . . . That the Gentiles should be fellow heirs, and of the same body, and partakers of his promise in Christ by the gospel:"

The Scriptures reveal that this present age is to come to an end.

Matthew 13:39, 40, 49 "The harvest is the end of the world (Greek; age)."

Matthew 24:3 "What shall be the sign of Thy coming and of the end of the world (Greek; age)."

Matthew 28:20 "I am with you alway, even unto the end of the world (Greek; age)."

3. **The Future Ages:** This term is used to refer to the ages beyond the second coming of Christ: those that are future to the present Messianic Age. The Bible does not give a full description of these future ages, but it does establish their reality by referring to them.

a. **The Age to Come**—This refers to the age immediately following the second coming of Christ. Many expositers speak of this as The Kingdom Age in its fullest earthly manifestation. However, there is a sharp division of opinion concerning this future age. The Scriptures do speak clearly of an age to come:

Mark 10:30 ". . . in the world (Greek; age) to come eternal life."

Luke 20:34-36 "The children of this world (Greek; age) marry . . . but they which shall be accounted worthy to obtain that world (Greek; age), and the resurrection from the dead, neither marry, nor are given in marriage: neither can they die any more: for they are equal unto the angels; and are the children of God, being the children of the resurrection."

Ephesians 1:21 ". . . not only in this world (Greek; age), but also in that which is to come."

Hebrews 6:5 ". . . and the powers of the world (Greek; age) to come."

b. **The Eternal Ages Future**—The eternal ages are referred to in Scripture as:

—the ages to come ***(Ephesians 2:7)***
—world without end ***(Ephesians 3:21)***
—forever and ever ***(I Timothy 1:17; II Timothy 4:18; Revelation 5:13, 14; 14:11; 20:10)***

The following Scriptures speak of the endless ages to come:

***Ephesians 2:7** "... that in the ages to come He might show the exceeding riches of His grace."*

***Ephesians 3:21** "Unto Him be glory in the church by Christ Jesus throughout all ages, world without end. Amen."*

The dominant thought in the Scriptures concerning eternity future is the eternal bliss of the righteous and the eternal torment of the wicked.

C. **Conclusions:** God as the eternal administrator of time has ordained its successive ages and therefore was also able to be the great chronographer of the ages, writing concerning them and their related events.

Thus, the literary method of *chronography* used in writing Scripture gives rise to the *Chronometrical Principle* of interpreting Scripture.

III. QUALIFICATION

A. The first step in using this principle is to determine whether the verse or passage under consideration has some time element in it.

B. The second step in using this principle is to rightly discern the tenses of the verbs in the verse to determine whether they are pointing to the past, the present, or the future. This necessitates consulting Hebrew and Greek study aids in order to realize the full force of the tense in each situation.

C. The next step is to determine to what period or age of time the verse is referring. To facilitate this one may ask the following questions:

1. Does it refer to the Eternal Ages Past?
2. Does it refer to the Age of Creation?
3. Does it refer to the Age of Re-creation?
4. Does it refer to the Age of the Patriarchs?
5. Does it refer to the Age of the Chosen Nation?
6. Does it refer to the Messianic Age?
7. Does it refer to the Age to Come?
8. Does it refer to the Eternal Ages Future?

D. In interpretation great care must be taken so as not to confuse God's time element, as set forth in this principle. The interpreter must not take that which belonged under the Law Age and was abolished at the cross, and bring it over into the Messianic Age. For example, animal sacrifices, the Aaronic priesthood, ceremonial laws, circumcision, and the keeping of Sabbaths were abolished at Calvary and should not be placed in the Messianic Age ***(Acts 15:1-11; Colossians 2:14-17).*** Neither should temporal things belonging to the present Messianic Age be carried over into the Age to Come or the Eternal Ages. Such things as marriage, mortality, and death do not belong to the Future Ages ***(Luke 20:34-36).*** Much confusion in Biblical interpretation is caused by attributing to a particular age that which belongs to another.

E. The interpreter must recognize that the ages are successive, each age making way for another. Each age is greater than the previous as it moves onto a higher level in the eternal purpose of God. The Age of Law was greater than the Age of Promise; the Messianic Age is greater than both the Age of Promise and the Age of Law; the Age to Come and the Eternal Ages will supersede all previous ages.

F. It is also to be recognized that within certain of these ages there are shorter periods of time referred to in Scripture. Some of these are:

1. Times
2. Seasons (this is often used in connection with "times")
3. Days
4. Weeks
5. Months
6. Years

7. Day of the Lord
8. The Jubilee Years
9. The Sabbaths—Weekly, Festival, Annual
10. The Last Days: The Latter Days
11. The Time of the End

Each of these should be considered on their own to discern their full significance.

G. This principle must be used in connection with the Election, Covenantal, and Ethnic Division Principles. Also consult Chapter 15, "The Dispensations Redefined."

IV. DEMONSTRATION

Ephesians 3:10, 11: "To the intent that now unto the principalities and powers in heavenly places might be known by the church the manifold wisdom of God, according to the eternal purpose which He purposed in Christ Jesus our Lord:"

This passage involves the Church as the instrument of God's eternal purpose in Christ. The Church is the instrument for manifesting God's wisdom because it is the instrument of fulfilling His purpose. The words "eternal purpose" appear in the Greek text as "the purpose of the ages." These ages include the past ages, the present age, and the future ages. In each of the successive ages of God's varied dealings with man, there has been but one purpose which God has been working to fulfill. His mode of operation has changed, but His purpose has remained constant. This purpose, proceeding forth from God's person, was centered in Christ Jesus and concerned the Church, His body. ***Romans 8:28, 29*** defines for us what this purpose has been: ***". . . to them who are the called according to His purpose. For whom He did foreknow, He also did predestinate to be conformed to the image of His Son, that He might be the firstborn among many brethren."*** The desire of the Father's heart has always been to have a family of sons conformed to the image of His only-begotten Son, who is the express image of the Father's person. This is the purpose of the ages. Each successive age has been a progressive step toward the ultimate fulfillment of this one Divine purpose.

Chapter 15
THE DISPENSATIONS REDEFINED

I. DEFINITION

A. **Dictionary Definition:** According to "Webster's Dictionary" the definition of "dispensation" includes:

1. An administrative system; management.
2. In theology:
   a. The ordering of events under divine authority; the dealing of God to His creatures.
   b. Any religious system; a system of principles and rites enjoined.

B. **Scripture Definition:** The Scriptural background for this word is as follows:

New Testament Greek			
OIKONOMIA	=	"administration (of a household or estate); specifically a religious economy"	
		Translated:	
		dispensation	***I Corinthians 9:17 — "a dispensation of the gospel"***
			Ephesians 1:10 — "in the dispensation of the fulness of times"
			Ephesians 3:2 — "the dispensation of the grace of God"
			Colossians 1:25 — "the dispensation of God"
		stewardship	***Luke 16:2 — "give an account of thy stewardship"***
			Luke 16:3 — "taketh away from me the stewardship"
			Luke 16:4 — "when I am put out of the stewardship"

C. **Theological Definition:** There has been much misunderstanding concerning the use of the word "dispensation." The confusion surrounding this word has centered around its application to ages of time. Certain dispensational schools have confined the various dispensations to limited periods of time. This confinement misses the emphasis of the meaning of the word. The term "dispensation" involves God's administrative dealings with man, but it contains *no direct allusion to the ages of time.* To maintain balance in interpretation this distinction must be constantly kept in mind. Therefore, in this chapter we are using the word "dispensation" not to refer to an age of time, but rather to an arrangement or administration of religious affairs.

II. CLASSIFICATION

God's plan of redemption is one, but through the ages His method of dealing with man in regard to his sin has varied. These various dispensations, or arrangements, cannot be separated from the divine covenants. They, in fact, find their very basis in the covenants. Each of these redemptive covenants was a particular arrangement between God and man, having its own distinctive emphasis. Therefore, the word "dispensations" as used here refers to the dealings of God with man under their respective covenants.

Each dispensation will now be placed in its appropriate covenantal setting:

The Dispensation of Innocence	The Edenic Covenant
The Dispensation of Conscience	The Adamic Covenant
The Dispensation of Human Government	The Noahic Covenant
The Dispensation of Promise	The Abrahamic Covenant
The Dispensation of Law	The Mosaic Covenant
The Dispensation of Grace	The New Covenant
The Dispensation of the Kingdom	The Everlasting Covenant

A. **The Dispensation of Innocence—The Edenic Covenant:** The Edenic Covenant included an arrangement between God and man characterized by man's innocence. The details of this arrangement are recorded in ***Genesis***

1:26-2:25. Man was created in the image and likeness of God. He was in a state of innocency, knowing neither good nor evil. He was placed in the garden of Eden and, having received one commandment, was put under a period of probation. The one commandment given to Adam was that he was not to partake of the Tree of the Knowledge of Good and Evil, lest he come under the death penalty. Man, having a free will and the power of choice, chose to partake of the forbidden fruit and brought himself, with the whole of mankind, under subjection to Satan, sin, and death. Thus, sin temporarily broke this arrangement and excluded man from its benefits.

B. **The Dispensation of Conscience—The Adamic Covenant:** The Adamic Covenant included the arrangement between God and man that was characterized by man's awakened conscience. The details of this arrangement are recorded in ***Genesis 3-7*** and ***Romans 1, 7.*** Though man did possess the faculty of conscience in his state of innocency, it was inoperative until the fall. Partaking of the Tree of the Knowledge of Good and Evil awakened man's conscience because it is, in itself, the discerner within man to distinguish between good and evil. Thus man came under the arrangement of conscience, and God's dealings with man was through his conscience ***(Romans 2:15).*** Though the conscience defines good and evil, it gives man no power to overcome evil, and therefore by itself is an inadequate arrangement between God and man. The judgment on Noah's generation confirmed this fact. The arrangement of conscience under the Adamic Covenant has continued to exist, just as the blessings and curses of the covenant are also still in effect.

C. **The Dispensation of Human Government—The Noahic Covenant:** The Noahic Covenant included the arrangement between God and man that was characterized by man being entrusted with governmental authority. The details of this arrangement are recorded in ***Genesis 8, 9.*** After the flood God placed in the hands of man the legal authority to execute murderers. This suggests the institution of human government, in that such an act is the highest function of government, and implies every lesser function. Though divinely instituted, human government has proved itself throughout history to be inadequate to produce divine order. The failure of human government was proven decisively in God's judgment at the tower of Babel ***(Genesis 10, 11).***

D. **The Dispensation of Promise—The Abrahamic Covenant:** The Abrahamic Covenant included the arrangement between God and man characterized by man receiving promises from God. The details of this arrangement are recorded in ***Genesis 12-50.*** God gave promises to Abraham and confirmed them to Isaac and Jacob. Their relationship to God was centered around these promises. These promises, involving the seed and the land, included temporal, national and spiritual blessings. They received the fulfillment of some of the promises in their day, but they died in faith, not having received certain other promises which were to be fulfilled under other arrangements ***(Hebrews 11:8-21, 33).*** This arrangement of promises was centered in the only begotten son of promise.

E. **The Dispensation of Law—The Mosaic Covenant:** The Mosaic Covenant included the arrangement between God and man characterized by man coming under the law of God. The details of this arrangement are recorded mainly in ***Exodus 19-49*** and ***Leviticus.*** In fulfillment of the promise to Abraham, Isaac, and Jacob, the children of Israel had become a great nation in Egypt, and had been delivered from it to possess the promised land. At Mount Sinai God brought the nation under the Mosaic economy. This arrangement included the moral, civil and ceremonial law. The ceremonial law included the Tabernacle, Priesthood, Sacrifices, Feasts and Sabbaths. However, the law arrangement also proved inadequate to accomplish the full purpose of God. This was proved to be true when those who were under the law rejected and crucified Him who was the fulfillment of the law. While Christ fulfilled and abolished the ceremonial law, the righteousness of the moral law finds its fulfillment in those who walk not after the flesh but after the Spirit ***(Romans 8:1-4).***

F. **The Dispensation of Grace—The New Covenant:** The New Covenant included the arrangement between God and man that was characterized by man receiving the grace of God. The details of this arrangement are recorded especially in the epistles of the New Testament. ***John 1:17*** declares that ***"the Law was given by Moses, but grace and truth came by Jesus Christ,"*** and ***Titus 2:11*** states ***"For the grace of God that bringeth salvation hath appeared unto all men."*** Jesus Christ is the grace of God personified who established the New Covenant in His own blood ***(Matthew 26:26-28).*** This is the new arrangement of grace by which all men may come into eternal fellowship with God by faith in the Lord Jesus Christ. This arrangement is abundantly able to accomplish the eternal purpose of God in relation to man.

G. **The Dispensation of the Kingdom—The Everlasting Covenant:** The Everlasting Covenant included the arrangement between God and man characterized by man's place of dominion in the everlasting kingdom of God. There has never been a time when the kingdom of God has not been in existence. The psalmist proclaims in

Psalms 145:13: "Thy kingdom is an everlasting kingdom." This is true because the King Himself is ***"eternal, immortal, invisible" (I Timothy 1:17).*** In relation to man on earth the kingdom of God has been expressed in different forms. Each of these forms provided a progressive expression of the eternal kingdom. This arrangement under the Everlasting Covenant is actually the beginning and the consummation of all the other arrangements under their covenants. This arrangement of the kingdom ushers in the eternal order ***(Revelation 20-22).***

> ***"Then cometh the end, when He shall have delivered up the kingdom to God, even the Father . . . that God may be all in all." (I Corinthians 15:24-28)***

III. CONCLUSION

In summary:

A. The dispensations find their proper foundation in the covenants in that they only refer to the different methods of God's dealings under these arrangements.

B. The dispensations, having no definite reference to time, do have a point of commencement. However, each arrangement was not abolished when another arrangement was ushered in (e.g., conscience was not abolished when human government was brought in; promise was not abolished when law was brought in).

Chapter 16
THE BREACH PRINCIPLE

I. DEFINITION

That principle by which the interpretation of a certain verse or passage of Scripture is aided by a consideration of certain breaches of promise and time.

II. AMPLIFICATION

Since this principle will be a ''new'' one to many interpreters a larger amount of space will be given to its development.

A. **Definition of a ''Breach'':** According to Webster's Dictionary, a ''breach'' is:

—A state of being broken; a rupture; a break; a gap.
—A hole or opening, as in a wall or fence, made by breaking or parting.
—An interruption of continuity; blank space.
—A break or interruption in friendly relations.

The following phrases are also defined:

—Breach of faith	a failure to keep faith.
—Breach of privilege	an act in violation of rules, order, privileges or dignity of a legislative body.
—Breach of promise	failure to fulfill a promise.
—Breach of the peace	a violation of the public peace.
—Breach of trust	a violation by fraud or omission of any duty imposed on a person in a position of trust.

This word has the following background in Scripture:

Old Testament Hebrew

BEDEQ = ''a gap or leak (in a building or a ship); fissure or rent.''
Translated:

breach(es)	***II Kings 12:5-8, 12***
calkers	***Ezekiel 27:9, 27***

BAQA = ''to cleave; generally to rend, break, rupture or open; to break through or into.''
Translated:

make a breach	***Isaiah 7:6; 22:9; Ezekiel 26:10***
break	***Genesis 7:11; II Chronicles 25:12; Proverbs 3:20; Isaiah 58:8***
cleave	***Genesis 22:3; Numbers 16:31; Judges 15:19; Psalms 74:15; Amos 6:11; Zechariah 14:4***
divide	***Exodus 14:16, 21; Nehemiah 9:11; Psalms 78:13***
rend	***Joshua 9:4; I Kings 1:40; Job 26:8; Ezekiel 13:11, 13***
tear	***II Kings 2:24; Hosea 13:8***

MIPHRATS = ''a break (in the shore); i.e., a haven.''
Translated:

breaches	***Judges 5:17***

PARATS = ''to break out, break through, break down, make a breach in, break into, break open, break up.''
Translated:

	make a breach	***I Chronicles 13:11; 15:13***
	break	***Genesis 38:29; Exodus 19:22, 24; II Samuel 5:20; II Kings 14:13; I Chronicles 14:11; Nehemiah 1:3; 2:13; Job 16:14; Psalms 80:12; 89:40; 106:29; Proverbs 25:28***
PERETS	= "a break (literally or figuratively), bursting forth, a breach." Translated:	
	breach	***Genesis 38:29; Judges 21:15; II Samuel 5:20; 6:8; I Kings 11:27; I Chronicles 13:11; 14:11; Nehemiah 6:1; Job 16:14; Psalms 106:23; Isaiah 30:13; 58:12; Amos 4:3; 9:11***
	breaking forth	***I Chronicles 14:11; Job 30:14; Psalms 144:14***
	gap	***Ezekiel 13:5; 22:30***
SHEBER	= "a fracture; figuratively a ruin; a breaking; breach; crushing." Translated:	
	breach	***Leviticus 24:20; Psalms 60:2; Proverbs 15:4; Isaiah 30:26; Jeremiah 14:17; Lamentations 2:13***
	breaking	***Job 41:25; Isaiah 30:13, 14***
	broken	***Leviticus 21:19***
	destruction	***Proverbs 16:18; 17:19; 18:12; Isaiah 1:28; Jeremiah 4:6, 20; Ezekiel 32:9***
TENUWAH	= "alienation; by implication, enmity; opposition." (root word = hinder, restrain, frustrate, forbid, dissuade, refuse) Translated:	
	breach of promise	***Numbers 14:34 (margin—altering of my purpose)***
	occasion	***Job 33:10***

Together these words provide us with a wide variety of applications, but the basic meaning that links them all is the thought of a division or gap. We will now proceed to consider various examples of breaches in Scripture.

B. **Breaches of Promise**

1. **Breach of Promise Concerning Entering the Land:** God had promised Abraham, Isaac and Jacob that their seed would inherit the land of Canaan ***(Genesis 15:13-21; 22:16-18; 28:13-15; Psalms 105:8-12).*** With the exodus, which came in fulfillment of prophecy, it was God's purpose to bring Israel into the promised land. This, God had confirmed to Moses their leader ***(Exodus 3:15-17).*** After two years, Israel came to Kadesh-Barnea on the border of Canaan. From there Moses sent twelve spies to search out the land and bring back some of its fruit. Forty days later they returned and ten of the spies brought an evil report saying that, though the land was good, the obstacles were too great to be overcome. This caused the whole nation to rise in unbelief and rebellion, and reject the land of promise. In so doing they turned their backs upon the Abrahamic Covenant ***(Numbers 13, 14).*** The New Testament records plainly that they could not enter into the promise because of their unbelief ***(Hebrews 3, 4).*** God clearly expressed His reaction and determination to Moses:

> ***"Doubtless ye shall not come into the land, concerning which I sware to make you dwell therein . . . And your children shall wander in the wilderness forty years, and bear your whoredoms . . . After the number of the days in which ye searched the land, even forty days, each day for a year, shall ye bear your iniquities, even forty years, and ye shall know my breach of promise." Numbers 14:30,33,34***

The marginal rendering indicates that the "breach of promise" refers to an altering of His purpose. The Amplified Version states that it was a revoking of the promise. In actual history this breach of promise was a time lapse in the fulfillment of the promise to the nation. This gap in time lasted forty years, during which the first generation that had come out of Egypt died in unbelief in the wilderness. Both the first and second generations experienced the breach caused by being out of covenant relationship with God. Circumcision was the seal of the Abrahamic Covenant ***(Genesis 17).*** For this reason the second generation had to be circumcised before they could enter into the blessings of the covenant ***(Joshua 5:2-9).*** Thus, the entering of the land was postponed by unbelief for forty years. This is known as "the breach period." This time spent in unbelief was lost time as far as Israel was concerned.

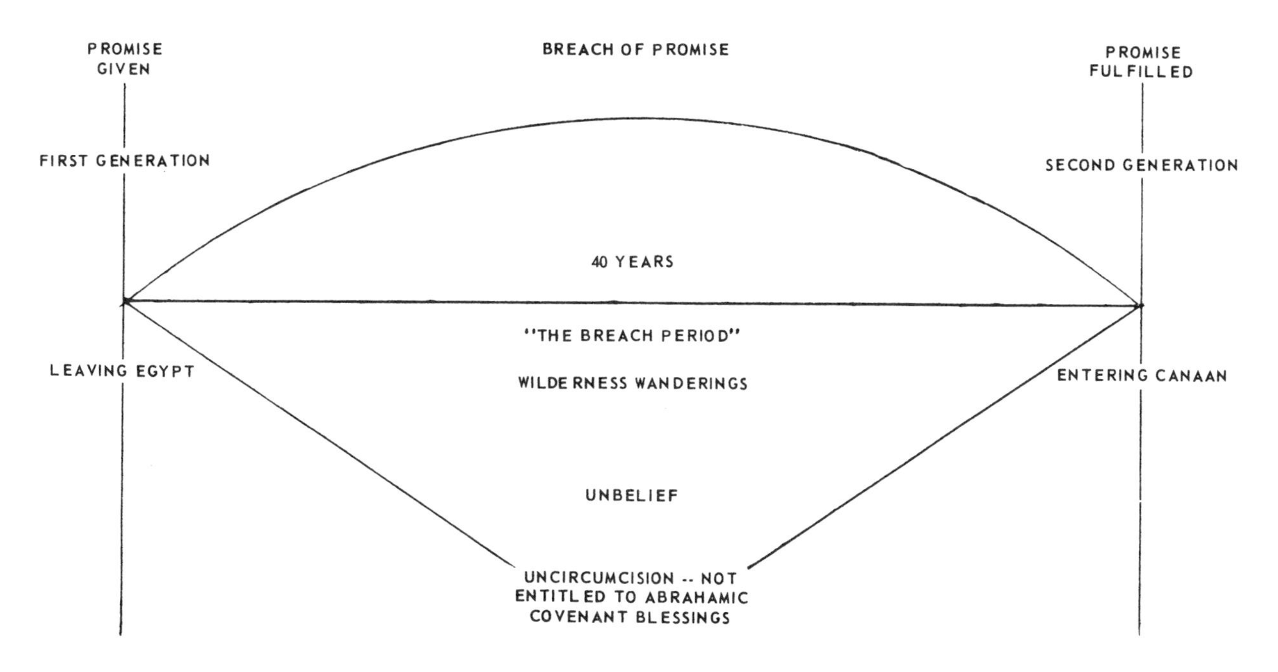

2. **Breach of Promise Concerning Dominion in the Land:** God had promised Abraham, Isaac and Jacob that their seed would also have dominion over the Canaanites ***(Genesis 15:18-21; 22:16-18; 24:60).*** This promised victory over their enemies was confirmed to the nation by Moses ***(Deuteronomy 28:14; 30:1-20).*** This dominion was contingent upon their obedience. The book of Joshua records the fulfillment of this promise when Joshua led Israel in the conquest of Canaan ***(Joshua 1:1-9; 21:43-45).*** However, the book of Judges records that after the death of Joshua another generation arose that, through not following the Lord, lost the dominion. They began to compromise with their enemies and lapsed into idolatry and immorality. Seven times during the period of the judges, Israel went through the cycle explained in ***Judges 2:11-19.***

—Departure from the Lord
—Servitude to their enemies
—Supplication to the Lord
—Saviour-Judge raised up
—Return to the Lord
—Death of the judge
—Departure from the Lord

The book of Judges covers approximately 450 years of Israel's history (see ***Acts 13:20***). About 111 years of this time were spent in servitude to various Canaanite nations. During these periods of bondage God's promise of dominion was not being fulfilled due to apostacy. These years were lost time to Israel. As such, they provide a solution for an apparent discrepancy in Biblical chronology. In ***I Kings 6:1*** we read that from the exodus to the building of the Temple 480 years elapsed. On the other hand Paul, in ***Acts 13:17-23,*** specifically mentions 530 years from within that same period, and implies at least 570 years. Paul fails to mention the years of the conquest in Joshua, the years between Joshua and Judges, and the early years of Solomon's reign, all of which fall within the boundaries of ***I Kings 6:1.*** These three time periods may be shown to be seven years, thirteen years and four years, respectively. Therefore, using Paul's years in conjunction with all the chronological references from Exodus to I Kings, the years covering this period come to a grand total of 594 years. The apparent discrepancy between this figure and the one given in ***I Kings 6:1*** is 114 years (594 - 480 = 114 years). Why then were these 114 years left out of the ***I Kings 6:1*** total? By totalling all the years which Israel spent in servitude to their enemies, including Abimelech's usurpation, we arrive at a figure of 114 years. Therefore, a possible solution to this discrepancy is that the ***I Kings 6:1*** reference left out the time that was lost when Israel was in bondage due to their disobedience. During these periods God's promise of theocratic dominion was not being fulfilled because they were not meeting its conditions. These servitudes were breaches of promise and gaps of lost time in Israel's theocratic history. The following charts will help to illustrate this.

Chronology of the Period from the Exodus to the Building of the Temple

	Years
1. The wilderness wanderings — ***Acts 13:17, 18***	40
2. The conquest of Canaan — ***Joshua 14:7, 10; Exodus 12:40, 41; Numbers 10:11, 12; 13:17-20***	7
*3. The Joshua-Judges connection (see below)	13
4. First servitude—Cushan — ***Judges 3:8***	8
5. Othniel — ***Judges 3:11***	40
6. Second servitude — Eglon — ***Judges 3:12-14***	18
7. Ehud — ***Judges 3:30***	80
8. Shamgar included in third servitude — ***Judges 3:31; 4:1; 5:6, 7***	—
9. Third servitude — Jabin — ***Judges 4:2, 3***	20
10. Deborah and Barak — ***Judges 5:31***	40
11. Fourth servitude—Midian — ***Judges 6:1-6***	7
12. Gideon — ***Judges 8:28***	40
13. Usurpation of Abimelech — ***Judges 9:22***	3
14. Tola — ***Judges 10:2***	23
15. Jair — ***Judges 10:3***	22
16. Fifth servitude—Ammon — ***Judges 10:8***	18
17. Jephthah — ***Judges 12:7***	6
18. Ibzan — ***Judges 12:9***	7
19. Elon — ***Judges 12:11***	10
20. Abdon — ***Judges 12:14***	8
21. Sixth servitude—Philistines — ***Judges 13:1***	40
22. Samson included in sixth servitude — ***Judges 15:20***	—
23. Eli — ***I Samuel 4:18***	40
24. Samuel (the Eli-Saul connection) — ***I Samuel 7:2, 13; 9:1, 2; 10:1***	20
25. Reign of Saul — ***Acts 13:21***	40
26. Reign of David — ***II Samuel 2:11; 5:4, 5***	40
27. Reign of Solomon — ***I Kings 6:1***	4
	594

*NOTE: For a further discussion of the chronology of this period see Martin Anstey's *Chronology of the Old Testament.*

3. **Breach of Promise Concerning Remaining in the Land:** God had promised Abraham, Isaac and Jacob that their seed would not only inherit the land and have dominion over their enemies, but would also remain in the land, having it for an everlasting possession ***(Genesis 17:8; 48:4).*** This promise was given certain conditions under the Mosaic and Palestinian Covenants ***(Deuteronomy 27-30).*** One of these conditions for Israel's remaining in the land was that they were to allow the land to keep its Sabbaths. In other words, they were to let the land lay fallow, not sowing or reaping, one out of every seven years. Also, every fiftieth year (7 X 7 = 49 + 1 = 50) was to be a jubilee year, which was an additional Sabbath for the land ***(Leviticus 25:1-22).*** Under these covenants God threatened to punish them for not keeping the Sabbaths.

> ***"And if ye shall despise My statutes . . . break My covenant . . . I will make your cities waste, and bring your sanctuaries unto desolation . . . And I will bring the land into desolation . . . And I will scatter you among the heathen . . . then shall the land enjoy her sabbaths, as long as it lieth desolate, and ye be in your enemies' land; even then shall the land rest, and enjoy her sabbaths. As long as it lieth desolate it shall rest; because it did not rest in your sabbaths, when ye dwelt upon it . . . If they shall confess their iniquity . . . if then their uncircumcised hearts be humbled . . . Then will I remember my covenant with Jacob . . . Isaac, and . . . Abraham . . . and I will remember the land." Leviticus 26:15, 31-35, 40-42*** (See also ***Leviticus 26:14-46; 18:24-30; 20:22-26; Deuteronomy 28:58-68.)***

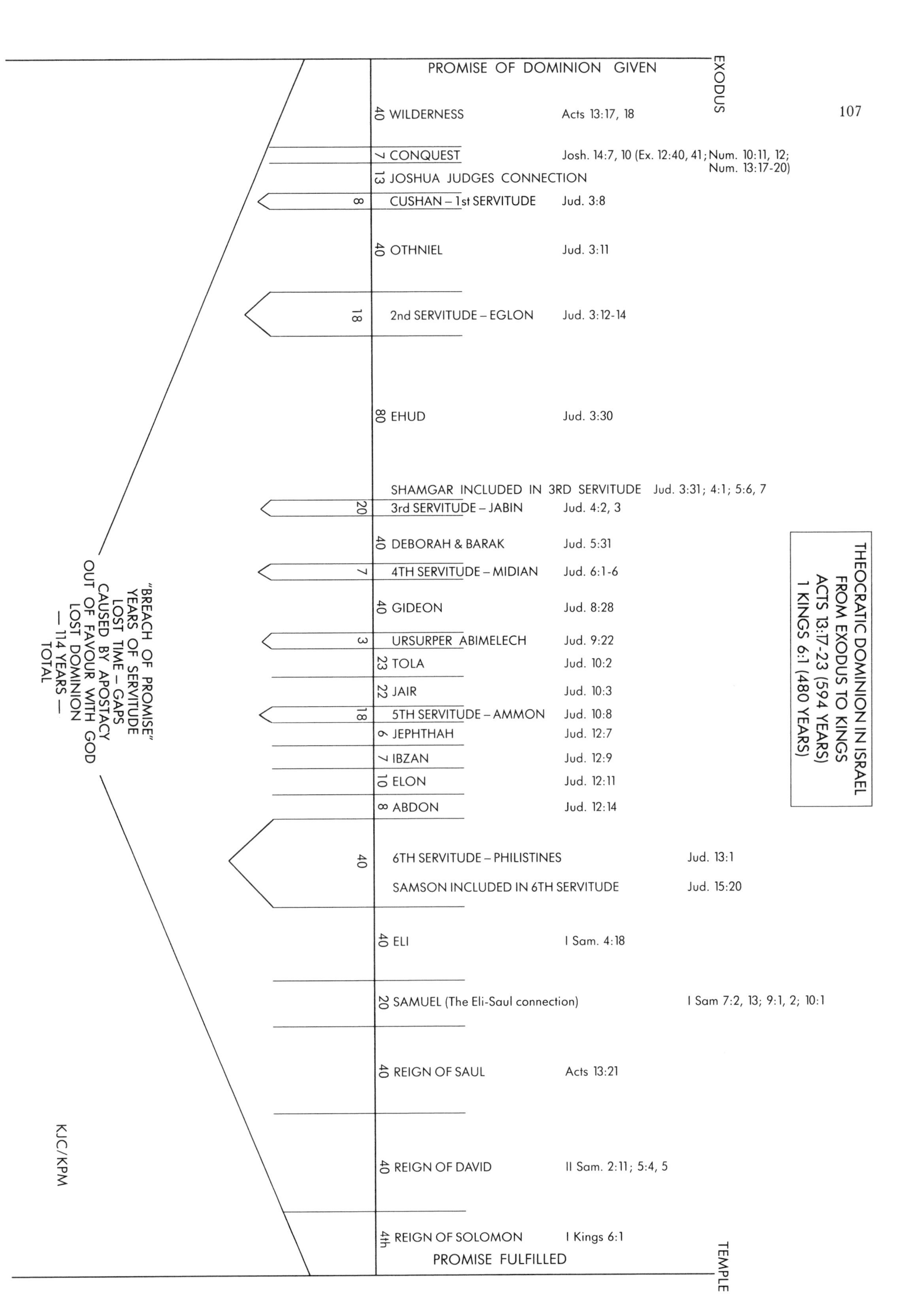
EXODUS
PROMISE OF DOMINION GIVEN
40 WILDERNESS Acts 13:17, 18
7 CONQUEST Josh. 14:7, 10 (Ex. 12:40, 41; Num. 10:11, 12; Num. 13:17-20)
13 JOSHUA JUDGES CONNECTION
8 CUSHAN – 1st SERVITUDE Jud. 3:8
40 OTHNIEL Jud. 3:11
18 2nd SERVITUDE – EGLON Jud. 3:12-14
80 EHUD Jud. 3:30
SHAMGAR INCLUDED IN 3RD SERVITUDE Jud. 3:31; 4:1; 5:6, 7
20 3rd SERVITUDE – JABIN Jud. 4:2, 3
40 DEBORAH & BARAK Jud. 5:31
7 4TH SERVITUDE – MIDIAN Jud. 6:1-6
40 GIDEON Jud. 8:28
3 URSURPER ABIMELECH Jud. 9:22
23 TOLA Jud. 10:2
22 JAIR Jud. 10:3
18 5TH SERVITUDE – AMMON Jud. 10:8
6 JEPHTHAH Jud. 12:7
7 IBZAN Jud. 12:9
10 ELON Jud. 12:11
8 ABDON Jud. 12:14
40 6TH SERVITUDE – PHILISTINES Jud. 13:1
SAMSON INCLUDED IN 6TH SERVITUDE Jud. 15:20
40 ELI I Sam. 4:18
20 SAMUEL (The Eli-Saul connection) I Sam 7:2, 13; 9:1, 2; 10:1
40 REIGN OF SAUL Acts 13:21
40 REIGN OF DAVID II Sam. 2:11; 5:4, 5
4th REIGN OF SOLOMON I Kings 6:1
PROMISE FULFILLED
TEMPLE
"BREACH OF PROMISE"
YEARS OF SERVITUDE
LOST TIME – GAPS
CAUSED BY APOSTACY
OUT OF FAVOUR WITH GOD
LOST DOMINION
— 114 YEARS —
TOTAL
KJC/KPM
THEOCRATIC DOMINION IN ISRAEL
FROM EXODUS TO KINGS
ACTS 13:17-23 (594 YEARS)
1 KINGS 6:1 (480 YEARS)

This actually came to pass in Israel's history when God sent Judah into captivity to Babylon for 70 years. The reason for the 70-year duration of this captivity is clearly stated in ***II Chronicles 36:21.*** For approximately 490 years (70 x 7) Israel had failed to meet the conditions for remaining in the land by not allowing the land to keep her Sabbaths. After removing His people for 70 years from the land so that it could have its overdue rest, God was able to allow them to return from captivity to dwell in the land once again ***(Jeremiah 25:12; 29:10; Daniel 9:2).*** This period was time lost in that it was a breach in the fulfillment of God's promise concerning Israel's remaining in the land.

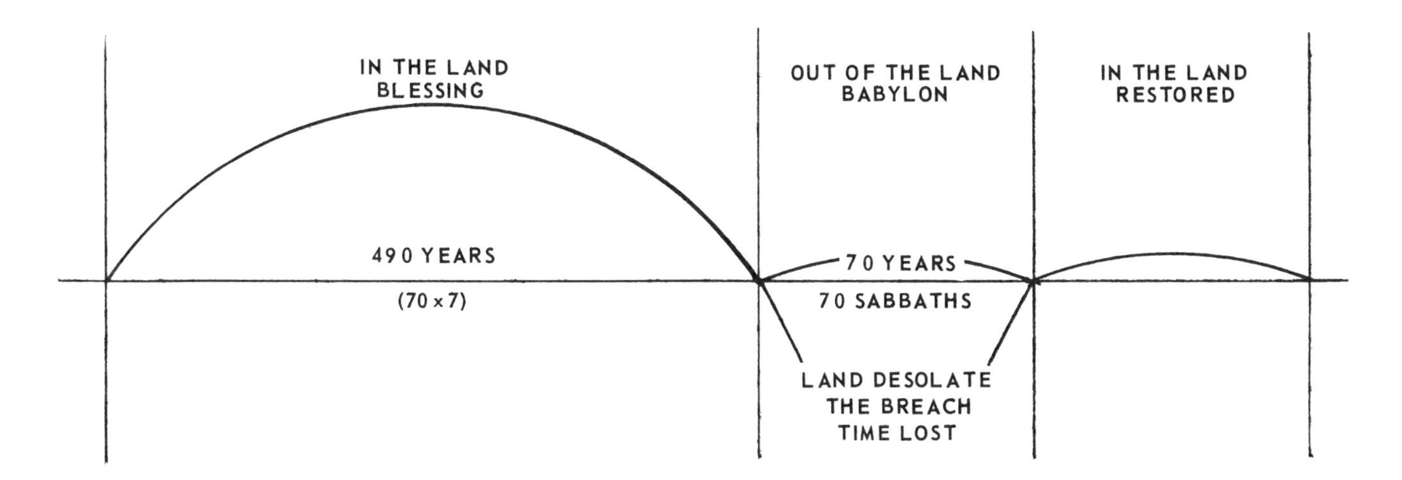

4. **Breach of Promise Concerning the Sceptre:** Jacob prophesied over his son Judah that ***"the sceptre shall not depart from Judah, nor a lawgiver from between his feet, until Shiloh come; and unto Him shall the gathering of the people be" (Genesis 49:10).*** The first king of Israel who came from the tribe of Judah was David. God confirmed to David the promise of the sceptre and the throne in the terms of the David Covenant ***(II Samuel 7; Psalms 89).*** This came in confirmation and fulfillment of Jacob's prophecy. There was an unbroken dynasty of Davidic kings reigning over Judah until Zedekiah, the last king to hold the sceptre. Zedekiah was dethroned approximately 600 years before Shiloh (Messiah) came. This sceptre and throne of David was promised to Jesus Christ ***(Numbers 24:17; Luke 1:30-33).*** The 600 years from Zedekiah to Christ was apparently a breach of promise concerning the sceptre.

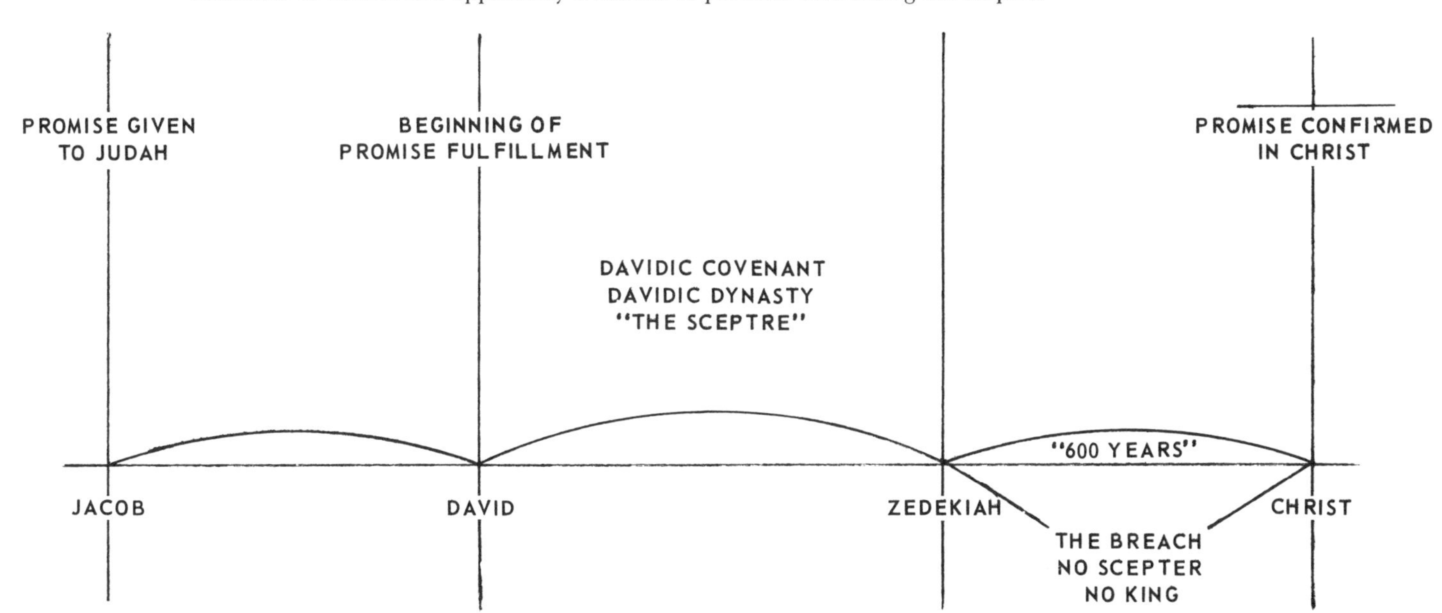

5. **Breach of Promise Concerning the Nazarite Vow:** In ***Numbers 6:1-12*** the laws concerning the vow of separation are recorded. This vow was a promise that a man or woman could make to God to show special consecration to Him. The vow was to be in effect for a period of time specified by the Nazarite. If he became defiled at any point during the days of his separation unto the Lord, all the previous days would be lost as far as the fulfilling of his vow was concerned.

"But the days that were before shall be lost, because his separation was defiled." Numbers 6:12

These lost days constituted a breach of his promise to the Lord. Samson, as a Nazarite defiling his vow, was an example of this ***(Judges 13-17).***

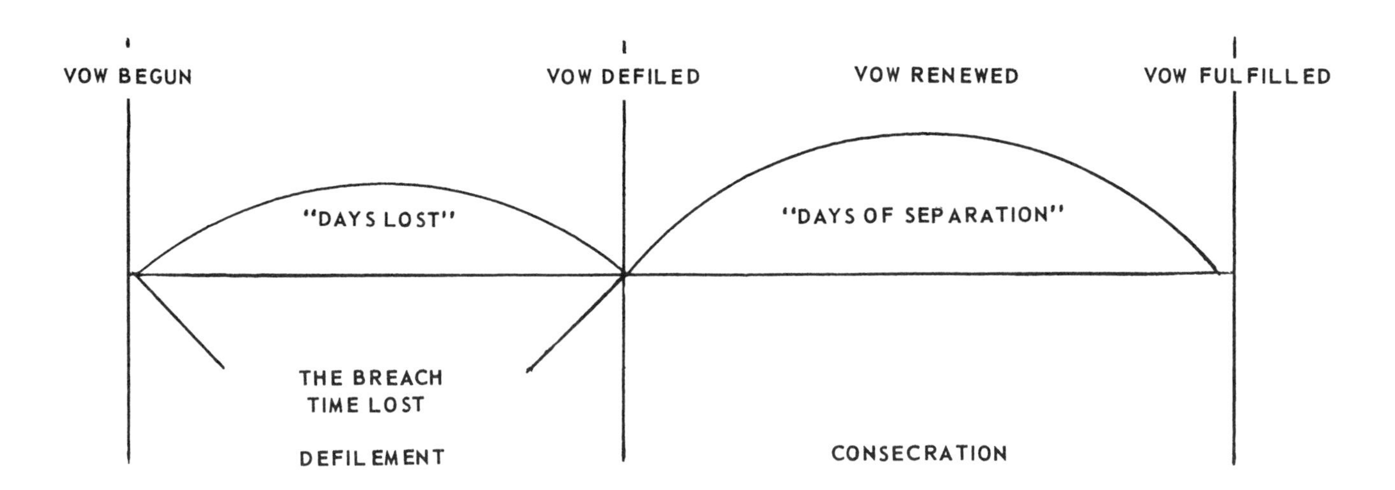

C. **The Breach of Time in Prophetic Fulfillment:** A consideration of certain prophecies concerning the future, both in the Old and New Testament implies a *breach of time* in their complete fulfillment. By "breach of time" we mean the span or period of time between the fulfillments of certain prophecies. This is not to say that "God's prophetic time-clock" stopped, for it never has. But because the prophets were often caught up in what is spoken of as "the prophetic perspective" they would group together in certain verses or passages events involving the past, present and future. Because God is the great I AM THAT I AM ***(Exodus 3:14-15),*** time past, present and future are as one eternal present before Him. Hence, when the prophets were in the Spirit, they saw things from God's eternal present. However, history which is the fulfillment of prophecy, shows that there was or is a "breach of time" or "time periods" for these prophetic details of events to unfold. Thus, *breach of time* is not to be confused with the *breach of promise.* It deals with a different type of breach altogether and must be kept in clear distinction.

The Old Testament prophets could not always understand their own utterances concerning the coming of Christ. They searched what was meant and what manner of *time* the Spirit of Christ which was in them did signify when it testified before hand the sufferings of Christ and the glory that should follow. It was revealed to them that their utterances were not just for themselves or their generation but unto another generation ***(I Peter 1:10-12).***

Various passages in the prophetical books view mountain peaks of events as being all together with no valleys between. Their historical fulfillment has proven that there is a "time gap" or a *breach of time* involved in their fulfillment. This is especially true concerning the events pertaining to the first and second comings of Christ. This area of "time element" is what makes the interpretation of prophecy so very difficult.

1. **The First and Second Comings of Messiah:** A comparison of ***Isaiah 61:1, 2*** with ***Luke 4:16-21*** implies the first and second comings of Christ. When Jesus entered the synagogue at Nazareth, He was given the book of Isaiah. He opened it to Chapter 61 and began to read. He read the clauses of verse 1 and read the first clause of verse 2, concerning "The acceptable year of the Lord." At this point he stopped reading and closed the book. It may be asked why He did not continue to read. The next clause speaks of "the day of vegeance of our God." These two clauses certainly imply the first and second comings of the Lord. The first coming was indeed *"the acceptable year of the Lord,"* and His ministry in the Gospels, from His anointing

in Jordan to His crucifixion, certainly fulfilled the clauses of verse 1 ***(II Corinthians 6:2*** with ***Isaiah 49:8).*** There was no vengeance in His heart then, for He asked His Father to forgive those who crucified Him. It is the second coming that is ***"the day of vengeance of our God" (Isaiah 63:4*** with ***II Thessalonians 1:7-9).*** Though the prophet Isaiah spoke of these two events together in the same passage, history proves that there is a *breach of time* between them, extending from the first to the second coming.

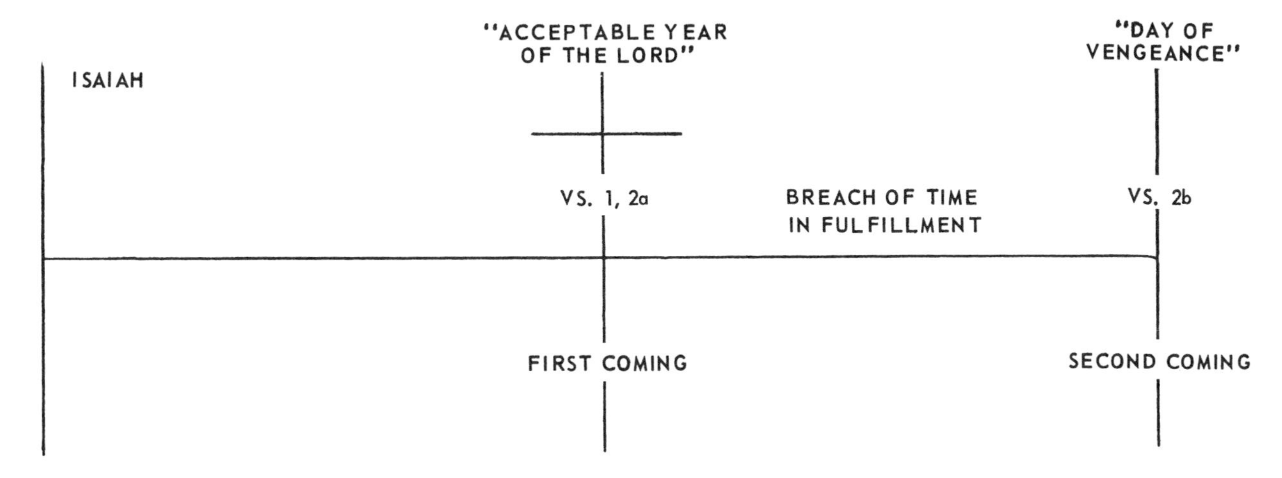

2. **The Pre-existence, Incarnation and Crucifixion of Messiah:** ***(Micah 5:1-2)*** These two verses of prophetic utterance from Micah include clauses that are Messianic. They run together as if they were to be fulfilled all at once. Yet the historical fulfillment of these verses shows that a *breach of time* is involved in their fulfillment. The primary Messianic elements of the prophecy are noted here:

   a. The Ruler in Israel had His goings forth from of old, from everlasting. This is a reference to Messiah's pre-existence, pointing out His eternity of being.

   b. The Ruler would come out of Bethlehem of Judah. The fulfillment of this phase shows it to be Messiah's incarnation. It speaks of His virgin birth ***(Matthew 2:1-6).***

   c. The Ruler or Judge of Israel was to be smitten with a rod upon the cheek. Historically this was fulfilled in the events pertaining to Messiah's crucifixion ***(Matthew 27:30).***

   This historical fulfillment of these clauses indicates a breach of time in their realization.

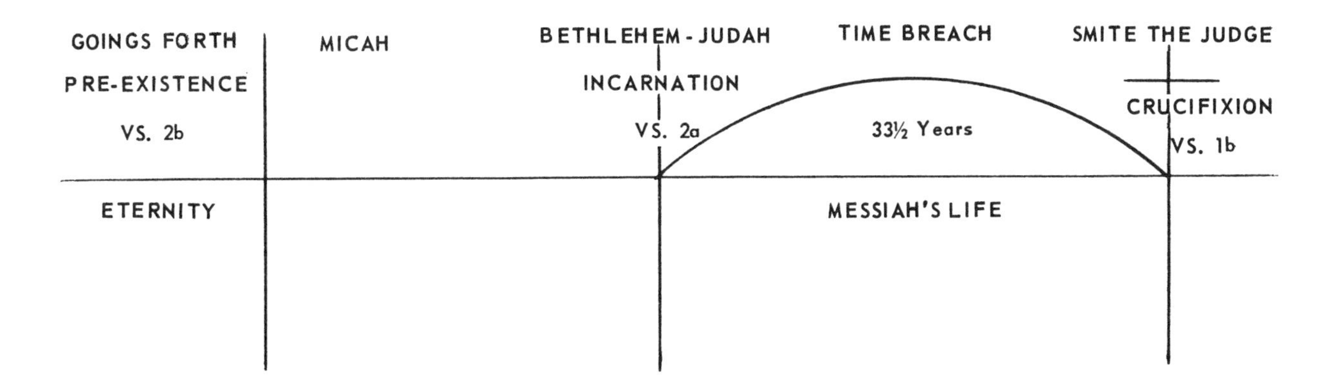

3. **The Day of the Lord:** The prophets spoke of "the Day of the Lord" that was to come. A consideration of any of these prophetic utterances, in the light of historical fulfillment, clearly shows that "the Day of the Lord," with its surrounding events, was used to refer to both the first and second comings of Christ. Nearly 2000 years have elapsed between these two comings, thus constituting a *breach of time.*

a. ***Malachi 3:1-2*** speaks of the Messiah's first coming as the Messenger of the Covenant, preceded by the ministry of John the Baptist (see also ***Mark 1:2***). It is spoken of as "The Day of His coming."

b. ***Malachi 4:1*** speaks of Messiah's second coming. This is also spoken of as "the day that cometh." It is a time of complete judgment upon the wicked.

Thus, between ***Malachi 3:1-2*** and ***Malachi 4:1,*** there is an intervening Messianic era — a *breach of time* between the first and second comings of the Lord.

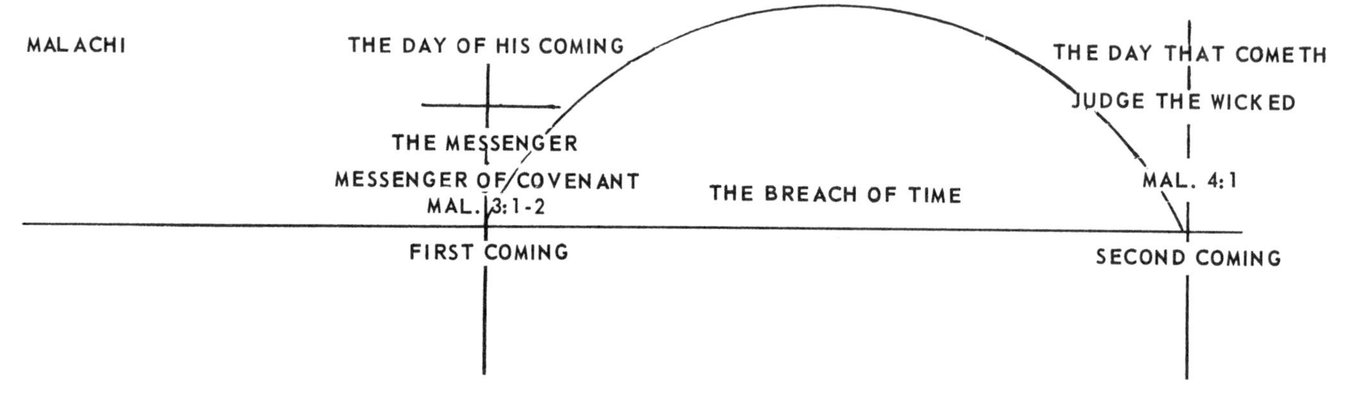

4. **The Two Resurrections:** There are several verses in Scripture which speak of the resurrection, both of the righteous and the wicked.

a. ***Daniel 12:2*** — Some shall awake to everlasting life.
Some shall awake to everlasting shame and contempt.

b. ***John 5:29*** — The resurrection of life.
The resurrection of damnation.

c. ***Acts 24:15*** — A resurrection of the just.
A resurrection of the unjust.

By referring to ***Revelation 20:5, 6,*** we discover that there are two resurrections:

The first resurrection — for the blessed and holy.
The second resurrection — for the rest of the dead.

This passage also explains that there is a "thousand years" between the first and second resurrection. Thus, there is a *breach of time* between the resurrections of the righteous and of the wicked. Though all the verses above speak of the resurrection of the just and the unjust, there is implied in them a *breach of time,* as is clearly stated in Revelation.

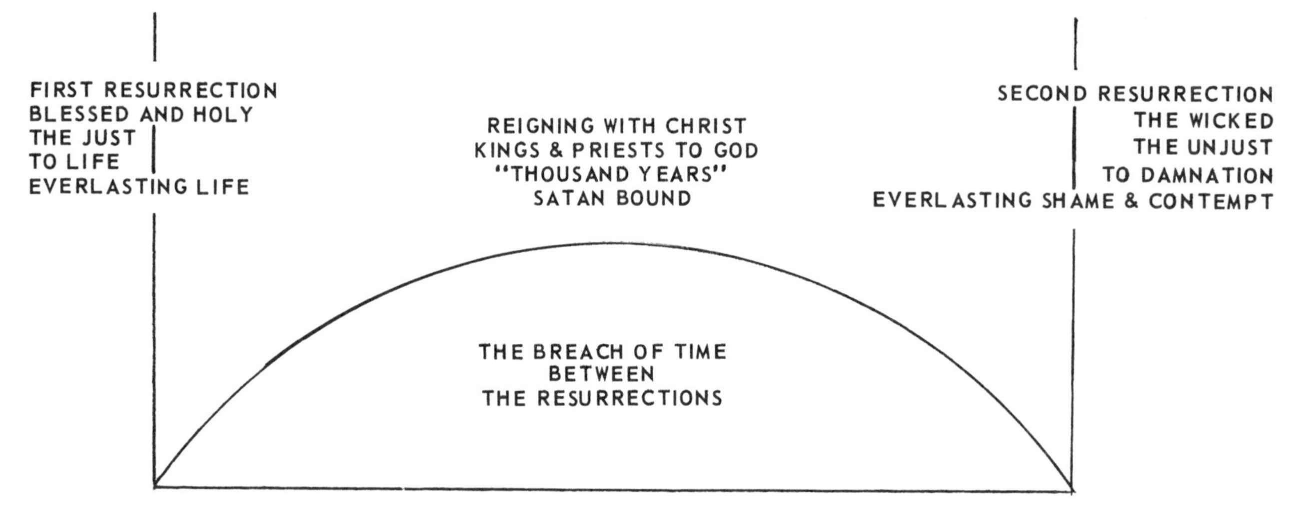

NOTE: Those who interpret the first resurrection to be spiritual and the second to be bodily, state that the "thousand years" between is symbolic of the period of time between the two advents of Christ. Therefore there is a *breach of time* between the resurrections, regardless how these two resurrections are interpreted.

D. **Summation of Breach Revelation:** That which is revealed in Scripture concerning the many breaches of time and promise only further substantiates and illustrates the fact that God both transcends and controls time. The breaches of time are not to be viewed as having caused the time clock of God's eternal purpose to stop running. Man's failures, as illustrated in the breaches of promise, did not alter God's scheduled purposes. Though it *was* time lost for man, it *was not* time lost for God. His purpose and promises are sure and so also is their fulfillment. In that God is eternal and has all of time laid out before Him, He was able to write concerning the various breaches of time and promise in history and prophecy. This He did skillfully, scattering the clues to many of these breaches throughout Scripture.

Thus, the *literary method of breach revelation* used in writing Scripture gives rise to the *breach principle* of interpreting Scripture.

III. QUALIFICATION

A. The first and most difficult step in using this principle is determining whether the verse or passage under consideration is in any way related to a breach.

B. If a breach is intimated, the interpreter must correctly discern the true nature of the breach, as well as its cause and boundaries.

C. There must be a clear distinction between breaches of promise and breaches of time in prophetic utterance. The breaches of promise are caused by unbelief, while the breaches of time are caused by the prophet's viewing separated events as one.

D. Due to the limited relevance of this principle to Scripture, the interpreter must be cautious in seeking to apply it.

E. Obviously, this principle must be used in harmony with all others.

IV. DEMONSTRATION

Romans 11:25 ". . . that blindness in part has happened to Israel, until the fullness of the Gentiles be come in."

It becomes apparent from even a superficial reading of this verse that there is a breach of sight involved. In other words, there is a period of time in which Israel is in a state of blindness. This breach of time is to last *until* the "fullness of the Gentiles be come in."

Jesus Christ came as the promised Messiah to the chosen nation of Israel, confirming the promises made to the fathers. However, according to the prophecy of Isaiah, the nation as a whole had ears and could not hear, eyes and could not see, and a heart that could not perceive ***(Isaiah 6:9, 10).*** Through the spiritual blindness of their unbelief they could not see Jesus as their promised Messiah ***(Matthew 13:14, 15; Acts 28:25-27).***

There was ***"a remnant according to the election of grace . . . and the rest were blinded" (Romans 11:5, 7).*** This state of spiritual blindness was to continue over a period of time, during which the Gentiles were to come into blessing through the Messiah. The context of this verse is dealing with the symbolism of the olive tree. The natural branches, Israel, were broken off through unbelief. The wild branches, the Gentiles, are grafted in through faith ***(Romans 11:19, 20).*** The only way that national Israel can be grafted back into the olive tree is if they do not remain in unbelief ***(Romans 11:23).*** The verse under consideration points out that this state of blind unbelief is to continue over a breach of time, during which the full number of the Gentiles will come in. It implies that there will come a time when the blindness shall be lifted and ***"all Israel shall be saved" (Romans 11:26).***

Although the coming of the Gentiles is a breach in God's dealing with Israel, it is not of secondary importance to God. The Church age is *not* a parenthesis in the ultimate purpose of God, but rather is a parenthesis in national Israel's faith in their Messiah. The Church, composed of Jew and Gentile, is the eternal purpose of God in Christ ***(Ephesians 3:10, 11).***

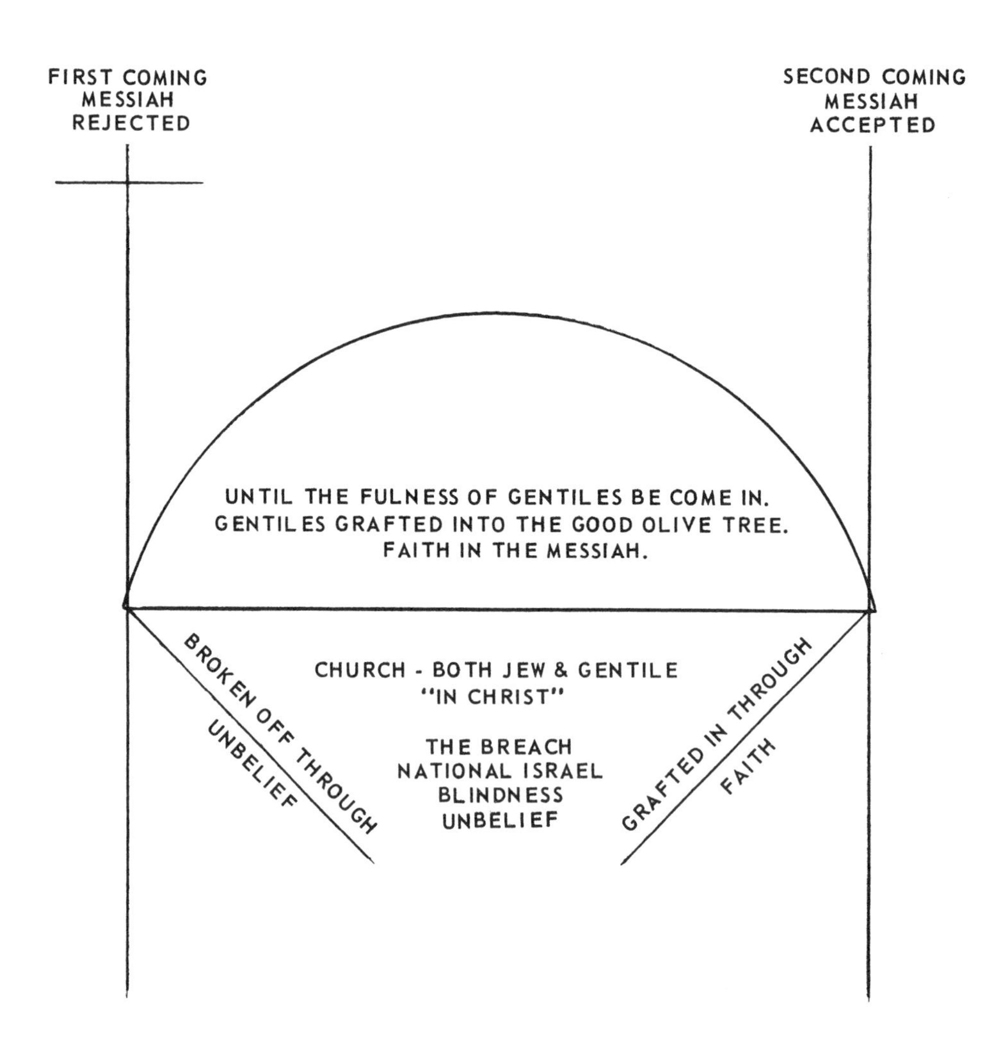

FIRST COMING
MESSIAH
REJECTED
SECOND COMING
MESSIAH
ACCEPTED
UNTIL THE FULNESS OF GENTILES BE COME IN.
GENTILES GRAFTED INTO THE GOOD OLIVE TREE.
FAITH IN THE MESSIAH.
CHURCH - BOTH JEW & GENTILE
"IN CHRIST"
THE BREACH
NATIONAL ISRAEL
BLINDNESS
UNBELIEF
BROKEN OFF THROUGH
UNBELIEF
GRAFTED IN THROUGH
FAITH

Chapter 17
THE CHRISTO-CENTRIC PRINCIPLE

I. DEFINITION

That principle by which Scripture is interpreted in relation to its center — Christ.

II. AMPLIFICATION

The basis for this principle is the fact that Christ is the central Person of the Bible. The entire written Word revolves around He who is the Living Word. His person and work is the theme of God's written revelation. In the wheel of divine revelation He is the hub, and all truths are as spokes relating to Him Who is The Truth. The truth of this is best expressed in the following verses:

Hebrews 10:7	*". . . in the volume of the book it is written of Me . . ."*
John 5:39	*"Search the Scriptures . . . they are they which testify of Me."*
Luke 24:27	*". . . He expounded unto them in all the Scriptures the things concerning Himself."*
Luke 24:44	*". . . all things must be fulfilled, which were written in the law of Moses, and in the prophets, and in the psalms, concerning Me."*
Acts 10:43	*"To Him give all the prophets witness . . ."*
John 1:45	*"We have found Him of whom Moses in the law, and the prophets, did write."*
NOTE ALSO:	*John 1:1, 14; 5:46, 47; Matthew 5:17, 18; Acts 3:18; John 14:6* with *17:17*

All of these Scriptures attest to the fact that the Bible is Christ-centered; He is the living embodiment of the Written Word.

In that God is the author of Scripture He was able to center all of its subjects around the person and work of His Son: *"that in all things He might have the preeminence" (Colossians 1:18).* We will now illustrate this in each of the major divisions of Scripture:

—The Old Testament Historical Books
—The Old Testament Poetical Books
—The Old Testament Prophetical Books
—The Gospels
—The Acts
—The Epistles
—The Apocalypse

A. **Christ in the Old Testament Historical Books**

Genesis	The Creator	*Colossians 1:16*
	The Beginning	*Revelation 1:8*
	The Seed of the Woman	*Matthew 1:23*
	The Ark of Salvation	*Luke 2:30*
	Isaac, Only Beloved Son	*John 3:16*
	Joseph, Beloved Son	*Matthew 3:17*
Exodus	The Deliverer	*Acts 5:31*
	The Mediator	*Hebrews 8:6*
	The Lawgiver	*Hebrews 8:10*
	High Priest	*Hebrews 2:17*
	Passover Lamb	*I Corinthians 5:7*
	Tabernacle of God with men	*John 1:14*
Leviticus	Sacrifice and Oblation	*Hebrews 10:12*
	Holy High Priest	*Hebrews 7:26*

	The Atonement	***Hebrews 9:14***
	Way of Approach to God	***Hebrews 7:25***
Numbers	The Tabernacle	***John 1:14***
	Sanctuary in Wilderness	***Ezekiel 11:16***
	The Nazarite	***Hebrews 7:26***
	The Son of Man/Serpent of Brass	***John 3:14***
	The Smitten Rock	***I Corinthians 10:4***
	The Star out of Jacob	***Matthew 2:2***
Deuteronomy	The True Prophet	***Deuteronomy 18:15-19; Acts 3:22***
	The Rock	***Deuteronomy 32:4, 18, 31; I Corinthians 10:4***
Joshua	Joshua (Jehoshua)	***Hebrews 4:8***
	Captain of our Salvation	***Hebrews 2:10***
	The Man with the Sword	***Joshua 5:13-15; Ephesians 6:12-18***
	Inheritance Giver	***Hebrews 4: Ephesians 1:3, 14***
Judges	Judge/Deliverer/Saviour	***Matthew 1:21-23***
Ruth	The Mighty Man	***Ruth 2:1***
	Lord of the Harvest	***Ruth 2:14-17***
	Kinsman Redeemer	
I Samuel	Anointed Prophet/Priest/King Intercessor	
	Sceptre/Throne/Kingdom Holder	***Luke 1:31-35***
II Samuel	The Son of David	***Matthew 1:1***
I Kings	King of Peace and Glory	
	The Wisdom of God	***I Corinthians 1:30***
	Temple Builder	***Ephesians 2:20-22***
	Greater than Solomon	***Matthew 12:42***
	The Prophet of God/Word	***John 1:14***
	King of Kings/Lord of Lords	***Revelation 19:16***
II Kings	The Righteous King	***II Kings 3:12***
	The Man of God	***John 1:14***
	The Word of the Lord personified	
I Chronicles	The Greather King David	***Matthew 1:1***
II Chronicles	Prophet/Priest/King Temple Cleanser	***Hebrews 9:10, 11***
	Reformer	***Hebrews 9:10, 11***
Ezra	Governor/Priest	***Hebrews 5:1-5; Matthew 2:6***
	Scribe and Restorer	***Isaiah 58:12***
Nehemiah	Governor of Judah	***Matthew 2:6***
	Man of Prayer and Work	***John 17; Matthew 16:18***
Esther	The Great King and His Bride	***Revelation 19:7***

B. **Christ in the Old Testament Poetical Books**

Job	Patient Suffering Priest	***Hebrews 5:1-5***
Psalms	The Beloved Shepherd/King	***John 3:16; Hebrews 13:20***
	The Sweet Singer	***Hebrews 2:12***
Proverbs	The Wisdom of God	***I Corinthians 1:24, 30; Colossians 2:3***
Ecclesiastes	The Preacher in Jerusalem	***Ecclesiastes 1:1***
	The Son of David	
	The Wisdom of God	***I Corinthians 1:24***
	The King "from above"	***Galatians 4:26***
Song of Solomon	King of Peace	
	Beloved Bridgegroom Lover	***Ephesians 5:32***

C. **Christ in the Old Testament Prophetical Books**

Isaiah	The Holy One of Israel	***Mark 1:24***
	Our Salvation	***Matthew 1:21***

	Our Righteousness	*I Corinthians 1:30*
	Our Comfort	*John 14:16, 18*
	The True Judge	*John 5:22*
Jeremiah	The Appointed Prophet	
	The Righteous Branch, the King	
	The LORD our Righteousness	*Jeremiah 23:4-6*
Lamentations	The Weeping Prophet	
	The Man of Sorrows	*Luke 19:41-44; Matthew 23:37, 38*
Ezekiel	The Son of Man	*John 1:51*
	The Shekinah Glory	*Ezekiel 43:1-4;*
Daniel	The Son of Man	*Daniel 7:13*
	The Crushing Stone	*Daniel 2:34-45; Matthew 21:42-44*
	The Kingdom of God personified	*Daniel 7:27*
	King of Kings/Lord of Lords	*Revelation 19:16*
Hosea	The Prophet of Law and Love	*Acts 3:22, 23; Matthew 5:17, 18; John 3:16*
Joel	Jehovah-God, Promiser and Baptizer with the Holy Spirit	*Luke 24:49; Acts 2:33; John 1:31-33*
Amos	Burden-bearer	*Isaiah 53:12*
	Judge and Punisher of Nations	*II Thessalonians 1:7-9*
	Builder of David's Tabernacle	*Matthew 16:18, 19; Acts 15:15-18*
Obadiah	Servant and Worshipper	*Hebrews 2:12*
	Executor of Divine Wrath	*II Thessalonians 1:6-10*
Jonah	The Greater than Jonah	*Matthew 12:39-41*
Micah	Heavenly Micah "like God"	*Hebrews 1:2-4*
	Rejected King of the Jews	*Micah 5:1; John 19:15*
	Establisher of His House	*Micah 4:1, 2; Hebrews 3:6*
Nahum	Prophet of Comfort and Vengeance	*John 14:16; II Thessalonians 1:8*
Habakkuk	The Judge of Babylon	*Revelation 17, 18*
	The Rewarder	*Hebrews 10:38; 11:6*
Zephaniah	The Jealous God	*Zephaniah 1:18; II Corinthians 11:2*
	Executor of God's Wrath	*Romans 2:5, 6*
Haggai	Prophet/Priest/Prince	
	Builder of the Lord's House	*Matthew 16:18; Hebrews 3:5*
Zechariah	One whom Jehovah Remembers	
	The Branch	*Zechariah 3:8; Matthew 2:23*
	Jehovah's Servant	*Zechariah 3:8; Philippians 2:7*
	The Smitten Shepherd	*Zechariah 13:7; Mark 14:27*
	King-Priest and Temple Builder	*Zechariah 6:9-12; Hebrews 5:5, 6*
	King over all the earth	*Zechariah 14:9; Revelation 19:16*
Malachi	The Messenger of the Covenant	*Matthew 26:26-28*
	Refiner/Purifier/Cleanser of the Temple	*Malachi 3:1-3; Matthew 3:11* *Matthew 3:11; John 2:13-17; Matthew 21:12-14*

D. **Christ in the Gospels**

Matthew	King/Lawgiver	*Matthew 2:2; Isaiah 33:22*
	Anointed, Son of David	*Matthew 3:16, 17; 1:1*
	Fulfiller of Law and Prophets	*Matthew 5:17*
Mark	The Son of God/Son of Man	*Mark 10:45*
	Suffering Servant who became Lord	*Mark 16:19*
Luke	Son of Man, Anointed Preacher, Saviour	*Luke 4:18, 19; 19:10*
John	The Word, the Eternal Son	*John 1:1; 3:16*
	The Life and the Light	*John 1:4, 5*

	The "I AM"	*John 8:56*
	The Way, The Truth, The Life	*John 14:6*

E. **Christ in the Acts**

Acts	Head of the Church, Baptizer in the Spirit	*Acts 2:1-4; 1:5-8*

F. **Christ in the Epistles**

Romans	The Salvation and Righteousness of God	*Romans 10:3-4*
	The Propitiation/Mercy Seat	*Romans 3:25*
I Corinthians	The Power and Wisdom of God Righteousness, Sanctification Wisdom and Redemption	*I Corinthians 1:24-30*
	The Love of God	*I Corinthians 13*
	The Resurrection and the Life	*I Corinthians 15*
II Corinthians	Comforter/Apostle	
	Sin-offering	*II Corinthians 5:21*
	The Glory of the New Covenant	*II Corinthians 3, 4*
Galatians	Faith, Righteousness, Life Redeemer, Seed of Abraham, New Covenant Mediator	*Galatians 3*
Ephesians	Fulness of God	*Ephesians 4:9-16*
	Head of the Church	*Ephesians 4:16*
	The Bridegroom	*Ephesians 5*
	Giver of the Ministries	*Ephesians 4:9-16*
	Grace and Peace of God	*Ephesians 1:2-3*
Philippians	Our Joy, Life, Mind, Goal and Strength	*Philippians 2, 3, 4*
Colossians	The Pre-existent, Pre-eminent, The Creator, Ruler, Redeemer, Head of the Body, Fulness of the Godhead Bodily	*Colossians 1:19; 2:9*
I Thessalonians	Our Sanctification	*I Thessalonians 5:23*
	Our Coming Lord	
II Thessalonians	The Avenger and Coming Lord	*II Thessalonians 1:6-10*
I Timothy	Elder, Deacon, Teacher who fulfills His Charge	*II Timothy 3*
II Timothy	Saviour, Seed of David, Righteous Judge	
	Lord of the Heavenly Kingdom	*II Timothy 4:1*
Titus	Saviour, Grace of God, and Redeemer	*Titus 1:3; 2:14*
Philemon	Intercessor, Advocate	
Hebrews	Angel of Jehovah	
	The Last Adam	
	The Prophet, the High Priest, Minister and Sacrifice, Author and Finisher of our Faith	*Hebrews 1-13*
James	Lord of Glory	*James 2:1*
	The Judge	*James 4:11, 12*
	The Lord of Hosts	*James 5:4*
	The Husbandman	*James 5:7*
I Peter	The Foreordained Lamb	*I Peter 1:19-20*
	The Chief Cornerstone	*I Peter 2:6*
	The Stone of Stumbling and Rock of Offense	*I Peter 2:8*

	The Example, The Chief Shepherd and Bishop	***I Peter 5:4***
II Peter	The Beloved Son	***II Peter 1:17***
	The Daystar and Coming Lord	***II Peter 1:19; 3:10***
I John	The Word, the Son, Advocate, Propitiation, Christ Who is Love, Light and Life	***I John 1, 2, 3***
II John	The Truth, the Son of God, the Christ	***II John***
III John	The Truth	***III John 4, 8***
Jude	The Coming Lord, Judge and Only Wise God our Saviour	***Jude 14, 25***

G. **Christ in the Apocalypse**

Revelation	Head of the Church, the Lamb	***Revelation 1, 2, 3, 4, 5***
	Lion of the Tribe of Judah	***Revelation 5:5***
	The Jehovah Angel	***Revelation 7:1-3***
	The Bridegroom	***Revelation 19:5-8***
	The Word, King of Kings and Lord of Lords	***Revelation 19:11-16***

Thus in writing Scripture God utilized the literary method of "central theme" in centering His written revelation around Christ.

The literary *method of making Christ the central theme* used in writing Scripture gives rise to the *Christo-centric Principle* of interpreting Scripture.

III. QUALIFICATION

A. The interpreter must recognize that the ultimate purpose of the written Word is to bring him to Christ, the Living Word.

B. This principle can be used only when the verse or passage under consideration speaks of Christ either:

1. Characteristically
   a. Typically
   b. Symbolically
2. Prophetically
3. Historically
4. Doctrinally

C. A verse should never be applied directly to Christ unless it possesses Christo-centric characteristics.

D. This principle should never be used when the resultant interpretation violates the actual literal sense of Scripture. In desiring to unveil the glories of Christo-centricity some have sought to relate every verse of Scripture *directly* to Christ, and in so doing have violated and missed the actual truths of those verses which do relate to Christ *indirectly*.

E. The Old Testament Scriptures which contain Christo-centric characteristics must be interpreted in the light of New Testament clear revelation of Christ. The clear historical and doctrinal must interpret the more obscure characteristic and prophetical.

IV. DEMONSTRATION

A. **Old Testament History—*Genesis 22:1-14:*** The subject of this passage is the historical account of Abraham, the father, being called to offer up his only son, Isaac, for a burnt offering on Mt. Moriah. This passage contains Christo-centric characteristics which are:

1. A Father/Son relationship
2. An only Son
3. The Son intended to be a sacrifice
4. Question of God providing a Lamb
5. Three days

Because of its Christo-centric characteristics this event can be interpreted as a typical foreshadowing of the Father God offering Christ, His Only Begotten Son, for the sins of the world. (Compare ***Hebrews 11:17-19*** with ***John 3:16.)***

B. **Old Testament Poetry—*Job 19:25-27:*** In these verses we have Job's confession of faith in the midst of extreme suffering. The Christo-centric characteristics of these verses are:

1. The living redeemer
2. Standing upon the earth in the latter day
3. Though flesh decays, flesh shall see God

These verses can be interpreted as pointing to Christ, the Living Redeemer who shall stand on the earth at His second coming and bring about the bodily resurrection of the dead.

C. **Old Testament Prophecy—*Jeremiah 23:5, 6:*** The prophecy of these verses concerns the Lord raising up unto David a King whose name would be "the Lord our Righteousness." This prophecy contains within it these Christo-centric characteristics:

1. Raising unto David a Righteous Branch
2. A King, reigning and prospering, executing judgment
3. Judah and Israel being saved
4. The Lord Our Righteousness

These verses are unmistakably prophetic of the coming of Jesus Christ, the Son of David ***(Matthew 1:1),*** the righteous King ***(Revelation 19:16; Matthew 2:2),*** who is the Lord our Righteousness ***(I Corinthians 1:30).***

D. **The Gospels—*John 6:1-65:*** The content of this chapter is the historical account of Christ's feeding the five thousand, followed by His teaching. The chapter is Christo-centric in that the purpose of the miracle of the multiplying of the fish and bread was to reveal by demonstration that Christ Himself was the Bread of Life.

NOTE: The four Gospels are Christo-Centric in that they present to us an actual, literal, historical account of Christ's ministry in word and deed.

E. **The Acts—*Acts 10:34-43:*** In this passage we have Peter's sermon to the Gentiles in the house of Cornelius. The whole of the sermon is Christo-centric in that it deals with the ministry, death and resurrection of Christ Jesus.

F. **The Epistles—*Hebrews 4:14-5:10:*** The subject of this passage is the High Priestly ministry of Christ. It is clearly Christo-centric because it is setting forth the doctrine of Christ's eternal Priesthood.

G. **The Apocalypse—*Revelation 19:11-16:*** This passage presents to us Christ's riding forth on the white horse to judge. It can be seen as Christo-centric because the following names are attributed to the rider:

1. Faithful and True
2. The Word of God
3. King of Kings
4. Lord of Lords

Chapter 18
THE MORAL PRINCIPLE

I. DEFINITION

That principle by which the interpretation of a verse or passage is determined by discerning the moral it contains.

II. AMPLIFICATION

Webster's Dictionary defines the word "moral" in its noun form as "the practical lesson taught by any story or incident; the significance or meaning: (plural) principles and practice in regard to right, wrong and duty; ethics, general conduct or behavior."

One of the chief purposes for the existence of the Bible is to instruct men in the way of righteousness. Most of its contents are written to teach man both what he should *be* and what he should *do* ***(II Timothy 3:16, 17).*** Many portions of Scripture are written as clear, concise instructions, such as in the Epistles and in the clear teachings of Jesus. On the other hand, much of Scripture contains indirect instruction and the moral of it must be drawn out ***(Proverbs 25:2).*** This can be illustrated in the following five areas of literary genre: (A) History, (B) Poetry, (C) Prophecy, (D) Proverbs and (E) Parables.

A. **History:** The historical sections of Scripture were written not only to record historical facts but also to teach spiritual lessons.

1. **The Death of Saul—*I Chronicles 10:13, 14:*** The life of Saul having been recorded in I Samuel, the writer of I Chronicles interprets for his readers the reason for Saul's death in an effort to exhort them not to follow his example.
2. **The Miracles of Jesus—*John 20:30, 31:*** After recording many of Christ's miracles, John points out that his purpose for recording them was ***"That ye might believe that Jesus is the Christ, the Son of God; and that believing ye might have life through His name."*** Behind the miracle was a moral. Though many missed it, the miracle was recorded to communicate the moral.
3. **The Exodus into the Wilderness—*I Corinthians 10:1-11:*** After summarizing the historical events recorded in the book of Exodus, Paul establishes the purpose for their record by saying in verse 11: ***"Now all these things happened unto them for examples: and they are written for our admonition, upon whom the ends of the world are come."***

Behind each historical event in Scripture lies a moral—a spiritual lesson—which it is designed to teach.

B. **Poetry:** The poetical sections of Scripture were also written for instruction purposes. Job exclaimed, ***"Oh that my words were now written! Oh that they were printed in a book!" (Job 19:23).*** At least thirteen of the psalms bear the title "Maschil," which means "instruction" ***(Psalms 78, 88, 89).*** The book of Ecclesiastes concludes with the moral of its contents ***(Ecclesiastes 12:13, 14).***

The divine purpose for Biblical poetry is to communicate spiritual principles.

C. **Prophecy:** The prophetical sections of Scripture are centered around divine principles. In the prophets God at times indicated that His purposes were instructional: ***"I am the Lord thy God which teacheth thee to profit, which leadeth thee by the way that thou shouldest go" (Isaiah 48:17); "Be thou instructed, O Jerusalem, lest My soul depart from thee" (Jeremiah 6:8).***

The utterances of the prophets are all based on divine principles, including the moralisms of the Law.

D. **Proverbs:** Most all of the proverbs in Scripture are to be found in the book bearing that name. These proverbs are "wise sayings" containing a moral. Their instructional purpose is clearly set forth in the opening passage of the book:

The proberbs of Solomon . . . To know wisdom and instruction; to perceive the words of understanding; to receive the instruction of wisdom, justice, and judgment, and equity; to give subtelty to the simple, to the young man knowledge and discretion. A wise man will hear, and will increase learning: and a man of understanding shall attain unto wise counsels: to understand a proverb, and the interpretation; the words of the wise, and their dark sayings (Proverbs 1:1-6).

E. **Parables:** Many of the parables in Scripture are found in the gospels and are taken from Christ's teaching. Though He taught in parables to conceal their truth from the proud. His purpose was also to teach the humble ***(Matthew 13:10-13). "And He began again to teach by the seaside . . . And He taught them many things by parables, and said unto them in His doctrine . . ." (Mark 4:1, 2).*** The moral of a parable is the key to its interpretation.

Thus, the literary *method of moralizing* used in writing Scripture gives rise to the *Moral Principle* of interpreting Scripture.

III. QUALIFICATION

A. This principle can be viewed as a system of interpretation on its own, in that it can be applied to almost all of Scripture.

B. Foundational to the use of this principle is a consideration of the literal sense of the passage. This would include an accurate discerning of such things as the facts of an event and their significance, and the interpretation of symbols and other figures of speech.

C. The interpreter must recognize that there may be more than one moral intended in a passage and that a moral may have various facets. Because of this, the moral of a passage may possibly be expressed in a variety of ways.

D. This method of interpretation must be kept in balance with others. The whole of Scripture was not intended to be only moralized. There is much more to be gained from it than just extracting lessons for our lives. A proper place must be kept for theological interpretation, which must never be contradicted by moral interpretation.

IV. DEMONSTRATION

A. **History—*I Chronicles 13:7-14; 15:1-3, 13-15: "And they carried the ark of God in a new cart out of the house of Abinadab."*** The ark of the covenant had been in captivity to the Philistines for several months. Because of divine judgments, they returned the ark to Israel on an ox-cart. When David became king his desire was to bring the ark out of the house of Abinadab into the tabernacle which he had pitched for it. He copied the Philistines' method by placing the ark on a new cart. For this, God brought judgment and death upon his efforts. David then searched the Law of Moses and discovered his error of not following the divine order. When he brought up the ark on the shoulders of the priests he was blessed for his efforts. The moral behind this historical event then is: God's work must be done in God's way in order to have God's blessing.

B. **Poetry—*Psalms 78:*** This psalm of instruction gives a panoramic view of Israel's history as recorded in the books of Exodus through I Samuel. The mercy of God was evident in the miracles He performed for them. Yet, in spite of God's blessing, they continually tempted and provoked Him with their unbelief and rebellion. This forced God to release the wrath of His judgment upon them. Thus, the cycle of events that is seen through this synopsis of history is: mercy — provocation — divine judgment. The moral that this psalm is teaching is: provoking God by despising His mercy will bring the wrath of His judgment.

C. **Prophecy—*Isaiah 1:10-17:*** Here the the prophet denounces the empty formalism of Israel's worship. He discounts their sacrifices, oblations, incense, new moons, Sabbaths and feasts as being hypocritical. Though God Himself ordained these forms of worship, they became an abomination to Him when they degenerated into merely an external religion. Thus, the moral of this prophecy is: external worship is an abomination to God when it lacks internal motivation.

D. **Proverbs—*Proverbs 14:4: "Where no oxen are, the crib is clean: but much increase is by the strength of the ox."***

Oxen are noted in this verse for their strength and productivity, but they must be fed regularly to maintain their strength. If there are no oxen, then the grain-crib can remain empty and clean and there is no work to be done around it. However, there can be no increase of harvest without using the strength of the ox. The moral of this proverb is: productivity makes work worthwhile.

E. **Parables—*Matthew 25:1-13:*** This is known as the parable of the wise and foolish virgins. The five wise virgins took extra oil with them in preparedness for the coming of the bridegroom. The five foolish virgins failed to take extra oil. When the bridegroom came the five virgins who were ready went into the marriage, while the five unready virgins had to go and seek to buy some oil. When they returned they were not admitted to the wedding. The moral of this parable is: believers must be prepared, watching for the coming of the Lord.

THE FIGURES OF SPEECH GROUP OF PRINCIPLES

Ch. 19 The Symbolic Principle
Ch. 20 The Numerical Principle
Ch. 21 The Typical Principle
Ch. 22 The Parabolic Principle
Ch. 23 The Allegorical Principle

These specialized principles may be grouped together because they deal with figures of speech or extensions of them. These certainly do not comprise all the figures of speech used in Scripture but are included as principles due to their prominence in Scripture and the difficulties they present in interpretation. The difference between symbol and type is defined in Chapter 21 and the difference between parable and allegory is handled in Chapter 23.

Chapter 19
THE SYMBOLIC PRINCIPLE

I. DEFINITION

That principle by which the interpretation of a verse or passage in Scripture containing symbolic elements can be determined by a proper interpretation of the symbol(s) involved.

II. AMPLIFICATION

According to Websters Dictionary, the word "symbol" is made up of two Greek words; "syn" meaning "together," and "ballein" meaning "to throw." It means literally "thrown together," and denotes an object used to represent something abstract: an emblem: using one thing to stand for or represent another.

Though the word "symbol" is not specifically used in the Bible, God caused the writers of Scripture to employ the literary method of symbolization throughout Scripture. They often used one thing to represent another because of common characteristics. This is what is meant by symbolization in which the link between that which is used as a symbol and that which is being symbolized is the characteristics common to both.

Things used as a symbol ← ← ← ← ← Common Characteristics → → → → → Things symbolized

God, in authoring the Bible, dealt with both creation and redemption. The first two chapters of Genesis contain the record of the creation of the natural realm: the rest of the Bible contains God's plan of redemption. In Scripture God uses the natural things He created to become symbols ***(Romans 1:19, 20)***. In other words, the language of creation becomes the language of the symbol which in turn becomes the language of redemption.

Basically, there are seven categories of symbols in Scripture: (A) Objects, (B) Creatures, (C) Actions, (D) Numbers, (E) Names, (F) Colors and (G) Directions.

A. **Symbolic Objects:** In Scripture God used inanimate objects, whether God-created or man-made, as symbols.

Hosea 7:8	***"Ephraim is a cake not turned."***
Psalms 18:2	***"The Lord is my Rock . . ."***
Proverbs 18:10	***"The Name of the Lord is a strong tower . . ."***
Deuteronomy 32:2	***"My doctrine shall drop as the rain . . ."***
Psalms 119:105	***"Thy Word is a lamp unto my feet . . ."***
Revelation 1:20	***"The seven stars are the seven angels . . . the seven candlesticks . . . are the seven churches."***

B. **Symbolic Creatures:** In Scripture God used living creatures, whether plants or animals, as symbols.

Daniel 7:17	***"These great beasts . . . are four kings."***
Hosea 7:11	***"Ephraim also is like a silly dove . . ."***
Luke 13:31, 32	***"Herod . . . that fox . . ."***
Isaiah 40:31	***"They that wait on the Lord . . . as eagles . . ."***
Luke 8:11	***"The seed is the Word of God . . ."***
I Peter 1:24	***"All flesh is as grass, and all the glory of man as the flower of the grass."***
John 1:29, 36	***"Jesus . . . the Lamb of God."***

C. **Symbolic Actions:** In Scripture God used actions to be symbolic.

Psalms 141:1, 2	***"The lifting up of my hands as the evening sacrifice."***
Genesis 25:23-26	***"Elder shall serve the younger . . . and his hand took hold on Esau's heal."***
Joshua 1:3	***"Every place that the sole of your feet shall tread upon, that have I given unto you . . ."***

Isaiah 31:1	***"Woe to them that go down to Egypt for help . . . they look not unto the Holy One of Israel."***

D. **Symbolic Numbers:** In Scripture God attributed symbolic significance to numbers.

II Corinthians 13:1	***"This is the third time I am coming to you. In the mouth of two or three witnesses shall every word be established."***
Revelation 13:18	***"The number of a man; and his number is six hundred threescore and six."***
Matthew 19:28	***". . . ye shall also sit upon twelve thrones, judging the twelve tribes of Israel."***
Genesis 14:4	***". . . in the thirteenth year they rebelled."***

NOTE: Refer to "The Numerical Principle."

E. **Symbolic Names:** In Scripture God used names to be symbolic both personally and nationally. In Scripture a name is generally significant of the nature, character, experience, or function of the person, place, or nation.

I Samuel 25:25	***"For as his name is, so is he; Nabal (Fool) is his name, and folly is with him."***
I Samuel 4:21	***"And she named the child Ichabod, saying, The glory is departed from Israel."***
Hosea 1:9	***"Then said God, Call his name Loammi: for ye are not My people, and I will not be your God."***
Matthew 1:21	***"Thou shalt call His name JESUS: for He shall save His people from their sins."***
John 1:42	***"Thou shalt be called Cephas, which is by interpretation A Stone."***

F. **Symbolic Colors:** In Scripture God attributed symbolic significance to colors.

Isaiah 1:18	***"Though your sins be as scarlet, they shall be as white as snow; though they be red like crimson, they shall be as wool."***
Mark 15:17, 18	***"And they clothed Him with purple . . . King of the Jews!"***
Revelation 3:4, 5	***"They shall walk with Me in white; for they are worthy . . ."***
Revelation 19:8	***"In fine linen, clean and white . . . the righteousness of saints."***

G. **Symbolic Directions:** In Scripture God attributed symbolic significance to directions.

Jeremiah 1:14	***"Out of the north an evil shall break forth"***
Ezekiel 43:1, 2	***"Toward the east: and, behold, the glory of the God of Israel came . . ."***
II Chronicles 4:4	The 12 oxen under Molten Sea, looked to *north, south, east, west.*
Daniel 8:4	The ram pushing *westward, northward* and *southward . . .*

It can be seen from the above illustrations that God, in authoring Scripture, utilized the literary method of symbolism. It is essential to recognize that since God is the virtual author of Scripture He was able to cause symbols to carry the same significance consistently throughout the Bible.

Thus, the literary *method of symbolism* used in writing Scripture gives rise to the *Symbolic Principle* of interpreting Scripture.

III. QUALIFICATION

A. The first step in using the Symbolic Principle is to rightly determine which elements of the verse under consideration are meant to be interpreted as symbols.

1. If the language of the verse makes no literal sense, then it must be interpreted as having symbolic sense (e.g., ***Revelation 12:1-4; 13:1-2;*** with ***Daniel 7:1-4).***

2. If it does make literal sense, then it can only be interpreted as having symbolic sense when the Scripture interprets or intimates this to be the case in other verses (e.g., The Tabernacle, ***John 1:14;*** e.g., The Temple, ***I Corinthians 3:17).***

B. The interpreter must recognize the three fundamental elements of symbolism:

1. The significance of a symbol is based upon the literal nature and characteristics of that which is being used as a symbol.

2. A symbol is meant to represent something essentially different from itself.
3. The link between that which is used as a symbol and that which it symbolizes is the characteristics common to both.

Thing used as a symbol	Common characteristics	Thing symbolized symbolized
(1)	(3)	(2)

C. The use of this principle must be in constant conjunction with the context-group of principles. Because many symbols are used more than once in Scripture, every usage of them, beginning with the First Mention, must be compared in order to gain a complete understanding of the *progressive* unfolding of their symbolic significance in Scripture.

D. Generally speaking, the Bible interprets its own symbols. Thus, the interpreter must search through Scripture for the interpretation of the symbol under consideration.

E. A study of the usages of the symbol in Scripture must be based on a consideration of the original languages (e.g., there are several different Hebrew words for ''lion'' each having its own significance).

F. The interpreter must keep in mind that something may be used to symbolize more than one thing in Scripture. The same symbol may represent different characteristic aspects. (e.g., gold — used to represent Divine nature, God, Wisdom, Faith, etc.) Also, some symbols may have both good and evil aspects to them (e.g., the Lion is used as a symbol of Jesus and His saints, as well as of the Devil. ***Revelation 5:5; I Peter 5:8;*** etc.).

G. When interpreting a symbol within a verse, its general Scriptural significance should be used unless there are clear indications otherwise.

H. If the symbol is uninterpreted in the Word, investigate the context thoroughly for the thought or idea set forth; check the concordance for other references, and consider the nature of the symbol used as it may give the clue (e.g., Lion, swine, lamb, etc.). The nature of such will give us the idea.

IV. DEMONSTRATION

A. **Symbolic Objects—*Matthew 16:18: ''Upon this Rock I will build My Church . . .''*** The symbolic element of this phrase is the ''Rock.'' By context and comparison we find that the Scriptures interpret the symbol of the ''Rock'' to be a reference to Christ.

Psalms 18:2, 31 — ***''The Lord is my Rock . . . who is a Rock save our God.''***
I Corinthians 10:4 — ***''That spiritual Rock that followed them: was Christ.''***
Deuteronomy 32:4, 15, 18, 30 — ***''God . . . the Rock'' (I Corinthians 3:10-12)***

Symbolic Object	→ Common Characteristics ←	Symbolized
The Rock	Solidity	Christ
	Stability	
	Strength	
	Foundation	

B. **Symbolic Creatures—*Genesis 3:1: ''The serpent was more subtil than any beast of the field.''*** The symbolic element of this phrase is the ''serpent.'' By context and comparison we find that the Scriptures interpret the symbol of the ''serpent'' to generally be a reference to Satan.

Revelation 12:9 — ***''That old serpent . . .''***
Revelation 20:2 — ***''That old serpent, which is the Devil, and Satan . . .''***
Genesis 3:14 — ***''The Lord God said unto the serpent . . .''***

Symbolic Creature	→ Common Characteristics ←	Symbolized
Serpent	Subtlety	
	Deception	
	Dangerous	

C. **Symbolic Actions—*Ephesians 2:6: "Sit together in heavenly places in Christ Jesus."*** One symbolic element in this verse is the action of "sitting." By context and comparison we find that the Scriptures interpret the symbol of "sitting" to be a reference to spiritual rest.

Psalms 110:1	***"The Lord said unto my Lord, Sit at My Right Hand."***
Mark 16:19	***"He . . . sat down on the right hand . . ."***
Hebrews 10:12	***". . . this Man . . . sat down on the right hand of God."***
Hebrews 12:2	***"Who . . . is set down at the right hand of the throne of God."***
Luke 17:7	***"Go and sit down."***

Symbolic Action	→ Common Characteristics ←	Symbolized
Sitting	Position Ceasing from labor	Spiritual Rest

D. **Symbolic Numbers—*Luke 10:1: "Appointed seventy . . . sent them two and two . . . into every city."*** One symbolic element in this verse is the number "two." By context and comparison we find that the Scriptures interpret the number "two" to be the number of testimony and witness.

Deuteronomy 17:6	***"At the mouth of two witnesses, or three witnesses."***
Deuteronomy 19:15	***"One witness shall not rise up . . . two witnesses . . ."***
II Corinthians 13:1	***"In the mouth of two or three witnesses shall every word be established."***

Symbolic Number	→ Common Characteristics ←	Symbolized
Two	More than one One with One Dependent on another Unity Testimony	Witness

NOTE: Refer to the Numerical Principle.

E. **Symbolic Names—*James 5:11: "The patience of Job . . ."*** The symbolic element in this verse is the name "Job." By referring to the book of Job and other study helps we find that Job's name means "persecuted." In Scripture a name is generally significant of the nature, character, experience or function of the person, place or nation. Thus we determine by context and comparison that Job's name was indicative of his experience.

Job 1:13-19	***Job's loss of animals, sons and daughters.***
Job 2:7-9	***Job's affliction and suffering under Satan, smitten with boils.***
Job 19:22-28	***Job's physical condition: "skin and bone," and persecuted by his friends.***

Symbolic Name	→ Common Characteristics ←	Symbolized
Job	Persecution Adversity Affliction Crying out of emptiness	Job's experience

F. **Symbolic Colors—*Revelation 6:2: ". . . a white horse . . ."*** One of the symbolic elements in this verse is the color "white." By context and comparison we find that the Scriptures interpret "white" to be symbolic of "righteousness." In Scripture "white" is mainly associated with God, Christ, Angels and Saints.

Revelation 3:4, 5	***"They shall walk with Me in white . . . He that overcometh . . . shall be clothed in white."***
Revelation 7:14	***"Washed their robes, and made them white in the Blood of the Lamb."***
Revelation 15:6	***"Angels . . . clothed in pure and white linen."***
Revelation 19:8	***"Fine linen, clean and white . . . fine linen is the righteousness of the saints."***

Symbolic Color	→ Common Characteristics ←	Symbolized
White	Purity Clean White	Righteousness

G. **Symblic Directions**—***Luke 10:30: ". . . A certain man when down from Jerusalem to Jericho."*** One of the symbolic elements in this verse is the direction "down." By context and comparison we find that the Scriptures interpret the direction "down" to generally be symbolic of "spiritual digression" (negative) or "humility" (positive).

Genesis 12:10-13:1	***". . . Abram went down into Egypt . . . went up out of Egypt."***
Isaiah 14:12, 15	***"Lucifer . . . brought down to hell, to the sides of the pit."***
Jonah 1:3, 5	***"From the presence of the Lord . . . and went down . . . down . . . down."***
Luke 10:15	***"Capernaum . . . shalt be thrust down to hell (unto Hades)."***

Symbolic Direction	**→ Common Characteristics ←**	**Symbolized**
Down	Lowered	Spiritual digression
	Descended	
	Reduced	
	Moved from higher to lower position	

Chapter 20
THE NUMERICAL PRINCIPLE

I. DEFINITION

That principle by which the interpretation of a verse or passage in Scripture containing numbers is aided by a recognition of the symbolic significance of the numbers involved.

II. AMPLIFICATION

It is impossible to read the Scriptures without noticing the continuous use of numbers. Nearly every page of the Bible contains some usages of numbers. God Himself is the Divine numberer and He has stamped His numerical seal upon the whole of creation. This same seal has been placed upon His book—the Holy Bible. In ***Daniel 8:13, 14,*** the saint who gives to Daniel the number of days concerning the cleansing of the sanctuary is referred to in a marginal rendering as Palmoni, "the numberer of secrets," or "the wonderful numberer."

Job 14:16	***"For now Thou numberest my steps . . ."***
Psalms 90:12	***"So teach us to number our days . . ."***
Psalms 147:4	***"He telleth the number of the stars . . ."***
Daniel 5:26	***"God hath numbered thy kingdom . . ."***
Matthew 10:30	***"But the very hairs of your head are all numbered . . ."***

These verses point out that God is indeed "the wonderful numberer." This is more particularly to be seen in His dealings with His chosen nation. Israel's way of life was governed by numbers. This was especially evident in the Tabernacle of Moses, the Feasts of the Lord, and the Ceremonial and Civil Laws ***(Exodus 25-40).***

Numbers, as used in the Word of God, are not used promiscuously, but rather take on spiritual meaning and significance. They are a special form of symbol in Scripture. There are basically two ways in which numbers are to be found in Scripture: by name and by implication. Genesis 15 contains both of these.

A. **Named Numbers:**	Verse 9	3 years
	Verse 13	400 years
	Verse 16	4 generations
B. **Implied Numbers:**	Verse 9	5 sacrifices
	Verse 10	8 pieces
	Verses 19-21	10 nations

The following is a brief interpretation of some of the numbers most often used in Scripture. These were interpreted by using the First Mention, Progressive Mention, Full Mention, and Symbolic Principles. The list is by no means complete and there are many shades of significance that could be added to it.

ONE

Number of God: Beginning, source, commencement, first
Genesis 1:1; Matthew 6:33
Number of Compound Unity:
Deuteronomy 6:4 (Hebrew—ECHAD); ***John 17:21-23; I Corinthians 12:12-14***
Numerical One:
Genesis 22:2 (Hebrew—YACHIYO); Only One, ***Zechariah 12:10; John 3:16***

TWO

Number of Witness, Testimony (1 with 1 = 2):
John 8:17, 18; Deuteronomy 17:6; 19:15; Matthew 18:16; Revelation 11:2-4; Luke 9:30-32
Number of Division, Separation (1 against 1 = 2):
Exodus 8:23, 31:18; Matthew 7; Genesis 19; Genesis 1:6-8; Matthew 24:40-41

THREE

Number of Godhead:
I John 5:6-7; Matthew 28:19

Number of Divine Completeness, Perfect Testimony:
Deuteronomy 17:6; Matthew 12:40; Ezekiel 14:14, 18; Daniel 3:23-24; Leviticus 23; Exodus 12:7; Exodus 3:6

FOUR

Number of Earth, Creation, World: Proceeds from three and is dependent thereon
Genesis 2:10; Leviticus 11:20-27; Jeremiah 49:36; Ezekiel 37:9; I Corinthians 15:39; Revelation 7:1, 2 (four seasons; four winds; four corners of earth)

FIVE

Number of the Cross, Grace, Atonement, Life:
Genesis 1:20-23; Five offerings, ***Leviticus 1-5;*** Five-fold ministry, ***Ephesians 4:11; Exodus 13:18*** margin; ***Joshua 1:14*** margin; The five "I will's" of Satan, ***Isaiah 14:12-14;*** The five wounds of Jesus on the cross, Five in the Tabernacle, ***Exodus 26:3, 9, 26, 27, 37; 27:1, 18***

SIX

Number of Man, Beast, Satan:
Genesis 1:26-31; Six generations of Cain, ***Genesis 4:17-18; I Samuel 17:4-7; II Samuel 21:20; Numbers 35:15***

SEVEN

Number of Perfection, Completeness:
Genesis 2:1-3; 5:24; Jude 14; Joshua 6; Leviticus 14:7, 16, 27, 51
Number of Book of Revelation:
Revelation 1:4, 11, 12, 16, 20; 2:1; 4:5; 5:1, 6; 8:2; 10:3, 4; 12:3; 15:1, 6-8; 17:9-11
(Seven is used about 600 times in the Bible)

EIGHT

Number of Resurrection, New Beginning:
Leviticus 14:10-11; Exodus 22:30; Genesis 17:12; I Peter 3:20; Matthew 28:1; John 20:26
(Numerical value of "Jesus" is 888)

NINE

Number of Finality, Fullness, Fruitfulness:
Genesis 17:1; Matthew 27:45
Number of the Holy Spirit:
Galatians 5:22, 23; (Nine fruits, nine gifts) ***I Corinthians 12:1-11***
(Nine months for the "Fruit of the womb")

TEN

Number of Law, Order, Government, Restoration:
Genesis 1; ("God said," 10 times) ***Exodus 34:28; Daniel 2*** (10 toes); ***Daniel 7*** (10 horns); ***Revelation 12:3***
Number of Trial, Testing, Responsibility:
Matthew 25:1-30; Luke 15:8; 19:13-25; Numbers 14:22; Revelation 2:10; Leviticus 27:32; Exodus 12:3

ELEVEN

Number of Incompleteness, Disorganization, Disintegration:
(One beyond 10, yet one short of 12)
Genesis 32:22; 35:16, 18; Matthew 20:6; Exodus 26:7; Deuteronomy 1:1-8
Number of Lawlessness, Disorder, The Antichrist:
Daniel 7 (the 11th "Little Horn")

TWELVE

Number of Divine Government, Apostolic Fulness:
Genesis 49:28; Exodus 15:27; 24:4; 28:15-21; Matthew 19:28; Luke 6:13 (12 Apostles); ***Revelation 12:1*** (Note number 12 in the "Holy City, New Jerusalem," ***Revelation 21:12, 21; 22:2)***

THIRTEEN

Number of Rebellion, Backsliding, Apostacy:
Genesis 14:4; 10:10 (Nimrod, 13th from Adam); ***Genesis 17:25; Esther 9:1***
Number of Double Portion:
Genesis 48 (Ephraim, 13th Tribe) (Judas and Paul, 13th Apostle)

FOURTEEN

Number of Passover:
Exodus 12:6; Numbers 9:5; Genesis 31:41; Acts 27:27-33

SEVENTEEN	Number of Spiritual Order: (10 + 7 = 17) ***Genesis 37:2; I Chronicles 25:5; Jeremiah 32:9; Genesis 7:11; 8:4; Acts 2:9-11*** ("Walk with God," ***Genesis 5:24; 6:9;*** Enoch the 7th and Noah 10th)
TWENTY-FOUR	Number of Priestly Courses, Governmental Perfection: (2x12 = 24) ***Joshua 4:2-9; I Kings 19:19; I Chronicles 24:3-5; 25; Revelation 4:4-10*** (Note in the "Holy City, New Jerusalem" ***Revelation 21, 22)***
THIRTY	Number of Consecration, Maturity for Ministry: ***Numbers 4:3; Genesis 41:46; II Samuel 5:4; Luke 3:23; Matthew 26:15***
FORTY	Number of Probation, Testing (Ending in Victory or Judgment): ***Numbers 13:25; 14:33, 34; Matthew 4:2; Acts 1:3; Exodus 34:27-28; Ezekiel 4:6; Acts 7:30; I Kings 19:4-8***
FIFTY	Number of Pentecost, Liberty, Freedom, Jubilee: ***Exodus 26:5, 6; Leviticus 25:10-11; (Acts 2:1-4) II Kings 2:7; I Kings 18:4, 13; Numbers 8:25***
SEVENTY	Number Prior to Increase, or Representative of a Multitude: ***Genesis 11:26; 46:27; Exodus 1:5-7; Numbers 11:25; Exodus 15:27; 24:1, 9; Luke 10:1***
SEVENTY-FIVE	Number of Separation, Cleansing, Purification: ***Genesis 12:4; (Daniel 12:5-13)***
ONE HUNDRED TWENTY	Number of the End of all Flesh, the Beginning of Life in the Spirit: ***Genesis 6:3; Deuteronomy 34:7; II Chronicles 3:4; 5:12; 7:5; Acts 1:5***
ONE HUNDRED FORTY-FOUR	Number of God's Ultimate in Creation: (12 x 12 = 144) ***Revelation 21:17; I Chronicles 25:7; Revelation 7:1-6; 14:1-3***
THREE HUNDRED	Number of Faithful Remnant: ***Genesis 5:22; 6:15; Judges 8:4; 15:4***
SIX-SIX-SIX	Number of Antichrist, Satan, the Damned: ***Daniel 3; I Samuel 17; Daniel 7; Revelation 13:18; 14:9-11***

Though the Bible was written by various men of God over many generations, there is a marvelous consistency and harmony in its use of numbers. This is because God Himself, "the wonderful numberer," was able, by inspiring the writer to shape and maintain the significance of the numbers He desired to be used.

The literary *method of numeration* used in writing Scripture gives rise to the *Numerical Principle* of interpreting Scripture.

For a fuller treatment of the significance of numbers in Scripture the reader is directed to the following publications.

Number in Scripture. Ethelbert W. Bullinger, Kregel Publications.
The Seal of God in Creation and The Word. F.C. Payne, Hunkin, Ellis & King, Adelaide, Australia.
Keys to Scripture Numerics. Ed. F. Vallowe, 528 Pine Ridge Drive, Forest Park, Georgia 30050.

III. QUALIFICATION

A. The first step in using this principle is to recognize the numbers involved in the verse or passage, whether named or implied. The only possible difficulty in this is determining the implied numbers.

B. The first mention of the number in Scripture generally conveys its spiritual meaning.

C. God is consistent, and generally the significance of a number will be maintained throughout Scripture.

D. The spiritual significance of a number is not always stated; it may be veiled or hidden. Its significance can be seen by comparing it with other Scriptures using the same number.

E. Generally there are both good and evil, true and counterfeit, God and Satanic, aspects in the significance of numbers.

F. The numbers from one to thirteen are the basic numbers having spiritual significance. Multiples of these numbers generally carry the same meaning, only intensifying the truth symbolized by them.

G. This principle should be used in connection with many others, such as the First Mention, Full Mention and Symbolic Principles.

H. This principle must be used with discretion and kept in balance with the other principles in order to avoid eccentric interpretation.

IV. DEMONSTRATION

Luke 10:1: "After these things the Lord appointed other seventy also, and sent them two and two before His face into every city and place, whither He Himself would come.

A. **The Number Seventy:** The first number mentioned in this verse is the number "seventy." By context and comparison we find that Scripture interprets the number "seventy" to be the number of imminent increase or representative of a multitude.

Genesis 46:27; Exodus 1:5	Seventy souls went down into Egypt and there became a great nation.
Exodus 24:1, 9	Seventy elders represent the multitude.

In this passage the seventy disciples sent out by Christ are representative of the multitude that followed Him, and they were sent out prior to the harvest increase of disciples.

B. **The Number Two:** The second number mentioned is the number "two." By context and comparison we find that Scripture interprets the number "two" to be the number of testimony and witness.

Deuteronomy 19:15	One witness is insufficient, there must be two.

C. **The Number Three:** The third number in this verse is there by implication, the number "three." By context and comparison we find that Scripture interprets the number three to be the number of Divine completeness and perfect witness.

Deuteronomy 17:6, 7 ***II Corinthians 13:1***	In the mouth of two or three witnesses shall every word be established

In this passage each city was to receive the testimony of two witnesses. Jesus sent them into every city and place whither He Himself, the third Witness, would come. Jesus gave divine testimony and was the completion of witness.

By using the Numerical Principle this verse may be interpreted as follows: Jesus sent out the seventy disciples to represent the multitude of believers and to indicate an imminent increase. He sent them two by two because their mission was to bear witness and give testimony of Him. He purposed to follow their witness with His own perfect Divine testimony.

Chapter 21
THE TYPICAL PRINCIPLE

I. DEFINITION

The principle by which the interpretation of a verse or passage of Scripture containing typical elements can be determined only through a proper interpretation of the type or types involved.

II. AMPLIFICATION

A. **Definition of Types:** Webster's Dictionary defines the word "type" as:

1. An emblem; a symbol that which has a symbolical significance; that which is emblematic.
2. An allegorical symbolic representation of some object, which is called the antitype; a symbol; a sign; theologically, the word is mainly applied to those prophetic prefigurings of the persons and things of the new dispensation, which occur in the Old Testament.

The word "type" comes from the Greek word **"TUPOS"** which means "The mark of a stroke or blow; a figure formed by a blow or impression; the impress of a seal, the stamp made by a die; a figure, image, form, or mold; counterpart; example to be initiated; a model, pattern; an anticipative figure."

It is translated:

Print	***John 20:25***
Figure	***Acts 7:43; Romans 5:14***
Fashion	***Acts 7:44***
Manner	***Acts 23:25***
Form	***Romans 6:17***
Example	***I Corinthians 10:6; I Timothy 4:12***
Ensample	***I Corinthians 10:11; Philippians 3:17; I Thessalonians 1:7; II Thessalonians 3:9; I Peter 5:3***
Pattern	***Titus 2:7; Hebrews 8:5***

For the purposes of defining the Typical Principle now under consideration we will define a "type" to be "a figure or representation of something to come; an *anticipative figure,* a *prophetic symbol.*" This necessitates a brief discussion of the distinction between types and symbols.

B. **Distinction Between Type and Symbol:** Types are to be viewed as a select group of symbols having prophetic and foreshadowing characteristics.

Symbol	—A representation, one thing standing for another.
Type	—A prophetic representation, one thing prefiguring another.

Types are to be viewed as prophetic symbols. This is not to say that all symbols used in prophecy are types. For example ***Daniel 7*** is prophetic of Gentile kingdoms which are symbolized in this passage as "beasts." These beasts are not types (prophetic symbols), rather are symbols used in prophecy. A type is prophetic in and of itself and does not depend upon prophetic language for its prophetic import (e.g., ***Genesis 22*** provides us with a type having prophetic import without prophetic language).

A Symbol	may represent a thing, either past, present or future.
A Type	is essentially a prefiguring of something future from itself.
A Symbol	is a figure of something either past, present or future.
A Type	is a figure of that which is to come.
A Symbol	has in itself no essential reference to time.
A Type	has inherent in itself a reference to time.

A Symbol	is designed to represent certain characteristics or qualities in that which it represents.
A Type	is designed to be a pre-ordained representation of something or someone to come.
A Symbol	to be interpreted, requires a pointing out of the characteristics, qualities, marks, or features common to both the symbol and that which it symbolizes.
A Type	to be interpreted, generally requires a setting forth of an extended analogy between the type and that which it typifies.

The *rock* in ***Psalms 18:2*** is a *symbol,* not a type.
The *candlesticks* in ***Revelation 1:20*** are *symbols,* not types.
The *Lamb* in ***John 1:29*** is a *symbol,* not a type.
The *rainbow* in ***Genesis 9:13-16*** is a *symbol,* not a type.
The *olive trees* in ***Zechariah 4:3*** are *symbols,* not types.
The color *white* in ***Revelation 19:8*** is a *symbol,* not a type.
The number *666* in ***Revelation 13:18*** is a *symbol,* not a type.
Adam in ***Romans 5:14*** is a *type,* not a symbol.
Animal sacrifices in ***Leviticus 1-5*** are *types,* not symbols.
The *offices of Prophet, Priest and King* in ***I Kings 1:34*** are *types,* not symbols.
The *Tabernacle of Moses* in ***Exodus 25-40*** is a *type,* not a symbol.
Jonah's experience in the fish in ***Matthew 12:39-41*** is a *type,* not a symbol.

It must be recognized that types may involve symbols but symbols, of themselves, are never types.

In ***Exodus 12*** the historical event of the Feast of Passover is a type of Christ and His Church. Within this type there are symbolic elements such as the lamb, the hyssop, the unleavened bread, and the bitter herbs, but these by themselves are not types.

In ***Exodus 17*** the historical event of the smiting of the rock is a type of the crucifixion of Christ. Within this type there are symbolic elements such as the rock and the rod, which by themselves are not types.

The above illustrations show the interrelatedness of type and symbols to be such that, while symbolism may be used in typology, the converse is never true.

C. **Classification of Types:** God, knowing the end from the beginning, was able to cause the writing of the Old Testament to be done in such a way that many of its elements were meant to be viewed as anticipative of that which was to come in the New Testament. The types of the Old Testament may be divided into four main classifications: Persons, Offices, Institutions and Events.

1. **Persons:** In the writing of Scripture God caused the recording of history to be such that certain persons are meant to be viewed as prefiguring another person to come. These persons can be seen as foreshadows in either their character, office, function or relationship to the history of redemption.

   Romans 5:12-21: Verse 14—". . . Adam . . . who is the figure (Greek; Type) of Him that was to come . . ."

   Here, Paul, in setting forth an extended analogy shows Adam to be a type of Christ.

2. **Offices:** In writing Scripture God meant for certain offices to be viewed as foreshadows of offices to come.

   Hebrews 5:1-10: Verses 4, 5—". . . as was Aaron. So also Christ . . ."

   The writer to the Hebrews here sets forth as extended analogy showing the Aaronic Priesthood to be typical of Christ's Priesthood.

3. **Institutions:** In writing Scripture God meant for certain institutions to be viewed as foreshadows of institutions to come.

   Hebrews 8:1-5: Verse 4—"Who serve unto the example and shadow of heavenly things . . . the tabernacle."

   The writer to the Hebrews gives an extended analogy showing the instituting of the Mosaic Tabernacle to be typical of the heavenly institution.

4. **Events:** In the writing of Scripture God caused historical events to be recorded in such a way that they may be viewed as foreshadowings of events to come.

 I Corinthians 10:1-11: Verse 6—"Now these things were our examples (Greek; Types) . . ." Verse 11—"Now all these things happened unto them for ensamples (Greek; Types) . . ."

 In this passage Paul refers to several historical events of Israel's wandering in the wilderness as being typical of events in the experience of the New Testament Church.

 NOTE: It should be recognized that these categories often overlap in Scripture. For instance: an event may include persons, offices, and institutions.

These illustrations show that God, in authoring Scripture, was able to cause it to be written in such a way that many of the persons, offices, institutions and events were meant to be viewed as types of things to come.

D. **Conclusion:** The *literary method of prefiguring* (typology) used in writing Scripture gives rise to the *Typical Principle* of interpreting Scripture.

III. QUALIFICATION

A. The first step in using the Typical Principle is to correctly discern what elements, if any, of the passage under consideration are meant to be viewed as types.

B. The use of this principle must be in constant conjunction with the context group of principles.

C. Because types generally involve symbols, the Symbolic Principle must constantly be used in connection with the Typical Principle.

D. The interpreter must ascertain the primary point of *resemblance* between the type and anti-type. Then he must realize the full correspondence between them by drawing out an extended analogy.

E. The typical sense of Scripture is always solidly based on the literal sense. Typical sense cannot be used to eradicate or contradict the actual sense.

1. The significance of a type is based upon the literal nature and characteristics of that which is being used as a type.
2. A type is meant to prefigure something essentially different from itself.
3. The link between that which is used as a type and that which it typifies is the extended analogy that can be drawn between both.

F. Generally speaking, the Bible interprets its own types, or at least gives us the *key* to their interpretation. Thus the interpreter must search through the Scripture to discover the key by which he unlocks the door into the full interpretation of the type. The only safeguard against the human imagination's interpreting types is to let the Scripture interpret its own types. The best interpreter of Scripture is Scripture itself. To the honest searcher for truth there is hardly a type used in the Old Testament which is not interpreted or its key given in the New Testament. Many times just one verse of the New Testament is the key to the interpretation of many verses or chapters of that which is typical in the Old Testament.

 e.g., ***John 1:14*** becomes the key to interpreting the many chapters devoted to the Tabernacle of Moses in the Old Testament.

 e.g., ***John 1:51*** becomes the key to interpreting the chapter concerning Jacob's ladder in the Old Testament.

G. There are types in the Old Testament that are neither interpreted nor have "keys" given in the New Testament. However, there are none of these that cannot be safely guided and governed in their interpretation by "example-types" that God gives us in Scripture.

 Ephesians 5:22-23 implies that Adam and Eve are to be viewed as types of Christ and His bride. This becomes a sample type by which we may interpret other Old Testament brides as types of the bride of Christ (Rebekah, Rachel, Ruth and Esther).

Hebrews 11:17-19, together with ***John 3:16,*** sets forth Abraham and Isaac as a type of the Father and Jesus in their Father/Son relationship. This becomes a sample type by which we may interpret the relationship between Jacob and Joseph as a type.

H. Often a type may have more than one facet to its interpretation.

O.T. Type	Point of Resemblance	N. T. Interpretation
Tabernacle of Moses	God's Dwelling Place	1. Christ — ***John 1:14*** 2. Church — ***Hebrews 3:1-5*** 3. Believer — ***Ephesians 3:17*** 4. Heavenly Sanctuary — ***Hebrews 8:1-5***

I. The interpreter must recognize that a type is generally to be viewed as a prophecy. Many times God instructed His servants to do typically what He would fulfill actually. For example, God the Father instructed Abraham to do typically that which He Himself planned to do actually ***(Genesis 22).*** In another instance God told Israel to do typically with the Passover lamb what He would fulfill actually with the True Lamb ***(Exocus 12).*** However, we must recognize that these were not types to those persons involved, but were actual circumstances. Thus God takes the actual to be typical, which then becomes a prophetical of another actual. All types are to be viewed as God-ordained, not originating with man. Because all types are God-ordained, they hold an important place with Him. (Notice Moses' punishment for spoiling a God-ordained type through his disobedience. ***(Exodus 17; Number 20; Psalms 106:33; I Corinthians 10:1-4.)***

J. No doctrines should be built on types alone, but types may be used to illustrate doctrines.

K. No type is to be interpreted by or with another type.

L. The interpreter must recognize that there is no such thing as a "perfect and complete type," for the very nature of the things used as types were all stamped with imperfection and incompleteness. However, God used the imperfect and incomplete as sign posts pointing to Christ, the Perfect and Complete One.

M. The interpreter must be careful not to force the typological principle upon unsuitable passages. Some interpreters desiring to personalize Scripture, to establish eschatological truth or even to find Christ in the Old Testament have forced this principle upon passages to the point of distorting their interpretation.

IV. DEMONSTRATION

A. **Persons—*Genesis 37-50:*** These chapters cover the life-story of Joseph. A consideration of his character and experiences leads us to view him as a type of Christ. The primary point of resemblance is to be seen in the son's relationship to the Father.

O. T. Type	Point of Resemblance	Antitype
Joseph	— Son's relation to Father —	Jesus

In the extended analogy below only some of the most prominent correspondences are given. A full interpretation of this type would involve many more.

Joseph	Analogy	Jesus
Genesis 30:22-24	A first born son	***Matthew 1:25***
Genesis 29:31	Miracle birth	***Isaiah 7:14***
Genesis 37:2, 3	Beloved son	***Matthew 3:16***
Genesis 37:2	A shepherd	***John 10:11***
Genesis 35:22-26	Hated by half-brothers	***Mark 3:31, 32***
Genesis 37:5-10	Revelation of exaltation	***Matthew 26:64***
Genesis 37:12-14	Sent by father to brethren	***John 5:24, 30, 43***
Genesis 37:18	Rejected by brethren	***John 7:3***
Genesis 37:28	Sold for silver	***Matthew 27:3-10***
Genesis 39:11-19	Falsely accused	***Mark 14:55-60***
Genesis 40:1-4	Suffered as criminal	***Luke 23:32***
Genesis 41:40, 41	Exalted in due time	***Acts 5:31***
Genesis 41:45	Given an exalted name	***Philippians 2: 9, 10***
Genesis 41:43	All bow the knee	***Philippians 2:10, 11***

Genesis 41:45	Receives a Gentile bride	***Ephesians 3:6***
Genesis 45:14, 15	Brethren reconciled	***Zechariah 12:10-14***
Genesis 47:1-7	Reunited with his father	***Mark 16:19***

B. **Offices—*Exodus 28; Hebrews 5:1-5; 8:1-4:*** These passages, together with many others, deal with the office of the High Priest. The qualifications and function of this office, as outlined under the Mosaic Covenant, support the fact that it is a type of Christ's own office under the New Covenant.

The primary point of resemblance is to be seen as Mediatorship.

O. T. Type	Point of Resemblance	Antitype
High Priest	— Mediatorship —	Christ's Priesthood

The following are only a few of the many correspondences within the extended analogy that can be drawn in the full interpretation of the type.

High Priest	Analogy	Christ's Priesthood
Numbers 3:12	Born a priest	***Zechariah 6:12, 13***
Exodus 28:1	Taken from among men	***Hebrews 2:17***
Hebrews 5:4	Called of God	***Hebrews 5:5***
Exodus 28:29, 38	Ordained for men	***Hebrews 5:5-10***
Exodus 28:41	Anointed for ministry	***John 1:41***
Leviticus 1:1-9	Offer sacrifice	***Hebrews 8:3***
Exodus 28:1-4, 41	Ministry to God	***Hebrews 7:22-26***
Hebrews 5:2	Compassionate	***Hebrews 2:17***

C. **Institutions—*Exodus 25-40:*** These chapters are devoted to the institution of the Tabernacle of Moses. The New Testament gives us the key ***(John 1:14)*** that enables us to interpret this institution as a type of Christ. The primary point of resemblance is to be seen in the fact that it is God's dwelling place.

O. T. Type	Point of Resemblance	Antitype
Tabernacle of Moses	— God's Dwelling Place —	Christ

The following are only a few of the many correspondences within the extended analogy that can be drawn in the full interpretation of this type.

Tabernacle of Moses	Analogy	Christ
Ark of the Covenant	***"God with us"***	***Matthew 1:23***
The Mercy Seat	Propitiation	***Romans 3:25***
Rod that budded	Resurrection	***John 11:25***
Golden Pot of Manna	Bread of Life	***John 6:48-51***
Tables of Law	Tables of Heart	***Psalms 40:8***
The Name	Lord Jesus Christ	***Acts 2:36***
Altar of Incense	Intercessor	***Hebrews 7:25***
Golden Candlestick	Light of world	***John 8:12***
Table of Shewbread	Table of Lord	***Matthew 26:26-28***
The Veil	His Flesh	***Hebrews 10:20***
The Door	The Door	***John 10:9***
The Gate	The Way	***John 14:6***
Brazen Altar	Blood Atonement	***Hebrews 5:9-11***
Brazen Laver	Cleansing	***Ephesians 5:26***

D. **Events—*Genesis 6-9:*** These chapters provide us with the historical account of the event of the Flood. The circumstance and activity of this event is taken by Jesus to be typical of the Last Days.

The primary point of resemblance is judgment upon wickedness.

O. T. Type	Point of Resemblance	Antitype
The Flood	Judgment upon wickedness	Last Days

The following are only a few ot the many correspondences within the extended analogy that can be drawn in the full interpretation of this type.

The Flood	Analogy	The Last Days
Genesis 6:1	Population explosion	
Genesis 6:2	Intermarriage	
Genesis 6:4	Great wickedness	
Genesis 6:5	Evil thoughts and imaginations	
Genesis 6:11, 12	Corruption	*Luke 17:26, 27*
Genesis 6:11, 13	Violence	*Matthew 24:36-41*
Genesis 6:8, 9	Godly remnant	*II Peter 2:5*
Genesis 6:3; I Peter 2:5	Spirit and Word at Work	
Hebrews 11:7	Ark of salvation	
Genesis 7:1-24	Judgment-Deluge	
Genesis 7:1-24	All wicked perish	

Chapter 22
THE PARABOLIC PRINCIPLE

I. DEFINITION

That principle by which any parable is interpreted by discerning its moral and interpreting its elements.

II. AMPLIFICATION

A. **Definition:** A parable is "a short simple story from which a moral lesson may be drawn." It is an earthly story with a heavenly meaning. The relevant terms in Scripture will now be considered.

Old Testament Hebrew
MASHAL = "properly a pithy maxim, usually of a metaphorical nature: hence a simile: a proverbial saying, parable, similitude, resemblance."

Translated:

parable	***Numbers 23:7, 18; 24:3, 15, 20, 21, 23; Job 27:1; 29:1; Psalms 49:4; 78:2; Ezekiel 17:2; 20:49; 24:3; Micah 2:4; Habakkuk 2:6***
proverb	***Deuteronomy 28:37; I Samuel 24:13; I Kings 4:32; II Chronicles 7:20; Psalms 69:11; Proverbs 1:1, 6; 25:1; Ecclesiastes 12:9; Isaiah 14:4; Jeremiah 24:9; Ezekiel 18:2, 3***

New Testament Greek
PARABOLE = "a similitude, a fictitious narrative (of common life conveying a moral); a placing of one thing by the side of another; a comparison of one thing with another; a narrative, fictitious but agreeable to the laws and usages of human life, by which either the duties of men or the things of God, particularly the nature and history of God's kingdom, are figuratively portrayed; a short discourse that makes a comparison; it expresses a single complete thought."

Translated:

comparison	***Mark 4:30***
figure	***Hebrews 9:9; 11:19***
parable	***Matthew 13; 15:15; 21:33, 45; 22:1; 24:32; Mark 4:13; 7:17; Luke 5:36; 6:39; 12:16, 41; 18:1, 9; 19:11; 20:9, 19; 21:29***
proverb	***Luke 4:23***

Theologically speaking, a parable is a fictitous, but true to human life, story that is designed to illustrate by way of comparison some spiritual truth.

B. **Purpose:** The use of parables was one of Christ's main methods of teaching. He indicated that His reason for using them was two-fold:

1. To *reveal* truth to those who were open and hungry-hearted. ***(Matthew 13:9-12, 16, 19)***
2. To *conceal* truth from those who were closed and hard-hearted. ***(Matthew 13:13-15)***

C. **Sources:** Jesus took His parables from two major sources:

1. The realm of Creation — using such symbols as seed, wheat and tares, fish, leaven, pearls, sheep, etc.
2. The realm of Human Relationships — using such relationships as father and son, servant and master, bride and bridegroom, friends, etc.

D. **Classification:** There is much difference of opinion among Bible scholars over the definition and classification of the parables in Scripture. Though a few accept only those parables designated by Scripture as such, most scholars allow for a broader definition. Most all agree that a parable is an extended simile, but there is much disagreement over where the boundary line should be placed between simile and parable. Thus, in tabulating parables there is among scholars a wide range of numbers. Though various scholars have suggested several ways of classifying parables, for the sake of simplicity we will classify them as follows: (1) Short Parables and (2) Extended Parables.

1. **Short Parables:** A short parable could easily be confused with a simile. For the purposes of distinction, the simile will be viewed as generally having only one pair of details that can be compared, while a short parable will be seen as having several such pairs. For example, ***"He was led as a sheep to the slaughter" (Acts 8:32; Isaiah 53:7),*** is a simile. ***"His eyes were as a flame of fire" (Revelation 1:14),*** is a simile. ***"My beloved is like a roe" (Song of Solomon 2:9),*** is also a simile. On the other hand, ***"Another parable put He forth unto them, saying, The kingdom of heaven is like to a grain of mustard seed, which a man took, and sowed in his field: which indeed is the least of all seeds: but when it is grown, it is the greatest among herbs, and becometh a tree, so that the birds of the air come and lodge in the branches thereof" (Matthew 13:31, 32),*** is designated a short parable. ***"Either what woman having ten pieces of silver, if she lose one piece, doth not light a candle, and sweep the house, and seek diligently till she find it? And when she hath found it, she calleth her friends and her neighbours together, saying, Rejoice with me; for I have found the piece which I had lost" (Luke 15:8, 9),*** is an undesignated short parable. And ***"There was a little city, and few men within it; and there came a great king against it, and beseiged it, and built great bulwarks against it: now there was found in it a poor wise man, and he by his wisdom delivered the city; yet no man remembered that same poor man" (Ecclesiastes 9:14, 15),*** is an undesignated short parable.

2. **Extended Parables:** An extended parable differs from a short parable primarily in its length and in the number of pairs of details which can be compared. A short parable will generally include from two to five such pairs while an extended parable will include more.

   An extended parable must also be distinguished from an allegory. (Refer to the Allegorical Principle.) Some examples of extended parables are: the parable of the sower ***(Matthew 13:1-8),*** a designated extended parable; the parable of the prodigal son ***(Luke 15:11-31),*** an undesignated extended parable; the parable of the vineyard ***(Isaiah 5:1-6),*** an undesignated parable.

E. **Conclusion:** The *literary method of parabolic communication* used in writing Scripture gives rise to the *Parabolic Principle* of interpreting Scripture.

III. QUALIFICATION

A. The first step in using this principle is to make certain that the passage under consideration is a parable, whether designated or not.

B. A parable, being an extended simile, has one main focal point of comparison, but it is the whole of the parable that is the comparison. It is a comparison between the natural realm and the spiritual realm. Each of the details given concerning the natural realm have their correspondence to the spiritual realm. However, they all are vitally related to the focal point of the comparison. This can be illustrated with the kingdom of heaven parable in ***Matthew 13:33.*** The following questions could be asked concerning this comparison:

Is the kingdom of heaven *like* unto leaven?
OR Is the kingdom of heaven *like* unto leaven which a woman took?
OR Is the kingdom of heaven *like* unto leaven which a woman took and hid?
OR Is the kingdom of heaven *like* unto leaven which a woman took and hid in three measures of meal?
OR Is the kingdom of heaven *like* unto leaven which a woman took and hid in three measures of meal until the whole was leavened?

C. Every parable is designed to conceal and reveal one fundamental spiritual truth. In order to perceive the point of the parable the significance of each of its parts must be recognized. In other words the whole cannot be interpreted apart from an interpretation of each of its parts. As with all of Scripture the interpretation of parables must move from whole to part and from part to whole. All the details of a parable find their significance in relation to its main point.

D. In interpreting the parts of a parable the interpreter must allow Scripture to interpret Scripture by using the Context Group, Moral and Symbolic Principles. Many times the key to the interpretation of the parable will be found in its immediate context. Parables often involve various symbols which must be properly interpreted before the lesson of the parable can be rightly discerned.

E. Since parables are drawn from the cultural background of their authors, the interpreter should research the manners, customs, and material culture involved in the parable he is interpreting.

F. Doctrine should not be founded solely upon parabolic teaching. Though parables primarily illustrate doctrine, any doctrine they do teach must be viewed in its harmony with the clearly defined teachings of the Scripture.

G. Distinction must be made between parable and allegory. Refer to "The Allegorical Principle."

IV. DEMONSTRATION

A. **Christ's Demonstration:** Jesus Himself demonstrated this principle when He interpreted the extended parable of the wheat and tares ***(Matthew 13:24-30, 36-43).***

Parable—*Matthew 13:24-30*	**Interpretation—*Matthew 13:36-43***
Kingdom of heaven like unto a man	Sower—Son of Man
Sowed seed	The good seed—children of the kingdom
In his field	The field is the world
The enemy	The devil
Sowed tares	Children of the wicked one
Wheat and tares grow together until the harvest	Harvest—end of the (age) world
The reapers	The angels
Tares bundled to burn	Wicked gather and cast into fire
Wheat gathered to barn	Righteous shine in the kingdom

Jesus stated the lesson to be that at the end of the age the wicked and the righteous will be separated unto their eternal destinies.

B. **Short Parables:** ***Matthew 13:52. "Then said He unto them, Therefore every scribe which is instructed unto the kingdom of heaven is like unto a man that is an householder, which brigheth forth out of his treasure things new and old."***

The key to the interpretation of this parable is found in Jesus' question to his disciples in verse ***51, "Have ye understood . . . .?"*** To interpret this undesignated parable we will interpret each of the parts that comprise it.

Parable	**Interpretation**
The man, householder	The scribe—disciple
The treasure-house	The heart ***(Matthew 12:35)***
Things new	New teachings of truth
Things old	Old teachings of truth

The moral lesson of this parable is: as every disciple has received instruction in the things of the kingdom, he must also instruct others in the same way.

C. **Extended Parables:** ***Matthew 21:33-41.*** The parable of the vineyard ***(Mark 12:1-9; Luke 20:9-16).***

To interpret this designated parable, first the parallel accounts in Mark and Luke must be compared, as has been done under the Comparative Mention Principle. Having gathered all the details we will now interpret them using the Symbolic Principle.

Parable	**Interpretation by Comparative Scriptures**
A certain householder	God the Father
Planted vineyard, hedged it	Israel; Nation—***Isaiah 5:1; Psalms 80:9***
Digged winepress, built tower	Winepress—***Isaiah 5:1-7***
Let out to husbandmen	Rulers, Kings, Priests, Elders of Israel
Far country	Heavenly country—***Hebrews 11:11-16***
Time of the fruit drew near	
Sent His servants	The prophets sent—***Hebrews 1:1; Jeremiah 35:15***
Husbandmen treated them evilly	Killed and rejected the prophets—***II Chronicles 24:21; 36:16; Matthew 23:34, 37; Acts 7:52***

More servants sent	More prophets sent (major and minor)
Treated them likewise	***Jeremiah 37:15; II Kings 17:13***
Last of all He sent His Son	***John 3:16; Hebrews 1:1-2; Mark 12:6***
Husbandmen killed the Heir	Heir of all things—***Psalms 2:8; Hebrews 1:2***
They caught Him	In Gethsemane—***Matthew 26:47-56***
Cast Him out of vineyard	Outside the City—***Hebrews 13:11-13; John 19:7***
Slew Him	Slew, hanged on a tree—***Acts 10:39-43***
Lord of husbandmen miserably destroy those husbandmen	Jerusalem destroyed in AD 70—***Luke 19:41-44***
Let out vineyard to other husbandmen to get fruits	Kingdom taken from Jewry, given to a Nation (Church, ***I Peter 2:5-9)*** who renders fruits—***Matthew 21:41-43***

The lesson of this parable is: In their deeds of unfaithfulness and in crucifying the Son, the leaders of Israel were to be destroyed and their responsibilities given to the Church.

Chapter 23
THE ALLEGORICAL PRINCIPLE

I. DEFINITION

That principle by which any allegory is interpreted by discerning its lessons and interpreting its elements.

II. AMPLIFICATION

A. **Definition of Allegory:** Webster's Dictionary defines an allegory as: "A story in which people, things, and happenings have another meaning, as in a fable, or parable; allegories are used for teaching or explaining: the presentation of ideas by means of such stories; symbolical narration or description." In Scripture the word allegory appears only once, in ***Galatians 4:24.*** The Greek word in that passage will be briefly considered.

New Testament Greek
ALLEGOREO = "To allegorize; to speak allegorically or in a figure; to speak, not according to the primary sense of the word, but so that the facts stated are applied to illustrate principles; so to speak, that another sense is expressed than that which the words convey.
Translated:
are an allegory ***Galatians 4:24***

Hermeneutically speaking an allegory is a figure of speech used to communicate truth by expressing one thing under the image of another. It is an implied comparison which is sustained through numerous corresponding details. It is a figurative treatment of one subject under the guise of another.

B. **Allegory and Parable:** An allegory is an extended metaphor, just as a parable is an extended simile. A *metaphor* is a figure of speech in which one thing is likened to another. In it one thing is spoken of as if it were the other. It is an implied comparison in which a word or phrase ordinarily and primarily used of one thing is applied to another (e.g., ***"The Lord is my rock"—Psalms 18:2; "Behold the Lamb of God"—John 1:29).*** A *simile* is also a figure of speech in which one thing is likened to another, but it is usually stated with words such as "like" or "as." It is a stated comparison in which explicit evidence is given that a comparison is being made (e.g., ***"As new born babes, desire the sincere milk of the Word"—I Peter 2:2; "His feet like unto fine brass"—Revelation 1:15).***

From these definitions one important distinction between allegory and parable can be drawn. An *allegory* contains implicitly within itself, or its context, its own interpretation, in that one thing is stated as being another. ***("I am the true vine"—John 15:1.)*** A *parable* will either state its comparison explicity ***("The kingdom of heaven is like to a grain of mustard seed"—Matthew 13:31),*** or not at all, and will require explanation outside of itself to know what is being compared ***("A sower went forth to sow"—Matthew 13:3).***

Most interpreters recognize the fact that it is difficult to make a perfect distinction between allegories and parables. Mickelsen (p. 213, 230) makes a worthwhile distinction between these two:

	Parable		Allegory
1.	Plurality of main verbs in past tense	1.	Plurality of main verbs and mixture of tenses
2.	Formal comparisons (stated)	2.	Direct comparisons (implied)
3.	Words used literally	3.	Words used figuratively
4.	One chief point of comparison	4.	Plurality of points of comparison
5.	Particular example, a specific occurrence	5.	Emphasis usually on timeless truths
6.	Imagery kept distinct from the thing signified	6.	Imagery identified with specific thing signified
7.	Story true to the facts and experiences of life	7.	Story blends factual experience with nonfactual experience to enable the narrative to teach specific truths

8. Explained by telling what the imagery stands for in the main point of the story	8. Explained by showing why the imagery is identified with the reality and what specific truths are being taught

C. **Examples of Allegory in Scripture**

1. Allegories in the Old Testament:

—Psalms 80:8-15	The vine out of Egypt
—Proverbs 5:15-18	The allegory of waters
—Ecclesiastes 12:3-7	The allegory of old age

2. **Allegories in the New Testament:**

—Matthew 5:13	The salt of the earth
—John 10:1-16	The good shepherd
—John 15:1-10	The vine and the branches

3. **Inspired Allegorization:** In a class of its own is Paul's "allegory of the two covenants" in ***Galatians 4:21-31.*** This passage is not an allegory as defined above, but rather is the only example in Scripture of inspired allegorization. In contrasting the Old and New Covenants Paul allegorizes certain Old Testament historical realities for the sake of illustration and emphasis. Because of this passage some have misconstrued Paul as a fanciful allegorist, while others have used him to justify their own allegorical abuse of Scripture. Both need to recognize that Paul himself indicated that this was an exceptional use of the Old Testament for illustration, that this is the only example of such in his writings, and that Paul fully supported the validity and literal meaning of the historical events.

D. **Conclusion:** The *literary method of allegorical communication* used in writing Scripture gives rise to the *Allegorical Principle* of interpreting Scripture.

III. QUALIFICATION

A. The first step in using this principle is to make certain that the passage under consideration is an allegory.

B. Being an extended metaphor, the chief points of comparison in the allegory must be identified.

C. To interpret the whole of the allegory each of its parts must be interpreted.

D. In interpreting the parts of an allegory the interpreter must allow Scripture to interpret Scripture by using the Context Group of principles, the Moral Principle and the Symbolic Principle. Many times the key to the interpretation of the allegory will be found in its immediate context. Allegories often involve various symbols which must be properly interpreted before the lessons of the allegory can be rightly discerned.

E. Since allegories are drawn from the cultural background of their authors, the interpreter should research the manners, customs, and material culture involved in the allegory which he is interpreting.

F. Doctrine should not be founded solely upon allegorical teaching. Though allegories primarily illustrate doctrine, any doctrine they do teach must be viewed in its harmony with the clear teaching of the Scriptures.

G. The interpreter must not confuse allegory with allegorization. Allegory is a legitimate way of teaching and illustrating truth by association. Allegorization forces a passage to communicate truth not intended by the original author through use of a point by point comparison. In the allegorical method a text is interpreted apart from its grammatical historical meaning. What the original writer is saying is ignored and what the interpreter wants to say becomes the only important factor. Allegorization is the arbitrary assigning of meaning to the Scriptures.

IV. DEMONSTRATION

A. ***Matthew 5:13: "Ye are the salt of the earth: but if the salt has lost his savour, wherewith shalt it be salted? It is thenceforth good for nothing, but to be cast out, and to be trodden under foot of men."***

The key to the interpretation of this allegory was given by Jesus when He said, ***"Ye are . . . ."*** To interpret this allegory, we will first interpret each of the parts that comprise it.

Allegory	Interpretation
Salt	Ye—disciples of Jesus
Of the earth	The world—mankind
Lost savour	Lost influence
Wherewith shalt it be salted	Influence hard to be regained
Good for nothing	Of no profit to the Kingdom
To be cast out	Excommunicated
To be trodden under foot of men	Despised by unbelievers

The moral lesson of this allegory is: the world's only influence for good, the people of God, must maintain that influence lest they come under judgment.

B. ***John 15:1-10:*** The allegory of the vine and the branches. The key to the interpretation of this allegory is stated in verses 1 and 5: ***"I am the true vine, and My Father is the husbandman . . . , ye are the branches."*** To interpret this allegory we will first interpret each of the parts that comprise it.

Allegory	Verse	Interpretation
The vine and the husbandman	1	The relationship of Jesus to His Father. The Father totally cares for the Son
Fruitless branches taken away, fruit bearing branch purged	2	Sets forth the judgment of fruitless believers, and the purging of the fruitful believer in order to bring more fruit
The Word cleanses	3	The cleansing process of Christ's word to those in Him
Branch must abide in the vine to bear fruit	4,5	The believer must be in union with Christ in order to be fruitful
The branch not in the vine withers and is burned	6	Those who are not in Christ suffer judgment
The branch connected to the vine receives its needs	7	The believer in Christ and with Christ's words in him has his requests granted
The husbandman glorified by fruit-bearing branches	8	The Father is glorified by disciples who are fruitful
The husbandman cares for the vine and the vine cares for the branches	9	The Father loves Christ, so Christ loves the believer. The believer is to abide in Christ's love
The branches abide in the vine as the vine abides in the husbandman's care	10	The believer, by keeping Christ's commandments, abides in His love, even as Christ abode in His Father's love by keeping His commandments

The above interpretation of this allegory presents the main lessons to be learned. However, it should be noted that these do not exhaust the many facets of truth that are latent therein.

Chapter 24
THE INTERPRETATION OF PROPHECY

Due to the unique nature of prophecy and the special problems involved in its interpretation, an entire chapter will be devoted to the subject. As a literary style, prophecy is far more complex than historical or poetical literature. In that it is characterized by ecstatic utterance, it presents the interpreter with a concentrated revelation which may vary greatly in its form. The interpretation of prophecy presents to the interpreter one of the greatest challenges in applying the science of hermeneutics. However, prophecy being Scripture, it is evident that it can be interpreted by applying valid Scriptural principles of interpretation.

I. THE DEFINITION OF PROPHECY

Webster's Dictionary defines prophecy as: "Prediction of the future under the influence of divine guidance; act or practice of a prophet; something predicted."

There are several words in Scripture used to refer to prophecy:

Old Testament Hebrew

CHAZAH = "to gaze at; mentally to perceive, contemplate (with pleasure); specifically to have a vision of; to see, behold with the eye; to see as a seer in the ecstatic state."

Translated:

behold	***Job 23:9; Psalms 17:2; 27:4***
look	***Isaiah 33:20; Micah 4:11***
prophesy	***Isaiah 30:10***
provide	***Exodus 18:21***
see	***Isaiah 1:1; 13:1; Ezekiel 13:6-8; Habakkuk 1:1; Zechariah 10:2***

MASSA = "a burden; specifically tribute, or abstractly porterage; figuratively an utterance, chiefly a doom, especially singing; mental, desire."

Translated:

burden	***Isaiah 13:1; 15:1; 17:1; 19:1; Jeremiah 23:33, 34, 36; Habakkuk 1:1***
carry away	***II Chronicles 20:25***
prophecy	***Proverbs 30:1; 31:1***
song	***I Chronicles 15:22, 27***
tribute	***II Chronicles 17:11***

NABA = "to prophesy; i.e., speak (or sing) by inspiration (in prediction or simple discourse); prophesy under influence of divine spirit, in the ecstatic state."

Translated:

prophesy	***I Samuel 10:11; Jeremiah 2:8; 26:11; Ezekiel 37:7; Joel 2:28; Amos 3:8***
make self a prophet	***Jeremiah 29:26, 27***

NEBUWAH = "a prediction (spoken or written)."

Translated:

prophecy	***II Chronicles 9:29; 15:8; Nehemiah 6:12***

NATAPH = "to ooze; i. e., distill gradually; by implication to fall in drops; figuratively to speak by inspiration; prophecy, discourse."

Translated:

drop	***Judges 5:4; Ezekiel 21:2; Amos 7:16***
prophesy	***Micah 2:6, 11***

Thus, in these Hebrew words we see prophecy as an ecstatic vision, a burden, a divinely inspired utterance, a written or spoken prediction, and a dropping down of inspired speech.

New Testament Greek
PROPHETEUO = "to fortell events, divine, speak under inspiration, exercise the prophetic office; to proclaim a divine revelation, prophesy, to foretell the future; to speak forth by divine inspiration; to break forth under sudden impulse in lofty discourse or in praise of the divine counsels."

Translated:

prophesy ***Matthew 15:7; Luke 1:67; 22:64; John 11:51; Acts 2:17, 18; 21:9; I Corinthians 14:1, 3-5; I Peter 1:10; Jude 14; Revelation 11:3***

In Koine Greek the concept of prophecy was solidified to the point that only one word was used to encompass it. In the New Testament prophecy meant to proclaim a divine revelation, to foretell the future, and to break forth under sudden impulse into inspired discourse.

II. THE NATURE OF PROPHECY

The nature of prophecy is basically two-fold: forth-telling and fore-telling. There are as well, different degrees of prophetic inspiration.

A. **Prophecy as Forth-telling:** This form of prophecy is in the realm of preaching: the prophet speaks for God to the people, communicating the mind of God for the present. Often the past will be used to deal with the present. This will include such things as exhortation, reproof, warning, edification, and comfort.

B. **Prophecy as Foretelling:** This aspect of prophecy is in the form of prediction: the prophet speaks for God, communicating His mind for the future. Often both the past and present will be used to deal with the future. Many times the purpose of prophetic prediction is to produce present godliness.

C. **Degrees of Prophetic Inspiration:** Scripture reveals that there are varying degrees of prophetic unction. These are:

1. **The Spirit of Prophecy**—This is defined in ***Revelation 19:10; "The testimony of Jesus is the Spirit of prophecy."*** The Spirit of prophecy is the Holy Spirit's ability to come upon men and cause them to speak forth inspired utterances. The Spirit of prophecy was evident in the Godly line from Adam to Moses.

   a. Adam prophesied concerning his bride and the marriage estate ***(Genesis 2:20-25).***

   b. Enoch prophesied of the second coming of Christ ***(Jude 14, 15).***

   c. Noah was a preacher of righteousness because the Spirit of Christ was in him ***(II Peter 2:5).***

   d. Abraham was spoken of as a prophet ***(Genesis 20:7).***

   e. Isaac and Jacob had the Spirit of prophecy upon them as they blessed their sons ***(Genesis 27; 48; 49; Hebrews 11:20, 21).***

   f. Joseph prophesied of the Exodus from Egypt ***(Genesis 50:24; Hebrews 11:22).***

   At time the Spirit of prophecy fell upon groups of people. In ***Numbers 11:24-30*** the Lord took the Spirit that was upon Moses and placed it upon the seventy elders of Israel and they prophesied. In ***I Samuel 19:20-24*** the Spirit of prophecy fell upon several groups of messengers, as well as upon King Saul.

2. **The Gift of Prophecy:** This is mentioned in ***I Corinthians 12:10*** as one of the gifts of the Spirit. It can be defined as the God-given ability to speak forth supernaturally as the Spirit gives utterance. It is seen as being an operation of the Spirit in the New Testament Church which must be exercised within Divine guidelines ***(I Corinthians 14:3, 25, 31; I Thessalonians 5:20).*** Philip's four daughters are a possible example of this gift, in that the Scripture simply states that they prophesied ***(Acts 21:9).***

3. **The Office of a Prophet:** In ***Hosea 12:10*** and ***Hebrews 1:1*** it is stated that God spoke to His people by the ministry of the prophets. A prophet was a person who was given the distinctive ministry of representing God before man. He did so by moving under the "prophetic mantle" that came upon him. The prophet was God's mouthpiece, or spokesman, through which the Word of God flowed, whether forth-telling or

fore-telling. There were many men of God throughout Scripture who held this office. These will be dealt with in the following section.

4. **The Prophecy of Scripture:** In ***II Peter 1:19-21*** the expression ***"prophecy of the Scripture"*** is used to refer to the prophetical books of the Old Testament. Because the Scriptures are the inspired Word of God, the prophecy therein must be regarded as inspired and infallible revelation ***(II Timothy 3:15, 16).*** This then is the highest degree of prophecy and requires the most careful and systematic interpretation.

III. THE MINISTRY OF THE PROPHETS

A. **Designations of the Prophets:** In all of the various periods of Israel's history in the Old Testament, there appears to be no greater or grander ministry than that of the prophets. The prophets were noble and holy men of God. They were the representatives of God to Israel, declaring His word, His mind and His will to the nation in times of prosperity or adversity. These prophets were known under the following designations:

1. **The Men of God—*I Samuel 9:6; I Kings 12:22:*** Morally and ethnically, the prophets were indeed men of God, following, declaring and upholding the ways of God.
2. **The Seers—*I Samuel 9:9; II Chronicles 33:18; 35:18; II Samuel 24:11; Amos 7:12; Isaiah 29:10:*** The prophets were first called seers because of the visions, insight and foresight which they received from the Lord for the people.
3. **The Interpreters—*Isaiah 43:27:*** The word **"teachers"** means "interpreters." The prophets were the interpreters of the Law of the Lord. They interpreted the history of the nation in the light of the Word of the Lord.
4. **The Messengers of the Lord—*Isaiah 42:19; Malachi 3:1:*** The prophets were the divine messengers, sent by God, bearing the messages of the Lord to the nation. They delivered the messages faithfully.
5. **The Servants—*Jeremiah 44:4:*** The prophets were also called the Servants of Jehovah. They were His slaves; love-slaves to the will and service of God.
6. **The Prophets—*Hosea 12:10:*** The most common designation is that of prophet. These men who were prophets were public expounders and preachers of the Word of the Lord. They spoke under inspiration of the Spirit. ***"Holy men of God spake as they were moved by the Holy Ghost" (II Peter 1:21).*** They prophesied through both preaching and prediction. They represented God's Word to Israel. They upheld the righteousness of the Law, the holiness and mercy of God, Divine sovereignty over the nations, and reproved the sinfulness of men.

B. **The Development of the Prophetic Office:** It is important to see the rise and development of the prophetic office. Two focal points are seen in the prophets Moses and Samuel.

1. **The Prophet Moses—The Letter of the Law:** Moses stands unique among the Old Testament prophets because of that which he represents before God and the nation of Israel. Moses was the prophet who received the Law of God on Mt. Sinai. He actually became the *foundational ministry,* and all succeeding prophets were tested by the Law given to Moses.

   The Lord communicated with Moses face to face and he became a type of the Messiah who would be ***"like unto him." (Numbers 12:6-8; Exodus 33:11; Deuteronomy 18:15-18; Acts 3:22-23; Isaiah 8:16-20; Luke 16:29).***

2. **The Prophets Samuel to Malachi—The Spirit of the Law:** It is under Samuel that we see a distinct development of the prophetic office. The Scriptures clearly mark Moses and Samuel as being key men in the prophetic ministry:

   "For Moses truly said . . ." (Acts 3:22)
   "Yea, and all the prophets from Samuel and those that follow after . . ." (Acts 3:24)
   "And after that He gave them judges about the space of 450 years, until Samuel the prophet . . ." (Acts 13:20)

   Samuel was the last of the Judges and the first of the line of the prophets. Thus, from Samuel to Malachi we have the ministry of the prophets. It seems evident from the Scriptures that Samuel, under direction of the Lord, gathered young men who were hungry after God into *"schools of the prophets."* Here they received education and instruction out of the Law of Moses and were taught how to respond to the Spirit of the Lord in worship and prophecy ***(I Samuel 19:20).*** The Scriptures speak of these centers, where the sons of the prophets would gather together in preparation for ministry. It seems that schools of the prophets were found in:

Ramah	***I Samuel 19:18-24***
Bethel	***II Kings 2:3***
Jericho	***II Kings 2:5, 7, 15***
Gilgal	***II Kings 4:38; 2:1***

The dominant purpose in the establishment of these "schools of the prophets" was to maintain the spirit of the Law.

If Moses stood for the *letter* of the Law, the prophets indeed stood for the *spirit* of the Law. The true prophets of God never contradicted the letter of the Law; they upheld it. But when it degenerated into a dead form and mere ritual, the Holy Spirit came upon them to inspire and revive the spirit of the Law.

C. **Prophets in Relation to the Kings:** Not only do we see the beginning of the prophetic office in Samuel, we also see the beginning of the kingly office. It was the prophet Samuel who anointed both Saul and David to their kingly ministry. From this period until the captivities of the House of Israel and the House of Judah, there is a distinct relationship between the prophets and the kings. Most of the kings of Israel and Judah had a prophet of God sent to them. God's purpose was to influence the government of the nation as a whole through the king by means of the prophetic word. The prophet represented the Word of the Lord to the kings, and the kings were judged according to their acceptance or rejection of the prophetic word.

In previous periods, men inquired of God through the Priest, but now inquiry of God was primarily through the prophet. Thus, most of the kings were privileged to have the ministry of the Word of the Lord through the prophets.

Saul and David had the ministry of Samuel
(I Samuel 9-10, 16)
David had Nathan and Gad also as prophets
(II Samuel 12; 24:11)
Solomon had the prophet Nathan
(I Kings 1:38)
Rehoboam had the prophet Shemiah
(I Kings 12:21, 22)
Ahab had Elijah and Elisha
(I Kings 17:1; 19:16)

The kings of the House of Israel and Judah had prophets sent to them. These are referred to as the major and minor prophets, and are spoken of in the opening verses of the books of the major and minor prophets. Examples are: ***Isaiah 1:1-2; Jeremiah 1:1-2; Hosea 1:1-2; Micah 1:1.*** An understanding of the character and times of the kings of Israel and Judah is necessary for an understanding of the nature of the Word of the Lord through the respective prophets of that period.

D. **Classification of Prophets:** For the purposes of this chapter we will classify the prophets under two groupings: non-writing prophets and writing prophets.

1. **Non-writing Prophets:** There are a number of prophets mentioned in Scripture who were not involved in the writing of Scripture. They ministered in the realms of guidance, forth-telling, foretelling, and words of wisdom and knowledge. God confirmed their ministries with signs and miracles. In the Old Testament there were men like Aaron, Nathan, Gad, Abijah, Elijah and Elisha. In the New Testament there were men such as John the Baptist, Agabus, and Silas.

2. **Writing Prophets:** Out of the prophets God chose certain men to be inspired writers of Scripture ***(II Peter 1:20, 21).*** These prophets wrote Scripture in different styles: historical, poetical and prophetical.

   a. **Prophets who wrote Historical Books**—Some prophets were primarily involved in writing history, Moses in writing the Pentateuch, and Samuel in writing the books of Judges, Ruth, I Samuel, are two such men.

b. **Prophets who wrote Poetical Books**—Some prophets were inspired to write poetry. Two such men are David, who wrote many of the Psalms, and Jeremiah, who wrote Lamentations.

c. **Prophets who wrote Prophetical Books**—Many prophets were inspired to record their visions and prophecies. Daniel, Ezekiel and Zechariah, especially were prophets of vision. These they received and recorded under inspiration as infallible prophecy, foretelling the future and destiny of the nations.

The prophetical books of the Old Testament have been referred to as the major and minor prophets. This distinction refers only to the volume of their contents. The major prophets are Isaiah, Jeremiah, Lamentations, Ezekiel and Daniel. The minor prophets are Hosea, Joel, Amos, Obadiah, Jonah, Nahum, Habakkuk, Zephaniah, Haggai, Zechariah and Malachi. All of these books include both forthtelling and fore-telling though with greater emphasis on the latter.

IV. THE CLASSIFICATION OF WRITTEN PROPHECY

In the writings of the prophets there can be found three major classifications of prophetic revelation. These are woven together throughout prophetic Scripture like a three-fold cord, and are often so closely entwined that they are difficult to separate. The three are: Local prophecy, National-destiny prophecy, and Messianic prophecy.

A. **Local Prophecy:** Local prophecy refers to instances when the prophet speaks to his own generation about their spiritual condition and God's desires for them. This is viewed primarily as preaching in which the timeless principles and truths of God's character and being are revealed and applied to the life-situation of the prophet's own generation.

Truth is eternal and remains the standard by which every generation is measured. Thus, truth is applicable to all generations and the truth applied to the prophet's day is also applicable today. However, before the interpreter can safely apply the prophet's message to present times he must be careful to accurately discern what the prophet was saying to his own generation. In order to do this the interpreter must thoroughly acquaint himself with the moral conditions of that day.

Some examples of local prophecy are ***Isaiah 40:18-31; 55:6, 7; Jeremiah 26;*** and ***Micah 6:8.*** These prophecies obviously include timeless principles applicable to all generations.

B. **National-Destiny Prophecy:** National-destiny prophecy is when the prophet speaks concerning the future history of nations. This is viewed primarily as prediction in which the prophet may use the nation's past history and its present condition as the stage upon which their future judgment and/or blessing is portrayed.

Though primarily concerned with the destiny of the chosen nation of Israel, the prophets also predicted the destiny of the Gentile nations.

Some examples of national-destiny prophecy concerning the nation of Israel are: ***Isaiah 11:11-16; 43:1-28; Jeremiah 30; Ezekiel 27*** and ***Romans 9, 10, 11.***

Some examples of national-destiny prophecy concerning the Gentile nations are: ***Isaiah 13-23; Jeremiah 46-51; Ezekiel 29-32; Daniel 2, 7; Amos 1, 2; Obadiah*** and ***Nahum.***

In interpreting this area of prophecy, the interpreter must use the Ethnic-Division Principle so as not to confuse the destiny of nations.

C. **Messianic Prophecy:** Messianic prophecy is when the prophet speaks concerning Christ and the Church. This is viewed primarily as prediction in which the prophet may use various elements of past history, the present local situation, and even the future national destiny to foretell the ultimate phase of God's purpose in the Messianic era. Messianic prophecy encompasses all that relates to Christ and the Church, from His first coming through His second coming.

It was spoken of by Peter as "the sufferings of Christ and the glory that should follow" ***(I Peter 1:10-12).*** Messianic prophecy may be divided into three groupings, based on three stages of fulfillment:

1. **The First Coming of Christ:** These prophecies deal mainly with the birth, growth, ministry, sufferings, and exaltation of the Lord Jesus Christ. Most of the Old Testament Messianic prophecies pertain to the first coming of Christ and its related events. Some examples of these are: ***Genesis 3:15; Deuteronomy 18:15-18; Psalms 2, 8, 22*** and ***40; Isaiah 7:14; 9:6; 40:1-8; 52:14; 53:1-12; 61:1-4; Jeremiah 31:31; Micah 5:1-2; Zechariah 11:12-13; 13:9.***

2. **The Church:** These prophecies deal mainly with that which was to be the fruit of Messiah's sufferings, even the glory of the Church ***(Ephesians 3:21).*** There are many Old Testament prophecies which deal with the coming of the Gentiles into the kingdom of the Messiah. The New Testament clearly shows that these prophecies were predicting the grafting in of the Gentiles into the olive tree so that both Jew and Gentile could become one Body in Christ ***(Psalms 18:49*** with ***Romans 15:9; Deuteronomy 32:43*** with ***Romans 15:10; Psalms 117:1*** with ***Romans 15:11; Isaiah 11:10*** with ***Romans 15:12; Romans 11:13-25; Ephesians 3:6; I Corinthians 12:13).***

   Some examples of Messianic prophecies concerning the Church are: ***Isaiah 9:6-7; 26:1-4; 35:1-10; 54:1-17; Jeremiah 31:33, 34; Joel 2:28-32; Zechariah 2:10, 11; Malachi 1:11.***

3. **The Second Coming of Christ:** These prophecies deal primarily with Christ's return to consummate that which He initiated in His first coming. Though there were only a few specific prophecies in the Old Testament concerning Christ's second coming, there are many which deal with its related events. Many of these prophecies deal with "the Day of the Lord" and its climactic judgments. It should be noted that the burden of New Testament prophecy is the second coming of Christ.

   Some examples of second coming prophecies are: ***Genesis 49:10; Isaiah 2:10-22; 13:6-16; 24:1-23; 30:26-33; 34:1-17; Daniel 2*** and ***Daniel 7; Joel 3; Zechariah 14; Malachi 4:1-4; Matthew 24; Mark 13; Luke 21; I Corinthians 15; I Thessalonians 4:14-18; II Thessalonians 2; II Peter 3:1-13; Revelation 19.***

V. GUIDELINES FOR THE INTERPRETATION OF PROPHECY

A. **Guidelines Based upon the Principles of Scriptural Interpretation:** Though prophecy is unique in its nature, the guidelines for its interpretation are to be primarily taken from the principles that are used to interpret the whole of Scripture. For this section the reader should refer back to the Principles discussed previously in this text, as these guidelines will be based upon them.

1. **The Context Principle**
   a. The first rule of hermeneutics, "Scripture interprets Scripture" must be applied to prophecy.
   b. Any verse of prophecy must be considered in the light of its Biblical, Testamental, and Book context.
   c. Caution must be used in interpreting a verse of prophecy in the light of its passage context. This is because the prophets, caught up in an ecstatic state, often did not weave together a context with a logical train of thought or a chronological treatment of events.
   d. In dealing with prophecy, the interpreter must work from whole to part and part to whole.
   e. The obscure passages should be interpreted in the light of the clear.
2. **The First-Mention Principle:** Recognizing the value of first-mention, the interpreter should be faithful to consult the first mention of the prophetic theme with which he is dealing.
3. **The Comparative Mention Principle**
   a. The interpreter should be diligent to search through Scripture for any possible fulfillment of the prophecy under consideration.
   b. In interpreting prophecy, all prophetic passages relating to the same subject must be brought together and compared.
4. **The Progressive Mention Principle**
   a. When dealing with a prophetic theme the interpreter must be aware of its progressive development throughout Scripture.
   b. The interpreter must not confuse the progressive development of the prophetic theme.
5. **The Complete Mention Principle**
   a. For the interpreter to understand all that the Scripture has to say on any given prophetic subject he must bring together all relevant prophetic passages.
   b. Each prophetic passage must be interpreted in the light of this whole.

6. **The Election Principle**

   a. The interpreter must constantly keep in mind the fact that God's elective purposes are the foundation of prophetic revelation.

   b. When interpreting national prophecy, the interpreter must keep in mind God's elective purpose for that specific nation.

   c. The distinction between temporal purposes and eternal purposes must be kept in sharp focus.

7. **The Covenantal Principle**

   a. All prophecy must be considered in the light of its covenantal background.

   b. The interpreter must determine which covenant was the basis for the prophet's ministry.

   c. The interpreter must have a thorough knowledge of the covenants in order to be able to discern the covenants referred to in various prophetic passages.

   d. The developmental progression and inter-relatedness of the covenants must be recognized when dealing with prophecy.

   e. All prophecy must ultimately be interpreted in the light of the New Covenant. Old Testament prophecy must be interpreted through the cross and must not be used to overrule the everlasting New Covenant.

8. **The Ethnic-Division Principle**

   a. To properly interpret prophecy the interpreter must have a thorough knowledge of God's appointed ethnic-divisions and their respective places in His purposes.

   b. In order to distinguish between these divisions the interpreter should ask himself the following questions:

      —Does this verse refer to the united nation, the whole House of Israel?
      —Does it refer to the ten Tribed House of Israel, the Northern Kingdom?
      —Does it refer to the two Tribed House (plus the Levites) of Judah, the Southern Kingdom?
      —Does it refer to the Gentile nations?
      —Does it refer to the Church, chosen out of every nation?

   c. What is spoken of one division must not be interpreted as referring to another division. The same is true also of certain divisions within these divisions.

9. **The Chronometrical Principle**

   a. It must be recognized that the prophets were not always aware of the time element in their own prophecies ***(I Peter 1:10-12).***

   b. The prophets were caught up into God's timeless perspective in which past, present and future were laid out before them. Thus, in transcending time, some prophetic passages involve a weaving together of the past, present and future. Often, in speaking to their own generations, the prophets would use the past as a stage upon which to foretell the future. To the reader the time elements seem to be confused. At times they utilized what is known as "the prophetic perfect tense" speaking of future events as though they had already occurred. Therefore the interpreter must move with extreme caution in assigning prophetic passages to specific time fulfillments.

   c. The interpreter should ask himself the following questions in order to distinguish the time element in prophetic fulfillment:

      —Was the prophecy fulfilled during the lifetime of the prophet who was speaking?
      —Was the prophecy fulfilled during the time of the captivity:
         of the house of Israel to Assyria?
         of the House of Judah to Babylon?
      —Was the prophecy fulfilled in the time of the restoration of Judah from Babylon at the close of the seventy years captivity?

—Was the prophecy fulfilled during the time of Judah in the land after the Babylonian captivity; during the inter-Testamental period?
—Was the prophecy fulfilled in New Testament times in relation to the Messiah, the Church or the Jewish nation?
—Is the prophecy being fulfilled in the Church age?
—Is the prophecy to be fulfilled in the final years prior to the second coming of Christ?
—Is the prophecy to be fulfilled at the second advent of Christ?
—Is the prophecy to find fulfillment in the future ages:
the Kingdom of God relative to earth?
the eternal state in the new heavens and new earth?

10. **The Breach Principle**

a. The interpreter must recognize that some prophetic passages deal with conditional promises. Because of this, the promise may be fulfilled in the prophet's generation if certain conditions are met. If the conditions are not met, the fulfillment of the promise may be postponed to another generation. With this in mind, the prophet ministers to the people, either exhorting them to fulfill the conditions, or pronouncing judgment upon them for having failed to do so. When these elements exist in a passage, the interpreter must be careful to interpret the passage in the light of them.

b. The interpreter must also recognize that the prophets often viewed future events as mountain peaks close together, with no valleys in between. Thus, in a given passage, a prophet may group together events whose fulfillments may occur centuries apart.

11. **The Christo-Centric Principle**

a. Since the prophets were men who dealt with human history from the divine perspective, and since Christ is the solution to the dilemma of human history, the message of the prophets concerns Him ***(I Peter 1:10-12).***

b. Though Christ is the center of the truth communicated by the prophets, the interpreter must discern whether each particular passage relates to Christ directly or indirectly.

c. The interpreter must be careful not to force Christo-centric interpretation upon a prophetic passage. Passages that do not relate to Christ should not be interpreted as such.

d. Prophecies containing Christo-centric elements must be interpreted in the light of clear New Testament historical and doctrinal revelation.

12. **The Moral Principle**

a. The interpreter must recognize that the principles of God are timeless. Thus, principles which are applied to one generation are actually applicable to all.

b. Many prophetic passages are simply inspired preaching (forth-telling) in which the prophet is applying timeless principles to his own generation. Before the interpreter can apply those principles to his generation, he must correctly discern how the prophet applied them to his own.

c. In moralizing a passage, the interpreter must be careful not to confuse the literal meaning, nor to violate the other principles of interpretation.

13. **The Symbolic Principle**

a. Symbols, used as well in types, allegories, and parables, are also a vital part of prophecy. Since the prophets many times are revealing the unknown in the terminology of the known, symbolism seems to be one of their favorite vehicles of expression.

b. The interpreter must recognize that in apocalyptic prophecy, fanciful, non-real symbols are often used (e.g., ***Daniel 7; Revelation 13***). Many times these symbols are non-real aggregates of real parts. In these special cases, great care must be taken to interpret the parts while interpreting the whole symbol.

c. In interpreting the symbols in prophecy the first rule of hermeneutics should be followed: let Scripture interpret Scripture. The basic qualifications of the Symbolic Principle must be followed.

14. **The Numerical Principle:** While the interpreter must recognize evident numerical significance in prophecy, he must be careful not to distort prophecy by forcing extreme numerical significances upon its interpretation.

15. **The Typical Principle:** The interpreter must recognize the distinction between the types found mainly in the historical writings and the symbolic-typical actions primarily confined to the prophets. Some examples of symbolic-typical actions in prophecy are: Isaiah walking naked and barefoot for three years ***(Isaiah 20:2-4);*** Jeremiah hiding his girdle by the river Euphrates ***(Jeremiah 13:1-11);*** Jeremiah putting a yoke upon his neck ***(Jeremiah 27:1-14);*** Ezekiel's miniature portrayal of Jerusalem's seige ***(Ezekiel 4);*** and Ezekiel's laying on his side for over a year ***(Ezekiel 4).*** These actions must each be interpreted in the light of their specific contexts.

16. **The Parabolic Principle:** There are relatively few parables to be found in prophecy ***(Ezekiel 17:1-21*** is one example). Thus, care must be used to distinguish them from other similar figures of speech (refer to Ch. 23). In interpreting them, their symbols must be interpreted and caused to directly relate to the fundamental lesson the parable is teaching. The basic qualifications of the Parabolic Principle must be followed.

17. **The Allegorical Principle:** As with parables, there are relatively few allegories to be found in prophecy ***(Isaiah 5:1-7*** and ***Ezekiel 23:1-49*** are examples). They also must be distinguished from other similar figures of speech (refer to Ch. 23). In interpreting them, the extended analogy must be drawn by interpreting the symbols involved so that the intended lessons may be discovered. The basic qualifications of the Allegorical Principle must be adhered to.

B. **General Guidelines in Interpreting Prophecy:** Because prophecy is unique in its nature, there are special guidelines to be followed in addition to those applied generally to the whole of Scripture. The following is a brief listing of some of these guidelines.

1. **The spiritual gap between the prophet and interpreter must be bridged:** In that the prophets were "in the Spirit" when they prophesied, the interpreter must be under the influence of that same Spirit when he seeks to interpret that prophetic word inspired by the Spirit.

2. **The natural gap between the prophet and interpreter must be bridged:** In that God utilized the prophet's own natural frame of reference, the interpreter must put himself into that frame of reference with appropriate studies in the fields of language, culture, geography, and history.

3. **The predictive and didactic types of prophecy must be distinguished:** Prophecy involves both forth-telling (inspired preaching for the present) and foretelling (predicting the future). These are sometimes woven together in a single passage and require skillful exegesis on the part of the interpreter to correctly divide them.

4. **The non-systematic character of the prophets must be kept in clear focus:** Prophecy may be non-systematic in basically two ways: (a) prophecies are not necessarily arranged in a progressive chain of thought, rather are often a compilation of fragmentary revelation; and (b) prophecies are not necessarily arranged as to their chronological order of fulfillment. In recognizing this problem the interpreter would do well to approach carefully the interpretation of prophecy, utilizing the context group of principles.

5. **The fulfillment of predictive prophecy must be determined:** In dealing with predictive prophecy the interpreter must ultimately come to grips with the problem of its fulfillment. He must answer the questions: "Who or what was the prophet actually speaking of?" and "When is the prophecy actually fulfilled?" The following are some suggestions in applying this guideline:

   a. If the prophecy has been fulfilled, it should be studied in connection with materials that clearly indicate its fulfillment.

   b. If the prophecy has been partially fulfilled, the interpreter should search for the reason. Could it be that the hearers were only partially obedient? Or could it be that the prophecy, though having only one sense, may have more than one fulfillment? Some prophecies of blessing or judgment seem to have several fulfillments through time, climaxing at the end of this present age.

   c. If the prophecy is yet unfulfilled, the interpreter must proceed with caution in determining its eschatological significance. To begin with, he should look for interpretive clues based on the clear teaching of the rest of Scripture. Then he should determine the time element by using the questions given in the Chronological Principle (Ch. 14). He should also determine the local application of the prophecy, as well as the fundamental idea yet awaiting fulfillment.

VI. A DEMONSTRATION OF APPLYING THE PRINCIPLES TO PROPHECY

As already noted, hermeneutics is both a science and an art. The writings of the prophets present one of the greatest areas of challenge to the applied skill of the interpreter. The reason for this is found in the great variety of elements which compose the prophetic writings. This often calls for a weaving together of a number of principles in order to arrive at a proper interpretation of the prophetic passage under consideration. This indeed tests the skill of the interpreter. Not every prophetic passage will require the use of exactly the same principles. Which principles are to be woven together will depend on the elements involved in the prophecy. Hence the interpreter should be fully cognizant of the prophetic elements which need interpreting and the principles to be applied.

As a demonstration of the weaving of some of the principles together in interpreting prophetic passages, certain verses have been chosen from Hosea Chapters 1 through 4. It is not our purpose to thoroughly exegete these chapters, for to do so would involve a lengthy study into the background of the book, a bridging of the foundational gaps, and a verse by verse exposition of the passage. Instead, our procedure will be to choose appropriate verses from these chapters to demonstrate most of the principles.

A. **The Context Principle**

1. **The Scripture:** ***Hosea 1:4 ". . . and will cause to cease the kingdom of the house of Israel."***
2. **The Principle Applied**

   a. **The Passage Context**—The passage context of this phrase is ***Hosea 1-3,*** in which God uses the prophet's domestic situation to illustrate His dealings with the House of Israel. The immediate context of the phrase is verses 2-5. Here the Lord commands Hosea to marry Gomer, an adulterous woman. When a son was born to them God commanded that his name be called Jezreel. Verses 4 and 5 are an explanation of the prophetic significance of Jezreel's name. This significance is to be found in the history of several generations preceding Hosea. Ahab and Jezebel, the wicked rulers of Israel, had slain Naboth to obtain his vineyard in Jezreel. For this God had pronounced vengeance upon them ***(I Kings 21).*** Within approximately fifteen years this vengeance was executed upon the house of Ahab in Jezreel. Jehu, chosen by God to avenge Naboth's blood upon the house of Ahab, went beyond God's decree and slew a number of other persons at Jezreel ***(II Kings 9, 10).*** For this reason God pronounced vengeance upon the house of Jehu for the blood of Jezreel. Hosea uses this vengeance, which was executed upon the descendants of Jehu in his lifetime, to prophesy of a greater vengeance that was to come upon the house of Israel, the Northern Kingdom.

   b. **The Book Context**—The book of Hosea sets forth Hosea's domestic life as an example of God's dealings with Israel: His union with the nation, her unfaithfulness to the marriage covenant, His chastisement of her, and His love and mercy in redeeming and restoring her to Himself. Thus, the phrase under consideration concerning judgment must be considered in the light of those in the rest of the book which speak of restoration.

   c. **The Testament Context**—The Old Testament unfolds God's choice of Israel as a nation, His purpose in choosing her, and His dealings with her throughout her history through blessings and judgments. Though God was faithful to the marriage covenant He made with Israel, she repeatedly proved herself unfaithful. After centuries of patient dealings with her, God was forced to cast her off and send her into captivity: the house of Judah to Babylon and the house of Israel to Assyria. However, scattered throughout the Old Testament prophets are prophecies of restoration for the nation through her Messiah. The phrase in Hosea under consideration fits into this panorama as a prophecy of the Assyrian captivity of the Northern Kingdom of Israel.

   d. **The Bible Context**—The whole of Scripture context includes the clear New Testament revelation that Israel's judgment was caused by their sin of unbelief and that only through faith in Christ will they be restored to blessing ***(Romans 9-11).***

B. **The First Mention Principle**

1. **The Scripture:** ***Hosea 1:1 "The Word of the Lord that came unto Hosea . . ."***

2. **The Principle Applied:** Though the first reference to God speaking is to be found in ***Genesis 1:3,*** the first use of the specific phrase is to be found in ***Genesis 15:1.*** There God spoke to Abram in a vision and confirmed the seed-promise of His covenant with him. The phrase ***"the Word of the Lord came"*** signifies a supernatural communication of a Divine revelation of God's mind to man. The phrase carries this same significance through each of its numerous usages in Scripture, including the book of Hosea. Thus, when the Word of the Lord came to Hosea, God was communicating His mind to the prophet concerning the spiritual condition and national destiny of Israel.

C. **The Comparative Mention Principle**

1. **The Scripture:** ***Hosea 1:6, 9, 10; 2:23 ". . . for I will no more have mercy upon the house of Israel . . . for ye are not my people, and I will not be your God . . . and it shall come to pass, that in the place where it was said unto them, Ye are not my people, there it shall be said unto them, Ye are the sons of the living God . . . and I will have mercy upon her that had not obtained mercy; and I will say to them which were not my people, Thou art my people; and they shall say, Thou art my God."***

2. **The Principle Applied:** By comparing these phrases with quotations of them in the New Testament, their meaning may be ascertained. In ***Romans 9:25, 26*** Paul quotes ***Hosea 2:23 and 1:10*** in dealing with the relationship between Jew and Gentile in Christ. In ***I Peter 2:10*** Peter takes elements from ***Hosea 1:6, 9 and 2:23*** to show that those outside of Christ can now obtain mercy through Christ. These New Testament verses interpret for us the prophetic statements of Hosea to mean that both Israel, who were rejected as the people of God, and the Gentiles, who never were the people of God, may both become the people of God through faith in Christ.

D. **The Progressive Mention Principle**

1. **The Scripture:** ***Hosea 1:10 "Yet the number of the children of Israel shall be as the sand of the sea, which cannot be measured nor numbered . . ."***

2. **The Principle Applied:** By noting the progressive mentions of "sand" in Scripture, the meaning of this verse may be substantiated.

Genesis 22:17	Abraham's seed to be as the sand on the seashore.
Genesis 32:12	Jacob's seed to be as the sand of the sea.
Joshua 11:4	The Midianites were as the sand in multitude.
I Kings 4:20	Judah and Israel as the sand in multitude.
Isaiah 10:22	Israel as the sand of the sea.
Jeremiah 33:22	Seed of David to be numberless as the sand.
Romans 9:27	Israel as the sand of the sea.
Hebrews 11:12	Abraham's seed as the sand.
Revelation 20:8	Hosts of Gog and Magog as the sand.

The above progressive mentions show that the sand of the sea is significant of the innumerable masses of Abraham's seed after the flesh and of earthly unregenerate mankind. Thus, though Hosea prophesies concerning the cessation of the Northern Kingdom of Israel, he confirms that the promise of the Abrahamic Covenant remains valid.

E. **The Complete Mention Principle**

1. **The Scripture:** ***Hosea 2:15 "And I will give her . . . the valley of Achor for a door of hope . . ."***

2. **The Principle Applied:** By considering every reference to Achor in Scripture, the interpretation of Hosea's prophecy becomes quite clear.

Joshua 7:24, 26	The valley of Achor was chosen as the stoning place for Achan and his family because he had "troubled" Israel by taking forbidden spoil from the city of Jericho. Achor means "trouble."
Joshua 15:7	The valley of Achor was on the border of Judah's inheritance.
Isaiah 65:10	The valley of Achor was to be a place for herds to lie down for the faithful seed of Judah.

These references show that for Israel the valley of Achor had originally been a place of national trouble, then became a part of the national inheritance, and was to become a place of blessing. The prophecy of Hosea encompasses the whole of this progressive revelation by promising that what was once the valley of troubling would become a door of hope. That which had hindered their entrance into their inheritance would become a doorway into it.

F. **The Election Principle**

1. **The Scripture:** ***Hosea 1:1, 2 "The Word of the Lord that came unto Hosea . . . the beginning of the Word of the Lord by Hosea . . ."***

2. **The Principle Applied:** The phrases above not only indicate the giving of a divine communication but also a calling to declare that communication. As noted in the Election Principle, there are basically two types of callings. The election of time refers to God's choosing of individuals or nations to fulfill His purposes in relation to time. God chose Hosea as the most suitable vessel to depict His relationship to Israel and call them to repentance.

G. **The Covenantal Principle**

1. **The Scripture:** ***Hosea 1:10 "Yet the number of the children of Israel shall be as the sand of the sea, which cannot be measured nor numbered; and it shall come to pass, that in the place where it was said unto them, Ye are not my people, there it shall be said unto them, Ye are the sons of the living God."***

2. **The Principle Applied:** This verse contains covenantal terminology. The language relates to four different covenants: the Abrahamic, Mosaic, Palestinian, and New Covenants. The "sand of the sea" involves the Abrahamic Covenant ***(Genesis 22:17).*** The phrase ***"Ye are not my people"*** implies the Mosaic and Palestinian Covenants ***(Deuteronomy 27:9; Jeremiah 31:32*** because the nation failed to keep the conditions of these covenants). The phrase "sons of the living God" points to the New Covenant ***(Romans 9:26).*** In the light of the covenantal revelation, this verse of prohecy shows the relationship between four covenants. Hosea confirms the seed-promise of the Abrahamic Covenant and affirms that, though Israel would be rejected as God's people and cast out of the land on the basis of the Mosaic and Palestinian Covenants, they would finally become the sons of the living God under the New Covenant.

H. **The Ethnic Division Principle**

1. **The Scripture:** ***Hosea 1:6, 7 "for I will no more have mercy upon the house of Israel; . . . but I will have mercy upon the house of Judah."***

2. **The Principle Applied:** These verses refer to the two houses within the ethnic division of Israel. After Solomon's reign the nation of Israel was divided into two separate nations. The Northern Kingdom was called the house of Israel and consisted of ten of the tribes. The Southern Kingdom was called the house of Judah and consisted of two of the tribes and the Levites. These two houses had their respective God-ordained destinies. Thus, Hosea could prophesy seemingly opposing destinies for them. At the time of Hosea's standpoint in history, judgment was about to fall upon Israel while God's mercy was yet to be extended to Judah.

I. **The Chronometrical Principle**

1. **The Scripture:** ***Hosea 3:5 "Afterward shall the children of Israel return, and seek the Lord their God, and David their king; and shall fear the Lord and His goodness in the latter days."***

2. **The Principle Applied:** The time period mentioned in this verse is ***"the latter days."*** By using the context group of principles, this term can be shown to refer to the Messianic era ***(Isaiah 2:2; Ezekiel 38:16; Acts 2:17; Hebrews 1:1-2).*** Once this term is interpreted, we then discover the time in which rejected Israel would return to their God and serve their Davidic king.

J. **The Breach Principle**

1. **The Scripture:** ***Hosea 3:4, 5 "For the children of Israel shall abide many days without a king . . . Afterward shall the children of Israel return, and seek the Lord their God, and David their king . . ."***

2. **The Principle Applied:** God had promised Israel that they would have kings to rule over them ***(Genesis 17:6, 16; 49:10).*** The fulfillment of this promise began with David. After the division of the nation, both

houses had their respective dynasties: the house of Judah having Davidic kings and the house of Israel having non-Davidic kings. In due time both houses experienced God's breach of promise concerning kingly rule and went into respective captivities. Hosea prophesies concerning the house of Israel's experience of this breach, abiding many days without a king. Then he immediately foretells their seeking after their Davidic king in the Messianic era.

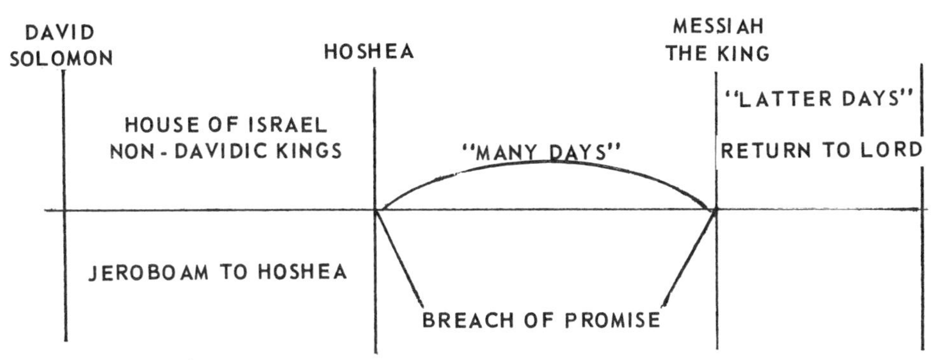

K. **The Christo-Centric Principle**

1. **The Scripture:** ***Hosea 2:16 "And it shall be at that day, saith the Lord, that thou shalt call me Ishi; and shalt call Me no more Baali."***

2. **The Principle Applied:** The nation of Israel had been the wife of Jehovah by the marriage covenant made at Mt. Sinai. The Lord declared that He had been a husband unto the people ***(Jeremiah 31:32).*** Over the years of Israel's history, the nation had played the harlot and had taken the names of Baal worship on her lips and was given a bill of divorcement ***(Jeremiah 3:8; Isaiah 50:1).*** Thus Israel became divorced from the Lord God. Hosea here prophesies that there would come a day in which the names of Baalim would be taken out of Israel's mouth and that the nation would call the Lord "Ishi," which means "My Husband." This signifies a restoration of the marriage state. The apostle Paul writes to those who know the law and tells them that they have become dead to the law by the body of Christ and that the old husband is dead; they can now be married to a new husband, Jesus Christ ***(Romans 7:1-4; II Corinthians 11:1-12).*** Hence, the husband is Jesus Christ and it is this which reveals the Christo-centric element in this verse of Hosea.

L. **The Moral Principle**

1. **The Scripture:** ***Hosea 4:6 "My people are destroyed for lack of knowledge: because thou hast rejected knowledge, I will also reject thee, that thou shalt be no priest to Me: seeing thou hast forgotten the law of thy God. I will also forget thy children.***

2. **The Principle Applied:** Originally the nation of Israel had been chosen to be a kingdom of priests unto God; to know the law of the Lord and to teach that knowledge to others ***(Exodus 19:3-6).*** However, over the years of Israel's history, the nation failed to learn the law of God; they forgot it and finally rejected the true source of knowledge. Because of this, God said through Hosea that He would do to them what they had done to His law; that is, reject them and forget them. Israel could no longer serve in priestly functions. The moral is applicable to all generations, for, any individual or nation who rejects God's law and the knowledge of God therein, will also be rejected of God.

M. **The Symbolic Principle**

1. **The Scripture:** ***Hosea 1:4, 6, 9 "Call his name Jezreel . . . Call her name Lo-ruhamah . . . Call his name Lo-ammi."***

2. **The Principle Applied:** Hosea was commanded of the Lord to take his wife Gomer unto himself. As a result of this union, in time there were born to the prophet three children. These were called by specific names which God gave to Hosea, each having symbolic significance. Jezreel means "it will be sown of God, seed of God, God will scatter," or "dropping of the friendship of God." This was symbolic of the scattering of the house of Israel. Lo-ruhamah means "not having obtained mercy," and this was symbolic of the

casting off of Israel into Assyrian captivity. Lo-ammi means "not My people," and this pointed to the rejection of the nation for its sins. Thus, Hosea's three children—two sons and one daughter—had symbolic names and were "signs and wonders" ***(Isaiah 8:18)*** declaring a message to the house of Israel.

N. **The Numerical Principle**

1. **The Scripture: *Hosea 3:2 "So I bought her to me for fifteen pieces of silver . . ."***
2. **The Principle Applied:** The Lord God, after describing Hosea's wife as adulterous, commanded the prophet to go and buy her back to himself for fifteen pieces of silver. Silver itself is symbolic of redemption money ***(Exodus 30:11-16)*** while the price of redemption was fifteen pieces, which is a significant number in Scripture. By comparing the Scripture references which speak of the number 15 it seems that this number is connected with "rest through redemption" ***(Leviticus 23:5-7, 34-35; Esther 9:20-22).*** (Also note that the number 15 is a multiple of 3 x 5. The number 3 is the number of God, and 5 is the number of grace or atonement. Together the numbers become significant of the grace of God revealed in the atonement.) Hosea bought his adulterous wife with this price of redemption, thus bringing her back again into union and rest with himself.

O. **The Typical Principle**

1. **The Scripture:** Read ***Hosea 1:2-9; 2:1-5, 14-23; 3:1-3.***
2. **The Principle Applied:** It is evident that the life-story of Hosea is symbolic and typical of the spiritual relationship of Jehovah to the nation of Israel. It is symbolic of Jehovah's past and present relationship with the nation and it is typical of His future relationship with her through the cross of Jesus Christ and the work of redemption.

Hosea was a prophet of tender, deep and pure love. He married Gomer, entering into the marriage covenant with her. She had been a "wife of whoredoms." Yet, Hosea took her to be his wife, according to the word of the Lord. He felt the union would be one of life-long happiness. To Hosea were born two sons and one daughter; Jezreel and Lo-ammi were the names of the two sons and Lo-ruhamah was the daughter's name. There names were symbolic. In the course of time, Gomer was found to be playing the harlot and with great sadness and according to God's law, Hosea was forced to divorce his adulterous wife. Yet God still gave promises of a new betrothal and covenant that would come. After a period of time, God commanded Hosea to buy his wife back to himself for 15 pieces of silver and 1½ homers of barley. Hosea did so, taking her to himself again with an exhortation to her that she was not to be for another man.

The whole story becomes symbolic and typical of Jehovah's relationship with the nation of Israel: Hosea represents Jehovah God; Gomer, his wife of whoredoms, represents Israel in her former idolatry in Egypt ***(Ezekiel 20:5-9).*** As Hosea took Gomer to himself according to the word of the Lord, so Jehovah took Israel to Himself under the Law Covenant. At Mt. Sinai He entered into a marriage contract with the nation and became a husband to her ***(Jeremiah 31:32).*** Children were born to the nation. However, just as Gomer played the harlot, so did Israel ***(Ezekiel 16: 23).*** Jehovah gave her a bill of divorcement ***(Jeremiah 3:8; Isaiah 50:1).*** It was after this that God gave promises of the coming New Covenant ***(Jeremiah 31:31-34).***

Hosea's buying back his wife with silver was typical of Jehovah's redeeming Israel by the price that Christ paid under the New Covenant ***(Hebrews 13:20).*** It was to be under this covenant that natural Israel, divorced and cast off under the Old Covenant, could be restored to a proper relationship with God through Christ.

Symbol/Type	**Symbolized/Antitype**
Hosea, the prophet	The Lord God
Gomer, wife of whoredoms.	Idolatrous Israel in Egypt
Hosea takes Gomer to be his wife	Jehovah takes Israel to be His wife at Mt. Sinai
Children born to them	Multiplicity of seed
Gomer plays the harlot	Israel plays the harlot
Hosea puts her away for many days	Jehovah divorces Israel for many years
Promises of new betrothal and covenant given.	Promises of new covenant given
Hosea buys his wife back for price of silver	Jehovah redeems Israel by the blood of Jesus
Gomer again becomes his, never to belong to another man	Israel becomes Jehovah's again, restored through the New Covenant, never to belong to another

CONCLUSION

It is a fitting conclusion to this text to remember that all men will give an account on the day of judgment for their every word ***(Matthew 12:36).*** The apostle James exhorts us not to be many teachers knowing that the heavier burden of accountability will be upon such ***(James 3:1-2)***. This surely becomes a challenge to all who seek to interpret the Divine revelation, the Holy Scripture. It is sadly possible to have the correct hermeneutical principles yet fail in interpretation because of the lack of proper union with Him who is THE Hermeneutician. To have all the hermeneutical principles without The Hermeneutician is to be like a ship without a helmsman. It is the prayer of the authors that teacher and student together will grow up into Jesus Christ in all things as we each seek to know Him who is life eternal. May this text be a helpful instrument towards that end. Amen.

BIBLIOGRAPHY

1. Berkhof, L., *Principles of Biblical Interpretation,* Grand Rapids, Michigan, Baker Book House, 1974.
2. Bullinger, E.W., *Figures of Speech Used in the Bible,* Grand Rapids, Michigan, Baker Book House, 1971.
3. Conner, Kevin J., *The Tabernacle of Moses,* Portland, Oregon, Center Press, 1974.
4. Dungan, D.R., *Hermeneutics,* Cincinnati, Ohio, The Standard Publishing Company.
5. Gesenius, William, *A Hebrew and English Lexicon,* Oxford, Claredon Press, 1974.
6. Green, Thomas Sheldon, *A Greek-English Lexicon to the New Testament,* Grand Rapids, Michigan, Zondervan Publishing House, 1973.
7. Habershon, Ada R., *The Study of the Types,* Grand Rapids, Michigan, Kregel Publications.
8. Hartill, J. Edwin, *Principles of Biblical Hermeneutics,* Grand Rapids, Michigan, Zondervan Publishing House, 1969.
9. Keach, Benjamin, *Preaching from the Types and Metaphors of the Bible,* Grand Rapids, Michigan, Kregel Publications, 1972.
10. Malmin, Ken and Kevin J. Conner, *New Testament Survey,* Portland, Oregon, Portland Bible College, 1974.
11. Malmin, Ken and Kevin J. Conner, *Old Testament Survey,* Portland, Oregon, Portland Bible College, 1974.
12. Mickelsen, A. Berkeley, *Interpreting the Bible,* Grand Rapids, Michigan, Wm. B. Eerdmans Publishing Company, 1974.
13. Orr, James, *The International Standard Bible Encyclopedia,* Wilmington, Delaware, Associated Publishers and Authors Inc., 1915.
14. Pamphilus, Eusebius, *Eusebius' Ecclesiastical History,* Grand Rapids, Michigan, Baker Book House, 1974.
15. Pink, Arthur W., *Interpretation of the Scriptures,* Grand Rapids, Michigan, Baker Book House, 1972.
16. Ramm, Bernard L., and others, *Hermeneutics,* Grand Rapids, Michigan, Baker Book House, 1972.
17. Ramm, Bernard L., *Protestant Biblical Interpretation,* Grand Rapids, Michigan, Baker Book House, 1970.
18. Roberts, Alexander and James Donaldson, *The Ante-Nicene Fathers,* Grand Rapids, Michigan, Wm. B. Eerdmans Publishing Company, 1972.
19. Strong, James, *Strong's Exhaustive Concordance,* Madison, New Jersey, 1890.
20. Thayer, Joseph Henry, D.D., *Thayer's Greek-English Lexicon,* Grand Rapids, Michigan, Associated Publishers and Authors Inc., 1885.
21. *The Englishman's Hebrew and Chaldee Concordance of the Old Testament,* Grand Rapids, Michigan, Zondervan Publishing House, 1973.
22. Thompson, Frank Charles, *The New Chain Reference Bible,* Indianapolis, Indiana, B. B. Kirkbride Bible Co. Inc., 1964.
23. Trench, Richard Chenevix, *Synonyms of the New Testament,* Grand Rapids, Michigan, Associated Publishers and Authors Inc.
24. Tan, Paul Lee, *The Interpretation of Prophecy,* Winona Lake, Indiana, BMH Books, Inc., 1974.
25. Terry, Milton S., *Biblical Hermeneutics,* Grand Rapids, Michigan, Zondervan Publishing House, 1974.
26. Unger, Merrill F., *Unger's Bible Dictionary,* Chicago, Moody Press, 1972.
27. Vine, W. E., *An Expository Dictionary of New Testament Words,* Old Tappan, New Jersey, Fleming H. Revell Company, 1966.
28. Walker, Williston, *A History of the Christian Church,* New York, Charles Scribner's Sons, 1970.
29. Webster, Noah, *Webster's New Twentieth Century Dictionary of the English Language,* New York, Rockville House Publisher's Inc., 1969.
30. Arndt, W. F. and F. W. Gingrich, *A Greek-English Lexicon of the New Testament* and other early Christian literature, Chicago, University of Chicago Press, 1969.
31. William Carey Library, *The New Englishman's Greek Concordance,* 533 Hermosa Street, South Pasadena, California, Associated Publishers and Authors Inc., 1972.

Other Resources Available by Kevin J. Conner

Kevin J. Conner

Church in the New Testament
The Book of Acts
Interpreting the Book of Revelation
Interpreting the Symbols & Types
The Epistle to the Romans
Feasts of Israel
Foundations of Christian Doctrine
The Tabernacle of Moses
The Tabernacle of David
The Temple of Solomon

Kevin J. Conner & Ken Malmin

The Covenants
Interpreting the Scriptures
New Testament Survey
Old Testament Survey

Ask for these resources at your local Christian bookstore.

City Bible Publishing
9200 NE Fremont
Portland OR 97220
503-253-9020
1-800-777-6057
www.citybiblepublishing.com